English Literature
and
Ancient Languages

KENNETH HAYNES

OXFORD
UNIVERSITY PRESS

OXFORD
UNIVERSITY PRESS

Great Clarendon Street, Oxford OX2 6DP

Oxford University Press is a department of the University of Oxford.
It furthers the University's objective of excellence in research, scholarship,
and education by publishing worldwide in

Oxford New York

Auckland Cape Town Dar es Salaam Hong Kong Karachi Kuala Lumpur
Madrid Melbourne Mexico City Nairobi New Delhi Taipei Toronto
Shanghai

With offices in

Argentina Austria Brazil Chile Czech Republic France Greece
Guatemala Hungary Italy Japan South Korea Poland Portugal
Singapore Switzerland Thailand Turkey Ukraine Vietnam

Oxford is a registered trade mark of Oxford University Press
in the UK and in certain other countries

Published in the United States
by Oxford University Press Inc., New York

First published 2003

British Library Cataloguing in Publication Data

Data available

Library of Congress Cataloging in Publication Data

Data applied for

ISBN 0-19-926190-3

3 5 7 9 10 8 6 4 2

Typeset by Regent Typesetting
Printed in Great Britain
on acid-free paper by
Biddles Ltd., King's Lynn, Norfolk

For

DONALD CARNE-ROSS

ἔχω γὰρ ἄχω διὰ σὲ κοὐκ ἄλλον βροτῶν

Contents

Introduction

IN THIS BOOK I am concerned with the presence of the Greek and Latin languages within English literature since the Renaissance, though to tell this story I must sometimes also consider their presence within French and German literature. The main subject is the influence of these ancient *languages* on English *literature*—not the influence of those languages on the English language, nor the influence of Greek and Roman literature on English literature, although those more familiar topics sometimes form part of the investigation. It is a study of the literary uses of the phenomena of language contact, of Greek and Latin in contact with English literature.

Three of these phenomena are treated here, from a literary perspective. The first one linguists call 'code-switching', which happens when a speaker changes to a foreign language in order to express or assert something—a concept, a social or professional status, shared intimacy, snobbery, solidarity, and so on. In the first chapter, this linguistic background provides a basis on which to investigate the literary question of why vernacular writers sometimes switch to Latin or Greek. Answers to the question vary greatly, and depend on the history of multilingualism as well as on the languages themselves and attitudes towards them at a given historical moment. The social status of those who have been taught Latin, for example, or the professional possibilities it promotes, its associations with particular domains within a culture, all influence the significance of writing or quoting it. Too often the Latin within a vernacular text has been seen exclusively as an ancient presence in a modern text, rather than as a contemporary language with important social implications. The modern history of Latin in its social, political, religious, and economic aspects is briefly surveyed in the first chapter. This is a prerequisite for attempting to understand literary examples in which authors, at whatever length, switch to Latin or (less often) to Greek. The rest of the chapter offers literary criticism of a variety of these examples; I have included famous examples from other European languages, in order to show how often multilingualism has been dramatized in literature and how frequently the social, political, and religious pressures motivating it have recurred.

Language purism is the second phenomenon of language contact surveyed in this study; it forms the background to the second chapter, which is concerned especially with the connections between register and vocabulary in English literature. These connections emerged in large part because of the pressures of language purism. The pressures were often in conflict; the two major kinds of purism in English literary history have had opposing influences on diction. A neo-classical purism that was easily embarrassed by low, vulgar, and common words created much anxiety about plain Saxon words; a purism in which Latin was seen as a foreign corruption of native English was equally a source of anxiety about latinate English words. Historically, the first purism came into English mediated by the French example of purism; the second, under the influence of German. The topic is tackled by asking questions about particularly obstinate examples of such diction, about latinate English diction which advertises its latinity (*irremeable, irriguous*) and about Saxon English which makes a statement through its Saxonness (*ugh, pox*).

To sharpen the focus, I turn to a particularly charged aspect of the English language, the monosyllable, in its perceived relation to the nature of English. From the fourteenth century, it has been claimed that the monosyllable is native to English, or that it expresses peculiarly English values. In English literature, statements about Englishness have self-consciously been made by deploying monosyllables. Interjections, cries, swearing, and short prayers all have monosyllabic versions, and they all have a particular weight in carrying the social and linguistic burden of authenticity. Some of this weight has been lent to the monosyllable, and the chapter discusses the literary handling of fraught monosyllables. The relation of the monosyllable to latinate English is further explored by attending both to writers who switch between a latinate English register and a monosyllabic one, and to writers for whom there is little tension between the two and who employ monosyllabic lines in latinate contexts. The chapter concludes by exploring the work of two authors who have written poems entirely in monosyllables (Chidiock Tichborne and William Loe).

A third phenomenon of language contact is 'interference'. This has a technical meaning in linguistics and refers to 'instances of deviation from the norms of either language which occur in the speech of bilinguals as a result of their familiarity with more than one language, i.e. as a result of language contact' (Uriel Weinreich, *Languages in Contact* (1953; The Hague: Mouton, 1967), 1). The term usually refers to a certain class of mistakes made by bilingual speakers and learners of foreign languages. However, to deviate from the norms of one language under the influence of the norms of another language is not something only tired speakers are liable to do. It may also be a deliberate attempt to dislocate one's language so that it conforms to a foreign paradigm: this is the subject of the third chapter. Milton's *Paradise Lost* and Joyce's *Finnegans Wake* are the two great monuments in English literature of this ambition. These are discussed in relation to the linguistic topic, along with a few other examples, in an effort to show that this apparently perverse method of writing is not a Miltonic and Joycean singularity but has led to a number of variously motivated, variously successful, works.

The chapter then covers the topic of highly latinate English and the animus such writing inspired. The fortunes of latinate English are broadly similar to those of Latin in the same period, attracting the same ambivalence of animus and desire, with animus more often in evidence than desire: no one uses *sesquipedalian* as a term of approval. Two key examples in the sixteenth century of animus against Latin are treated: the dispute between Gabriel Harvey and Thomas Nashe and the controversy over the Rheims New Testament. In both cases, a highly latinate style came in for critique, Harvey's as the style of a pompous ass, and the Rheims as obscurantist. However, the controversies were not only about style. Harvey was a man who tried to use a very latinate English to rise above his class status, and in the Rheims New Testament latinate English ('give us this day our supersubstantial bread') is used to make a statement about Catholic values. These controversies were so heated because of the passions involved in maintaining the social and religious structure. The chapter concludes by focusing on a single latinism: the *sunt qui*, the *there are who*, a latinism which occurs in Jonson, Milton, Wordsworth, and many others, and which provides an opportunity to study the presence of Latin in poetry at the level of syntax.

Unlike Latin, ancient Greek has been present only intermittently in English social history and English literature. Even among the Victorians, among whom Greek was a crucial means of forming and marking the governing class, it never matched Latin's linguistic importance to English. Greek influence on English is more diffuse and requires a different kind of description. In three respects, English poetic language has at times aspired to emulate Greek rather than Latin: compound epithets, privative adjectives, and metres. These form the subject of Chapter 4. In the Renaissance, the poverty of compound epithets in Latin was regretted, and Greek's facility for readily forming them was praised. After surveying briefly a history of the compound epithet, I turn to three pre-eminent examples—in Milton, Keats, and Hopkins—where the epithets are not only (in part) derived from, and imitations of, the language of Greek poetry, but are themselves attempts to represent or reject Greek paganism. These adjectives are most like Greek when they celebrate the beauty of the natural world. For Milton as for Hopkins, they make genuinely seductive the dangerous temptation of beauty; for Keats, they are an essential means to make real the Greek 'religion of beauty', as he understands it. Dependence on negative adjectives (which in English often begin in 'un-' or 'dis-') is also highly characteristic of both Greek and English high poetry. In addition to imitating particular Greek words, the English poets who make the most use of them (Milton, Wordsworth, Shelley) do so for their own varied purposes, Milton and Wordsworth often to invoke a pre-lapsarian state, Shelley sometimes to enact a 'lifting of the veil' from sensory reality, consistent with his commitment to Greek philosophy. It was in the nineteenth century that Greek metres were most productive for English poets. Their understanding of Greek prosody, though now obsolete and even then flawed, stimulated innovations in English metres. That three nineteenth-century terms describing aspects of Greek prosody provided an active stimulus for English poets is the argument of the final third of the chapter.

German and British hellenism is treated more broadly in the last chapter. Since the Renaissance, Rome played many roles in literature, was variously idealized, embodied, or rejected; Greece, however, was imagined as a distinct, autonomous alternative to Rome only toward the end of the eighteenth century, and in the course of the nineteenth it tended to assume one of only two guises, to be a model either of classic harmony or of tragic genius. The 'two Greeces' dominated German hellenism and would eventually be called 'Apollonian' and 'Dionysian' by Nietzsche. Their literary representation was rooted in two different aesthetic ideals derived from Greek literature. The Greece of 'sweetness and light' derives from the work of Winckelmann and his history of art; in literary terms, it placed a premium on harmonies imputed to Homer and Sophocles; during Goethe's most classicizing phase, it attained a distinctive form, in the *Iphigenie auf Tauris*. Specifically in Germany, however, an alternative literary version of Greece evolved, in Hölderlin above all, who created a late style of rupture and leaping, which he had studied and reproduced in translating Pindar.

In England, although there was no theoretical elaboration of the Dionysian or chthonic Greece before Pater late in the century, the influence of paratactical styles derived from Pindar and Aeschylus was a potent force on writers like Shelley, Swinburne, and Hopkins, all of whom found Aeschylus to be a supreme poet. These writers found in the Greek dramatist a way to embody certain of their key concepts and fascinations. Shelley's splintering of unity into diversity, Swinburne's experience of division, and Hopkins's abrupt selfhood are all indebted to their understanding of Aeschylean parataxis, a style of poetry which continued to be influential even among some modernist poets, long after the 'sweetness and light' which Arnold had imputed to Greece was discredited. In particular, the study of Aeschylus stimulated Ezra Pound's experiments in free verse and collage.

Part of what we mean by understanding a literary work is to be able to see why it is as it is and not otherwise: that was Coleridge, attributing to the work itself its own principle of sufficient reason. His formulation has invited scepticism on the grounds that it does not leave room for contingency in the artwork and in our response to it, and that in practice it emphasizes formal considerations to the exclusion of all the other reasons why an artefact is as it is. We can grant those objections, however, and still insist that understanding something will often mean seeing it in relation to an 'otherwise'. The point of this study is to explore a particular way in which literary works might have been otherwise: in their language choices. The tendency of so many native English speakers to see English as natural has prevented them from acknowledging the scope of an entire dimension in which English literature moves, namely across languages. Linguists and social historians of language have long known the importance of language contact, but literary critics have only just begun to study it. In his recent book, *Milton's Languages* (Cambridge: Cambridge University Press, 1997), John Hale examined 'the impact of multilingualism on style', and investigated Milton's language choices with great sensitivity. Very recently J. N. Adams and Simon Swain have investigated the multilingual environment of ancient Greece and Rome and in particular described the literary style in the context of that environment. As multilingualism is a general phenomenon, so too is its impact on literary style. These essays are meant to give an initial survey of a very rich topic; it can hardly be hoped that they will do justice to it.

I have quoted texts in their original spelling with the following exceptions: I have lightly modernized sixteenth-century English writing; I have transmitted only the more elementary of Hopkin's diacritical marks; I give neo-Latin texts spelled in conformity with modern scholarly conventions; German appears in modern spelling, and French after the sixteenth century does too.

Rosalie Anders, Geoffrey Hill, and Christopher Ricks read and improved each chapter. Two readers from Oxford University Press made helpful comments on the book. My greatest debt is to Donald Carne-Ross.

CHAPTER ONE

Multilingualism in Literature

LANGUAGES OVERLAP, IN life and in literature. Hardly any adult speaker is exclusively a monoglot, entirely without a scrap of another language, some equivalent to the familiarity of an English monoglot with *sushi* or *Gesundheit* or *hola*. A language without loanwords is inconceivable. A literary work of any length that gives no evidence whatever of foreign influence may be a work of self-conscious linguistic purism, itself a response to multilingualism. Languages interact, and various kinds of prejudice, desire, and anxiety mark the interaction.[1]

Multilingualism is found whenever a person is brought into sustained contact with someone speaking another language. This may be the result of adventure, marriage, trade, curiosity, proselytizing, education, colonialism, the desire for social status, political power or economic advancement, or the simple fact of having been born into an environment where many languages are spoken; no list could be complete. Most of us are multilingual to some degree, from a smattering to native fluency; and in other times and places, multilingual fluency has been a vastly more common phenomenon.

It becomes common when not merely individuals but entire groups speaking different languages come into sustained contact. Lemuel Gulliver offers a fine analysis of bilingualism on both Lilliput and Blefuscu:

from the great intercourse of trade and commerce between both realms, from the continual reception of exiles, which is mutual among them, and from the custom in each Empire to send their young nobility and richer gentry to the other, in order to polish themselves, by seeing the world, and understanding men and manners, there are few persons of distinction, or merchants, or seamen, who dwell in the maritime parts, but what can hold conversation in both tongues.

Swift identifies the part bilingualism plays in training the cultural elite, in commerce, and in the conduct of a government's foreign affairs. Had Gulliver been successfully persuaded to reduce the Empire of Blefuscu to a province of Lilliput and destroy all Big-Endian exiles and heretics, the story would have resembled less the relation of French to English than that of Gaelic, Occitan, and Catalan to English, French, and Spanish. Languages, like rivers, both unite and divide.

Sometimes languages are shared not only across a single linguistic divide but across several such borders. These take many forms: the broken jargon found along trade routes (like the original 'lingua franca'); languages that have helped maintain a religious or ethnic identity among dispersed members speaking different languages (Hebrew, Yiddish, Latin); languages spoken in courts of international law, or for the conduct of international affairs (French as the language of diplomacy in the eighteenth century and after), or to participate in high finance (Italian as a language of banking in the nineteenth century); languages accompanying military conquest or economic domination; languages for the administration of empires (Persian for the Mughal Empire, Quechua for the Incan Empire, German for the Habsburg Empire); languages known by one social class and not others (French in England, Holland, Prussia, and Russia). Historians have recently brought systematic attention to bear on the social history of language and to the diverse political, religious, military, cultural, and economic reasons behind language choices.[2]

Attitudes about the suitability of languages for specific functions arise with multilingualism and in response to the particular historical pressures acting on languages and their speakers. Charles V is recorded to have said, 'I speak Spanish to God, Italian to women, French to men and German to my horse'.[3] In the nineteenth century, a contemporary of Pushkin joked, 'We philosophize in German, joke in French, and use Russian only for praying to God and scolding our servants'.[4] The Austrian dramatist Grillparzer allocated languages in yet another way: Italian was for singing, German to say something, Greek for making an impression, Latin for speeches, French for gossip, Spanish for lovers, and English for boors.[5] Even now it is possible that an English speaker might use French for the purpose of politeness, or to show one is in control of an embarrassing situation, or to be a snob, or when English lacks the *mot juste*. An American English speaker might take advantage of the demotic appeal possessed by Spanish, to be cool or to assert a generational identity, like the teenage girl who told her parents that she was 'one hungry *muchacha*'. As the language of commerce, tourism, or science, English, in its turn, may be chosen by a French or Spanish speaker. This language-switching (which linguists sometimes call code-switching) among multilingual speakers has been studied by sociologists and linguists; it will also be valuable to consider multilingualism more generally in literary contexts.[6]

Bilingualism has a long history in the West and around the Mediterranean. It has not been always limited to individual speakers or to a few groups; some languages, pre-eminently Aramaic, Greek, Latin, and Arabic, have been learnt by speakers of many local languages, often leaving a lasting imprint on them. (Other languages that were extensively used, for example Phoenician or Egyptian, had a much more limited impact, generally because the nature of the language contact was narrower.) The widespread adoption of those languages was instrumental in creating such unity as existed in the Mediterranean. The reason Paul, who spoke Aramaic, could convert the Roman governor in Cyprus, who spoke Latin, was that they both spoke Greek. The Epistle to the Romans and the Epistle to the Hebrews were written with equal confidence that the language would not be a barrier to the Romans and the Hebrews, the conjectured audience of the latter epistle.[7]

Bilingualism among the Romans set an influential precedent in Western education and letters. Though the Latin language bears within it witness to its contacts with other languages (Etruscan and Celtic in particular), it was bilingualism in Greek that mattered most in Roman history and culture. The demise of Magna Graecia did not cause Greek to cease being spoken in Southern Italy, and in addition to that persistent Hellenic presence, Greek artisans and freed slaves became increasingly numerous in the Italian urban centres from the third century. The Greek they spoke had a very low status. On the other hand, the language enjoyed high status among the nobility, for whom Greek was inescapable: they were to be *utraque lingua docti*, and instruction in it began early in their lives. Greek was simultaneously a language of high and low prestige, a reflection of the Roman ambivalence towards the Greeks.[8]

Latin literature can scarcely be considered apart from Greek. Among early writers, Ennius freely adapted Euripides, while Livius Andronicus translated Homer both faithfully and with great ingenuity, to judge from the few fragments that survive.[9] Even Plautus' plays, with their lively colloquial Latin and popular appeal, some-times incorporate Greek, as in the *Bacchides*. Naturally there was a counter-reaction, but even Cato the Censor, who despised the Greeks ('nequissimum et indocile genus'[10]), knew their language well.

The greatest Latin writers of the Golden Age were fluent in Greek. Cicero and Horace went to Greece as part of their education, and Virgil had many opportunities to speak with educated Greeks in Italy. Their work shows the continual presence of Greek, as in Cicero's quotations, or Virgil's and Horace's emulation of their models. Horace boasts that he is the first to make Latin poetry move to Greek measures (*Odes* 3. 30), and in *Epistles* 2. 1, he writes that the Roman capture of Greece (militarily) had the happy result that the brutish victor was taken captive (culturally).

Even among later Roman writers hostile to Greeks, the language preserved much of its social and cultural importance. Juvenal com-plains about Greek in particular because it disgraces the old women who speak it, though he also feels that it would be nicer if young women spoke it less (*Satires* 6). Augustine's hatred of the Greek studies of his childhood (*Confessions* 1. 13) seems to be a new attitude.

Bilingualism was never as common in the eastern half of the Roman Empire. Moreover, in contrast to the relative openness of Romans to Greek, Greek writers, from about AD 50, began to remove the Latin presence within Greek and to prescribe strict classicizing rules. The Greek language had been remarkably resistant to foreign influence even before this time (in sharp contrast to other aspects of Greek culture, which borrowed widely from Near Eastern sources), and the language had been central in the self-definition of the Greeks; now, however, writers adopted a deliberate programme for writing in a single, pure, atticizing style. This was part of a larger effort to reinvent the glory of Athens, with the political and social implications of distancing educated speakers and writers from other citizens as well as appealing to the taste of philhellene Roman emperors.[11] Language purism recurs throughout the history of language contact; I will return to it in the second chapter.

Both the Roman and the Greek literary responses to language contact reveal a high degree of linguistic and historical self-consciousness, which would return to Western and Central Europe after the success of the Italian humanists. Bilingualism and sometimes multilingualism were essential features of the European Middle Ages.[12] Both Latin and French were widespread, Latin as the language of the church, state, and school, and French as the language of chivalry and, in some regions, of the ruling class and legal system. England became trilingual after the Norman Conquest: clerics spoke Latin, the aristocracy French (or Anglo-Norman), others Middle English. The three greatest medieval English poets can be read adequately only with an awareness of languages in contact: Chaucer, 'grant translateur', gave us English versions of Boethius' *Consolation of Philosophy* and part of the *Roman de la rose*; Gower wrote books in Latin and French as well as English; and Langland, an editor of *Piers Plowman* argues, creates a 'macaronic sublime' in which the language of sacred speech and theological depth is commingled with the homely realities of the vernacular.[13]

However, it is during and after the Renaissance that the specifically Roman experience of bilingualism served as a model for later writers. An English humanist could invoke the example of Cato in recommending the knowledge of Italian.[14] Once French had replaced Italian as the international language of cultural distinction, the analogy with Roman bilingualism was correspondingly adjusted and renewed. One of the most famous appeals to Roman bilingualism is Pope's imitation of Horace, *Epistles* 2. 1, in which Horace declared that a new elegance and refinement came into Roman poetry with the conquest of Greece. It provided Pope with the ground for his deepest meditation on English poetry, impressive not for its elegantly strained history ('We conquer'd France, but felt our captive's charms') but for the synthesis of the opposed principles of masculine energy and feminine refinement, represented by Latin and Greek for Horace and by English and French for Pope.

In Western and Central Europe, Latin has been the language of greatest moment. Joseph de Maistre claimed that 'the European sign is Latin', and Françoise Waquet, in her study of Latin in Europe since the Renaissance, has made sense of this claim.[15] Latin was essential to a shared set of institutions—churches, schools and universities, and the republic of letters—and had a similar destiny despite its diverse vernacular settings. Latin is inextricably part of the cultural meaning that Europe acquired after the Renaissance, a remarkably unitary meaning that was shared by *literati* across the continent. Waquet's study is divided into three parts: first, she outlines the institutions which supported Latin and the colossal labour that went into educating men in the language, a labour which, despite occasional resistance to it, continued into the middle of the twentieth century; second, she notes that the proficiency attained in Latin was generally mediocre, though with brilliant exceptions, and moreover that after the eighteenth century the language largely disappeared as a serious literary vehicle and as an oral medium; last, she accounts for this discrepancy between intention and achievement by studying the symbolism and cultural significance that became attached to the language, the passions that were involved in retaining it, and the uses to which it was put in supporting the social order.

It is not yet possible to offer a comprehensive social history of Latin in modern Europe. Still, with the help of Waquet's study and others, key moments in that history can be outlined. This history moves from the more strictly Latin humanism of the early Renaissance to a humanism concerned with both Latin and the vernaculars in the later Renaissance, to a Latin grown polite in the course of the seventeenth century, to the death of Latin in certain key respects in the eighteenth century, to the revivals and defences of Latin in the nineteenth century, to the end of that history in the mid-twentieth century. The dates vary from country to country; moreover, the historical changes themselves overlap and are not necessarily sequential. Still, even a rough outline of this history will give the context which must be known in order to understand the different meanings and implications that Latin has acquired since the Renaissance.

Latin at the start of our period is closely tied to Italian humanism and the new humanistic concerns; however, in its role as the language of the affairs of church and state, and in the university disciplines of theology, medicine, and law, Latin preceded humanism and would survive its demise. Official correspondence and state business was conducted in Latin, as it had been for centuries; now, however, a new value was attached to a revived classical Latin, although it remains unclear how and why, exactly, the transformation from the medieval *ars dictaminis* to the Renaissance *studia humanitatis* took place. We may note that the orations and correspondence of a city or state were a powerful opportunity to press for diplomatic advantages. By the beginning of the sixteenth century, Italian superiority was acknowledged throughout Europe, and other regions adopted humanist ideals, both in order to compete and because the humanists were mostly successful in pressing for their own interests at home.

The growth of the state in early modern Europe created opportunities for latinists. Naturally, there were variations in the kind of Latin that was taught, depending on the quality of the school, the professional options available to the students and their social status, and the date when humanist reforms were introduced; as there were variations in the purposes to which Latin was put, with more theology in the north and more law in Italy; none the less, the Latin that was taught gradually became more or less classical across Europe.[16]

One scholar contrasts this 'Latin humanism', whose international heyday ran from about 1480 to 1530, with the late humanism of the second half of the sixteenth century, which he calls 'Latin and vernacular humanism'. The vernaculars were consistently used alongside Latin in international communication by the 1530s and 1540s, and very often classical and vernacular texts circulated together as part of the polyglot environment of the time. Vernacular cribs started to appear in the colleges of Oxford and Cambridge by the 1570s and 1580s.[17]

It is sometimes said that the vernaculars had essentially replaced Latin by the seventeenth century. Consider, for example, the following statistic: at the beginning of the sixteenth century, about 90 per cent of the books published in Paris were in Latin; by mid-century, about 80 per cent; and by the end of the century, less than 25 per cent. None the less, it is a mistake to infer too much from this crude fact. First, the proportion of Parisian Latin titles stabilized in the first half of the seventeenth century, averaging around 20 per cent, before dropping in the second half. Elsewhere, Latin held on longer: the majority of books exchanged at the Frankfurt book fair were in Latin until the 1680s.[18] Second, Latin was firmly entrenched in particular areas, especially theology, science, and textbooks. Third, the fame of Galileo's and Descartes's vernacular works and the success of the new science should not obscure the fact that both Galileo and Descartes also published in Latin. The language chosen had to do with readership; Latin increased the potential audience for scholarly works. Besides, other figures (Huygens, for example) aspired to more traditional humanist goals, and it has been argued that humanism survived into the next century by pragmatically adapting itself—and the Latin which it taught—to the new circumstances of the times.[19]

None the less, in several respects Latin did decline during the seventeenth century. For example, even some eminent figures

(Fracastoro, Sigonius) were apologetic about their lack of facility in speaking Latin. The Latin spoken in the universities was occasionally denounced as barbaric; in the classroom, instruction in Latin would often be followed by explanations in the vernacular. The most consequential change, however, was the new status of Latin: it was 'ennobled', that is, it became identified with a liberal education and its increasing uselessness consolidated its symbolic force. This was the period when the pedant would be mocked, often depicted as a social climber who lacked civility and quoted too much—a theme that had its origin in Italy in the sixteenth century, occupied Montaigne in his essay on pedantry, was a constant anxiety of Gabriel Harvey (his *Pedantius* was published in 1581), and which was a particular concern of French literature in the seventeenth century (Cyrano de Bergerac's *Le Pédant joué*, Molière's *Les Femmes savantes*). Eliminating displays of pedantry, and of erudition, allowed Latin to be incorporated into polite society. Waquet, inspired in part by Pierre Bourdieu's study of social distinction as well as by Thorstein Veblen's classic analysis of the leisure class, sees the reign of Louis XIV as the critical period when Latin changed from a 'useful or even utilitarian subject needed for a few rather unglamorous professions' to a class-marker that would define 'the gentleman in England and the bourgeois in France, by ostentatiously expressing membership of a class that could "waste" money, time and energy on learning something that, in professional terms, had limited practical utility'. Because of this new association between class and Latin, actually knowing Latin became far less important than having studied it as a boy.[20]

In almost every respect, the living tradition of Latin came to an end in the nineteenth century. It largely faded away as an oral language by mid-century, instruction now being given regularly in the vernacular. The percentage of books printed in it became very small. Scientific publications mostly abandoned Latin, although a few influential works were published in it (the number theory of Gauss, the anatomy of Caldani). Latin was replaced by French as the language of diplomacy. Prominent neo-Latin works of literature were no longer written, and Latin poetry was largely given over to schools, amateurs, and hobbyists. Having ceded its practical usefulness to the vernaculars, Latin had begun to be assailed in the eighteenth century—especially in America—for its uselessness, its taking time away from the study of modern subjects, its inhibiting of creativity and promoting awkward affected styles, its nurturing of anti-democratic tendencies, and so on.

However, Latin was also vigorously defended as it was attacked, and in the nineteenth century the study of classics was substantially revived in secondary education. In the Prussian Gymnasium (where Greek had originally been given the leading role in education), Latin became the main discipline by mid-century. In England, ancient languages came to represent up to three-quarters of the instruction at some public schools. There also emerged, in France, a new and distinctive apologia for Latin, which had its roots in Chateaubriand's *Génie du christianisme* (1802) and was taken up by Joseph de Maistre in his defence of the absolute power of the pope, *Du pape* (1819). The symbolic, emotional, and mysterious efficacy of Latin was adduced in its defence. (In contrast, no one at the Council of Trent had argued that Latin possessed some kind of sacred quality.[21]) Although this particular apologia for Latin was limited to Catholic regions, other defences had a broader appeal. As an example, consider Kipling, whose story 'Regulus' is set in a classroom in which it is precisely through tedious and rote translation and quite apart from any comprehension of Horace that the Latin instructor builds the moral character of his students, who in any case are unlikely to retain more than a few tags from what they read. This belief in the moral efficacy of Latin grammar was shared, though also contested, throughout Europe.

From the middle of the nineteenth to the middle of the twentieth century, Latin instruction was supported whenever it was opposed, and vigorous polemics accompanied every threat to cut it back. Finally, in the mid-twentieth century, the language vanished rapidly when it was no longer supported by the institutions that had given sense to it.

A social history of Latin, concerned with the question of who knows Latin and why, complements its cultural history, more concerned with the vicissitudes of Latin literary style and the polemics which accompanied them, from the Ciceronianism of the Renaissance to the Tacitism of the Baroque, from the return of patristic Latin in the Counter-Reformation to the return of medieval Latin among Romantic writers. That is, there are occasions when the Latin used by writers ought to be seen not only in relation to others who wrote in Latin but also to those excluded from the language. By the nineteenth century, the question of access to classical languages became an explicit theme in literature, as in nineteenth-century fiction (Alessandro Manzoni's *I promessi sposi*, Thomas Hardy's *Jude the Obscure* and *A Pair of Blue Eyes*, George Eliot's *Romola* and *Middlemarch*).

The significance of Latin and the status of its speakers kept changing over the last five centuries. To choose to write Latin during the Renaissance was very different from that choice in the nineteenth century because the role of the language in society changed drastically during this time. Milton wrote Latin for an international audience, Johnson for the most part wrote for himself and his friends, and Landor wrote it in order to assert, loudly, his amateur status and disdain for unfit readers. The choice of Latin was often motivated by the social functions it performed. For example, it could be used to display professional qualifications (doctor, lawyer, scholar); to discuss sensitive and especially sexual matters; to exclude, impress, or intimidate women, or the masses, or colonial peoples (though at times members of these groups gained access to Latin education); or to indicate religious and doctrinal inclinations. Literary works that are written in Latin, quote Latin, or have Latin titles, as we will see, involve themselves in these functions.

Even a tentative overview of the social history of classical Greek in the West since the Renaissance is hardly possible; too much research remains to be done. A few points should be underlined at the outset. First, original composition in Greek never approached the level of facility and accomplishment found in neo-Latin. Of Greek poems by English poets, for example those by Herbert, Milton, Crashaw, Marvell, Johnson, Swinburne, we might say (hoising them with Johnson's petard) that they are like a dog walking on his hind legs; though not done well, we are surprised to see them done at all. But this would be glib (though not necessarily untrue): Greek verse by English poets has not received the critical and editorial attention that are essential to evaluate them adequately by relevant and historically informed criteria; the same is true for almost all the Greek verses produced in the West since the Renaissance. Even less known are compositions in Greek prose: letters (for example, by Filelfo or by Budé), translations (in England, for example, some of Virgil was translated into Greek, as were theological works in Latin by Alexander Nowell and John Jewel[22]), and essays (including Bembo's youthful essay in defence of Greek literature, Budé's preface to his *Commentarii linguae graecae*) are virtually unobtainable. The Greek verse composed at Eton in the eighteenth century, as well as the mass of English verse and prose translated into Greek at schools, universities, and clubs in the nineteenth century, are only slightly better known.[23] It is none the less obvious, even despite our ignorance, that writing Greek never had the practical uses that writing in Latin once had, and that reading Greek was always far more common than writing or speaking it. The sheer quantity, as well as diversity, of neo-Latin material eclipses its Greek (neo-Greek?) cousin.

Second, there were at least two periods when reading and translating Greek mattered very much to Western Europe: in the Reformation and in the nineteenth century. Mattering is hard to quantify. There are many expressions of the importance of Greek in both periods, but such cultural expressions cannot be taken to imply that the language was actually known. Take one example: the statutes of St Paul's School explicitly refer to the value of Latin and Greek literature, but the available evidence points to periods of Greeklessness after its foundation.[24] Moreover, it is very difficult to know at any time how much of a subject students actually learn in classes. There is a difference between being taught Greek and learning Greek; between having a rule that schoolchildren must always speak Latin or Greek and the observance of this rule; as there is between printing books in Greek and selling them, or buying Greek books and reading them. Cultural history can tell us that the importance of Greek was frequently and vigorously asserted at these two periods in European history, but many other kinds of history—economic, social, educational, etc.—are necessary in order to answer how much Greek actually mattered then. In the absence of much of this history, I offer a guess: it seems likely that it was only in the mid-nineteenth century in England and Germany that the level of literacy in Greek was high enough for interests of large segments of literate classes to be crystallized around it.

Thirdly, two myths are routinely denounced in the study of Greek in the West after the fall of Rome: the myth that Greek was unreadable in the Middle Ages and the myth that Greek was restored to the West in 1453, after Constantinople fell to the Turks. As myths go, these may not be grossly misleading, but we should none the less recall that Greek was studied in Naples and at the papal curia and elsewhere in the Middle Ages, and we may agree that 1423 (say) has a better claim than 1453 to be a key date of the turning point in Western access to Greek.[25]

The recovery of Greek was a necessary part of the Italian Renaissance, since the emulation of Rome could not be accomplished without Greek. In Italy it was Leonzio Pilato and, far more, Manuel Chrysoloras, who along with their students made Greek part of humanistic studies. Even so, it is difficult to evaluate how great a part it played in humanism, how significant it was in the period.[26] The Italian hostility to contemporary Greeks, frequently expressed and often reciprocated, worked against a close attachment to their language. On the other hand, Greek has been seen as a key to the Renaissance, especially in the nineteenth century when the rebirth of Greek studies in Italy was sometimes connected to a pagan interpretation of the Renaissance.

With a few exceptions, the Italian engagement with Greek studies was not very deep. In general the Italians contributed very little to Greek scholarship, and mostly left it to the Greeks who had recently arrived in Italy. Politian and Valla are the obvious exceptions, but Politian died young, and the great work of Valla on the text of the New Testament was little known until Erasmus published it in 1505, more than fifty years after Valla's death. Perhaps the recovery of Plato and in particular Ficino's commentaries on Plato constitute the most distinctive Italian contribution to the reception of Greek literature.[27] In the Cinquecento, Greek was more often seen as a useful supplement to Latin. Whatever Pietro Bembo's youthful attachment to Greek, by the time of his most influential work he was valuing Greek as a way to give added distinction to one's command of Latin.[28] The view of Greek as supplementary is also implicit in Castiglione's advice that the courtier 'have not only the understandinge of the Latin tunge, but also of the Greeke, because of the many and sundrye thinges that with greate excellencye are written in it'.[29]

There is some evidence for Greek as an oral medium during the Italian Renaissance. Guarino and Filelfo learnt Greek in Constantinople and so had that active skill, though Guarino's effectiveness in transforming classroom ideals into practice has been challenged. Politian, who composed Greek verses, boasted that Florentines were speaking pure Attic Greek. In Venice, the circle around Aldus Manutius dreamt, at least, of exclusively using Greek for oral communication. When Baptista Mantuan's brother returned from Venice, he not only spoke with a Venetian accent, but also showed off some knowledge of spoken Greek. Burckhardt reports that Popes

Paul III and Paul IV spoke Greek.[30] How much real knowledge of classical Greek was involved in or implied by these boasts is difficult to determine, but they invite scepticism; as the scholar best informed about the subject argues, 'Even in Rome at this time men were increasingly unwilling to speak Latin, let alone Greek; so an obligation to speak only the latter cannot be intended seriously'.[31]

North of the Alps, Greek had further-reaching consequences. Humanism in general was a more polemical affair in the north, where humanists and theologians were housed in the same institution, the university. On no issue were the polemics fiercer than on the status of Greek. Erasmus (whose name, like Melanchthon's, is the hellenized form of his vernacular name) had galvanized European attention with his edition of the Greek New Testament (1516). Humanist claims for the value of Greek were sharply contested by traditional theologians, and though reformers were willing to make use of Greek when it served their ends, they were often hostile to Greek literature. The humanist devotion to antiquity and to Greek in particular was nearly impossible to sustain in the midst of the conflict of the languages that was at the heart of the imminent religious crisis.[32] In the first third of the sixteenth century in Northern Europe, virtually every opinion about the relative merits of Greek, Latin, Hebrew, and the vernacular was expressed or imputed to one's enemies. Sometimes it was Latin that was resisted, for example by Martin Bucer, who planned a school from which Latin would be excluded in favour of Greek and Hebrew, since he saw the Latin of the Catholic Church as a grab for political power.[33] More often it was Greek, knowledge of which was criticized as unnecessary, exhibitionist, and threatening.[34] (It was Hebrew, of course, that aroused the fiercest passions; the goal of Reuchlin's opponent Johann Pfefferkorn was to confiscate and destroy Hebrew books.)

Perhaps it was in France that both enthusiasm for Greek and hostility to it were most evident.[35] For several generations of French humanists, Greek had been a major preoccupation, and scholarship in Greek, translations from it, and the printing of it flourished in France. It has been asserted that even a superficial acquaintance with Greek was enough to secure the appointments of several of Francis I's bishops and diplomats.[36] Soon after its endowment the Collège de France became a college of the three languages (Greek and Hebrew in 1530, Latin from 1534), like the *collegium trilingue* established at Leuven in 1517, modelled in its turn on the trilingual college at the

University of Alcalá. None the less, resistance to Greek, usually emanating from the Sorbonne, was fierce. The zealous doctors of orthodoxy condemned both Erasmus' translation of the New Testament into Latin and Lefèvre d'Étaples's translation into French. Rabelais's books in Greek were so suspect to his Franciscan superiors that they confiscated them. The persecution Robert Estienne encountered in printing the folio Greek Testament of 1550 decided him to move to Geneva, where Henri Estienne continued the Greek scholarship and printing of his father. The son had a particularly strong attachment to Greek, believing he had found in it a means for France to escape the cultural dominance of Italy. In his *Conformité du langage françois avec le grec* (1565), he attempts to reveal the innate similarity of Greek and French; if French would cultivate its affinity with Greek, it would gain superiority over Italian, to the same degree that, 'as all men acknowledge', Greek surpasses Latin.[37] By this time in France, however, the opinion was unusual, and enthusiasm for Greek was rapidly declining.

This cultural and perhaps proto-nationalist appeal to Greek was to be fully developed in Germany in the nineteenth century; in France, Estienne's proposal fell into oblivion, philhellenism became rarer, and instruction in Greek was reduced in the course of the seventeenth century.[38] For one thing, it acquired an aura of Jansenism, or heresy more generally. For another, it was at odds with the way the literature developed. Boileau would rebuke the muse of Ronsard for speaking Greek and Latin, and Molière would be able to present the knowledge of Greek as the *ne plus ultra* of pretentiousness. In *Les Femmes savantes*, Trissotin introduces his friend Vadius to the learned ladies:

> TRISSOTIN:
> Il sait du grec, Madame, autant qu'homme de France.
> PHILAMINTE:
> Du grec, ô Ciel; du grec! Il sait du grec, ma sœur!
> BÉLISE:
> Ah! ma nièce! du grec!
> > ARMANDE:
> > Du grec! quelle douceur!

In addition to heresy, Greek now bore with it the presumption of pedantry.

In Johnson's England, knowledge of Greek might be displayed without fear of heresy because the Anglican Church was the major institutional support of the language. Greek scholarship 'was regarded as a suitable adornment for clergymen outside the ranks of the universities and schools, and a fit and proper ground for promotion to high ecclesiastical dignity'.[39] The connection between the Church of England and Greek would last well into the nineteenth century; it was fame and ambition that drove Crabbe's curate to weigh the Greek page, add note on note, and dream of his Euripides' edition (*The Borough*, letter iii, ll. 206–11). Even outside the church, Greek had a certain social cachet in the eighteenth and early nineteenth century. Dr Johnson remarked that Greek is like lace, and every man wants as much of it as he can get. Lord Chesterfield insisted that his son learn Greek: 'It is Greek that must distinguish you in the learned world, Latin alone will not' (letter cxxii, 1750). Yet we should not infer that knowledge of Greek was widespread. Parson Adams of *Joseph Andrews* loves the language, but Fielding makes it clear that such loving proficiency in Greek was not usual: even the name 'Aeschylus' is beyond the gentleman who sought to test Adams's classical knowledge (book iii, chapter 2). In the introduction to *A Journey from this World to the Next*, the narrator relays Adams's opinion that nothing was commoner 'for Men now-a-days to pretend to have read *Greek* Authors, who have met with them only in Translations, and cannot conjugate a Verb in *mi*'. It was rare to quote Greek in Parliament, and when Viscount Belgrave did so in 1788, he was mocked for it.[40]

In Germany in the eighteenth century writers are repeatedly urged to imitate Greek, and the innate affinity between Greek and German is repeatedly affirmed.[41] Greek became a way of asserting German independence from French (and therefore Latin) cultural models; by the nineteenth century, it had become tied to German national aspirations. In sharp contrast with British hellenism, a peculiar intensity marked the German engagement with classics. Christopher Stray offers this comparison:[42]

The upper-middle-class social groups in Germany who carried the ideology of romantic Hellenism were politically weak, widely scattered members of a society which was not yet a nation. Against the Roman classicizing of the Gallic tradition they constructed a Hellenic ideal whose utopian nature reflected their own distance from the sites of power and the political fragmentation of Germany. . . . In England the less precarious situation of a prosperous middle class led to a variant of classics which was engaged with existing social forms rather than with a transformative mission. The resulting emphasis on manners and style, the acquisition of social markers which made social recognition easier, led to the development of a domesticated Hellenism which was more at home in the world of ordinary appearances and social style.

Gradually the German sense of mission did become domesticated. When Wilhelm von Humboldt initiated his university reforms, he made Greek an integral part of academic life, in the belief that such knowledge would not only provide Germans with the ability to free themselves from the French cultural dominance but would also lead to national unity and personal wholeness. Things did not work out exactly as planned, and an elaborate bureaucratic structure developed around the university to house and reward the study of Greek; *Altertumswissenschaft* replaced *Gräkomanie*.[43] It was not until mid-century that competent instruction in Greek reached a sufficient number of people that a social group could be defined by its ability to read Greek, it seems, the 'Homer-reading lawyers and Sophocles-quoting merchants'; even among them, instruction in Latin had been a more central aspect of their education.[44]

In England from the second half of the eighteenth century, Greece started to be perceived in new ways. A visual dimension was restored to it: Stuart's and Revett's classical archaeology, the new Doric style in architecture, the Greek Revival generally, Winckelmann's philosophical aesthetics rooted in Greece and his history of Greek art, the Elgin Marbles displayed in the British Museum from 1816, enabled a public to envisage ancient Greece. Other factors, too, were at work in drawing the public's attention to Greece: the Greek war of independence, a newly emergent Romantic hellenism, and the enthusiasm of radical democrats who equated Athens with liberty.[45] Greece emerged from a generalized sense of antiquity, of 'Greece and Rome', to become an autonomous object of interest in its own right.

Yet to focus on, say, the hellenic enthusiasms of Byron, Shelley, or Keats gives a misleading picture of the age. Greek continued to be poorly taught in the universities and schools,[46] and it remained largely the province of Anglican churchman and amateur gentleman until mid-century. Thomas Gaisford is notorious for having encouraged the study of Greek literature 'which not only elevates above the vulgar herd, but leads not infrequently to positions of considerable emolument', but as Christopher Stray has pointed out, the statement expressed a simple truth: the Anglican Church had livings at its disposal for which knowledge of Greek was thought indispensable.

Stray carefully plots the transformation of the social underpinnings of classics, and especially Greek, in the course of the century: it changed, gradually and contestedly, from being the concern mainly of Anglican churchmen and amateur gentlemen to being the means to form academics and the civil service elite. Throughout the educational system, instruction in English, Latin, and Greek would be pressed into service as a means to delineate social distinction and social class.[47] The social transformation of Greek was accompanied by a cultural one: ancient Athens, especially after the publication of Grote's history, would come to serve as a model for Britain's imperial democracy.[48] Even the system of accentuating ancient Greek could be made to serve a social function: it became a way of excluding women from male intellectual life, or at least of intimidating them. Elizabeth Barrett Browning has Aurora Leigh's cousin Romney remark scornfully of 'lady's Greek without the accents'. In *Middlemarch*, Casaubon is dismissive of Dorothea when she asks him about Greek accents, and as a result she suffers 'a painful suspicion that here indeed there might be secrets not capable of explanation to a woman's reason'.[49] Greek had joined Latin as a means to solidify group identities.

In the twentieth century, the demise of Greek as a social badge came very rapidly. Take two statements by J. W. Mackail: 1911, 'The position of Greek as a factor in culture has never been more assured than it is now', 1923, 'Times change; fashions vary; beliefs alter . . . fifty years ago, when I was a schoolboy, the value of Greek was taken for granted . . . Now we are in a new world. Nothing stands still'.[50] Compulsory Greek had come to an end in Cambridge in 1919.

In England as in Germany, the range of responses to Greece and to Greek in writers was very wide. The literary responses to Greek cannot simply be equated with the social functions of Greek, but they are connected, even in those writers who resist them, like Browning, Eliot, and Hardy. We become better readers of the vernacular when we realize that Greek, like Latin, is not a language whose history came to an end in antiquity; the presence of Greek and Latin in modern literature is not only an allusion to the ancients but also comments on contemporary readers of the ancients.

To insist that medieval and Renaissance literature ought to be considered in a bilingual environment, that is, of Latin and at least one vernacular, is not controversial; [51] such an acknowledgement cannot be avoided since Gower, More, Bacon, Campion, Hobbes, Herbert, Milton, and Crashaw all wrote books in Latin (to take examples from English writers alone), and since so many poets wrote some Latin verse, until at least the end of the eighteenth century. However, multilingual literature did not come to an end in 1700, and moreover the entire range of readers' and writers' linguistic abilities in other languages, from a masterly command to a smattering, is involved in their reading and writing.

One end of the range is the full, native proficiency in more than one language. Skill in neo-Latin very occasionally reached this level. The most famous example is Montaigne, whose father not only placed him in the care of a German tutor with excellent Latin and no French but also learnt (along with the rest of his household) enough Latin so that the boy was always addressed in that language ('De l'institution des enfans'). Though he fell out of the active practice of Latin while still in school, he still refers to it as his maternal language. Very high claims about his bilingualism have been made. Ann Moss, for example, believes that because of it Montaigne 'can move his French over the linguistic divide and make it speak from the position of ancient culture', and through this imaginative projection comes to recognize that culture 'as alien and indeed as incommensurate with one's own native culture'. Montaigne, she argues, is therefore able to write sympathetically about ancient homosexual practices despite what he calls the just abhorrence of his society towards that culture. She suggests that bilingualism gave Montaigne a certain 'cognitive flexibility' which is evident in his scepticism and in his awareness of the limitations of European culture. With bilingualism, one is able 'to inhabit two radically different conceptual schemes imaginatively', while translation is 'at best an inadequate, at worst an aggressive act'.[52]

I believe Moss is in error when she describes, not Montaigne's scepticism, but his bilingualism. It is not only the ancient world to which Montaigne's Latin gave him access; Latin was also a part of his own social order. From one perspective his Latin may have allowed him a certain cognitive flexibility; from another, Latin was a limit to Montaigne's imagination. In his time Latin was the monopoly of clerics and gentlemen, and Montaigne vehemently supported this monopoly, believing that the licence to spread religious opinions, or the Bible itself, in the vernacular was more dangerous than useful, and further believing that those of the lower sort would be unable to use the fruits of such knowledge wisely.[53] By seeing Latin solely in reference to antiquity rather than as a language with contemporary social implications, Moss mistakes Montaigne. He was a gentleman, and his entitlement formed part of a secure ground from which he was able to range his sceptical intelligence so freely, so penetratingly, over his society in other respects. If this is a limitation, it may be a limitation inherent in scepticism.

Moss's vocabulary about bilingualism is anachronistic. The notion that languages embody unique conceptual schemes is a Romantic view of language, and if you take the phrase 'conceptual scheme' seriously enough, it is obviously untrue (how could you possibly know that somebody has a conceptual scheme different from yours, or a conceptual scheme at all, if you can't translate it into terms you know?).[54] At any rate, the notion became far more influential centuries later when national and political identities were more closely connected to cultural and linguistic ones. Charles d'Orléans (this is Leonard Forster's example[55]) spent twenty-five years in an English prison, passing his time learning English and creating a parallel poetic œuvre in English. He had no sense of disloyalty to France in writing English, and this was typical of an age when the relations between language, country, and identity were looser than in later times. Language loyalty has been most intense whenever it has been enjoined by the political forces of nationalism. Forster dates the shift in attitudes about language loyalty to the nineteenth century, sometime between 1784, when Beckford wrote *Vathek* in French (which did not seem particularly odd to the public, especially when compared to the rest of his behaviour) and 1895, when Wilde wrote *Salomé* in French, which was thought to be a scandal.

We should describe bilingualism in terms less exalted than Moss's. It gave writers the option to choose a language in order to reach, or to elude, a particular audience; Latin, in particular, was available both to enlarge one's audience in one respect (as when religious controversialists like Luther, Calvin, Milton, and many others chose the international language) and to restrict it in another (by excluding the Latin-less from discussions of sensitive matters). It also provided writers the opportunity to emulate in one language desired features of the literature in another, as vernacular authors did when they imitated Latin during the Renaissance, a time when Latin literature offered writers new literary possibilities, from the magnificence of the high style to the urbanely bawdy, and models that ranged from ornate declamations to friendly chats.

I have, so far, been concentrating on the high end of proficiency within literary multilingualism. Yet even the best neo-Latin writers had a restricted Latin, and often a very restricted Latin, if we compare their Latin with that of the ancient Romans. Multilingual knowledge is not like a key which a writer either does or does not possess; it has gradations; we must consider the entire range of bilingualism or else neglect many literary aspects of the phenomenon. The topic of literary multilingualism is large; I would like to offer an initial taxonomy arranged according to the proportions of the languages in the works, from an œuvre balanced in two or more languages at one end to works including foreign words or phrases at the other end. To organize the material by the proportion of the foreign language has the advantage of being objective, independent of our analysis of the examples; moreover, it keeps different kinds of linguistic phenomenon distinct and makes the lines of historical development clearer. My goal has been to choose examples which are familiar, not obscure, and which are rewarding to consider in the light of their language choices. I am not attempting to provide a comprehensive catalogue but to provide examples suggestive of the range and importance of literary multilingualism.

Even among multilingual writers, those who produce a multilingual œuvre are a minority, and within that group the number of those whose literary work is memorable in more than one language is tiny. Anyone in Latin? Milton wrote some of the greatest neo-Latin poems ever, but his poetry (unlike the controversial writings) is better discussed not in the category of the multilingual œuvre but in that of the multilingual work. Du Bellay is a better example:[56] in 1558 his *Poemata* appeared along with *Les Regrets* and the *Antiquitez de Rome*. In a poem from the Latin collection, he refers to his French Muse as his wife and his Latin Muse as his mistress;[57] actually, his French and Latin poems are on much better terms than that comparison ordinarily implies. His lyric cycles in French take some of their substance from his Latin poetry, generally written first. Even if we should agree with many literary critics that the French poems are more deserving of our admiration (no one has preferred the *Patriae desiderium* to 'Heureux qui, comme Ulysse, a fait un beau voyage'), paying attention to the interplay between the French and Latin versions helps us to understand not only particular poems but also the integrity of lyric cycles, as poems are recast to fit in a new context. Self-translation is a phenomenon unique to multilingualism; it requires readers to have a pragmatically flexible notion of what makes a work or what counts as an original.[58] This is as true of Beckett or Nabokov as of Du Bellay; as on a smaller scale it is true of Marvell, whose 'The Garden' and 'On a Drop of Dew' exist alongside 'Hortus' and 'Ros', and of Cowper, who wrote a Latin translation of 'The Cast-away', and others.

When authors choose the language in which they write, their choices should be investigated because the choice implies that the language of a work could have been different, and one of the things literary criticism may do is answer the question of why a work is as it is and not otherwise. Some of the reasons motivating language choices are the same as they have ever been. Both French and English now, as Latin in the past, have been a way for writers to reach a larger audience, or to work in a medium of greater literary prestige. Writers, like everyone else, are subject to the economic, social, religious, and political forces that displace people and may make them multilingual. Writers, like everyone else, may discover elective affinities with languages. Other motivations for choosing a language may change over time, generally to be replaced by other sorts of choices; for example, social exclusion in English now takes place more often by changes in register (high or low, either choice may express social exclusivity) than by switching to Latin or French (*pas devant les enfants*). In other linguistic environments, diglossia (the situation in which two varieties of a language are spoken) may have social implications analogous to those of multilingualism. What matters is to be aware that language choices are sometimes statements of allegiance to values. Leonard Forster reads Rilke's late French poems as a declaration of the value not of French culture or the French literary tradition, but of the countryside of the Canton Valais, where he spent his last years. Rilke's early French poems are minor exercises; the later French poems, on the other hand, are written in the mature style which we recognize from the great German sequences. During his walks in the Swiss countryside, these poems came to him unbidden, Rilke writes, like the more famous German works. He was concerned with finding the voice of the landscape, and he heard that voice speaking French.[59]

Having studied the multilingual œuvre, let us next consider the multilingual book, which comes in many guises. An obvious one is

the bilingual text, as for example a text with a facing-page translation. This includes books like the volumes of the Loeb library, but it
can also be used more playfully, as in Pope's *Imitations of Horace*.
These poems, no less great and hardly more Horatian than the *Moral
Essays* of the same decade, have a dynamic, lively relation to the
Latin poems, sometimes taking no more than a cue from Horace that
is then developed by giving a modern story in place of the Roman
one. The Latin *en face* to Pope's English invites readers to mark the
constant interplay between them, especially since Pope even goes to
the trouble of arranging the Latin on the page so that the sections in
the Latin poems are located at the same height as the corresponding
English sections on the facing page. In the words of James
McLaverty, 'Pope's parallel texts balance the general equivalence of
Latin and English created by the typography with particular detailed
comparisons'.[60]

Another bilingual format is adopted by books containing poems in
different languages where the poems are arranged by language, not
en face. As recently as 1943, Douglas Young published *Auntran
Blads*, in which he added German, Greek, French, and Latin poems
at the end. The most famous example, however, must be Milton's
Poems of 1645, that is, *Poems of Mr John Milton, both English and
Latin, Compos'd at several times*. The Latin poems constitute a book
within this book, with their own title-page, commendatory notices,
and page numeration; the arrangement is preserved in the edition
of 1673. The English part of the book includes Italian sonnets, and
the Latin part includes some Greek ones. The critic John Hale has
offered the most sensitive analysis of Milton's multilingualism,
pointing out that bilingual volumes by a single author were rare and
that Milton's volume was unique in offering a bilingual work equi-
pollent in two languages. Milton plays his humanist role seriously,
and serious playing (*serio ludere*), Hale reminds us, is one reason
why Milton tries out varied linguistic masks: Italian for the love
sonnets (his lady spoke Italian), and Greek as evidence of the breadth
of his humanist education (and, as two Greek poems follow immediately after 'Ad Patrem', they may be taken as a vindication of his
father's support of his studies). The Latin poems are opportunities to
assume other masks, variously self-revealing: the ambitious, perhaps
boastful humanist (the title page announces that most of the poems
were written before he was 20); a man committed to Italian humanist values; the poet commemorating the loss of a friend, with whom

he used to communicate in Latin; an Ovidian; Virgilian; patriot; Christian.[61]

However, I would also remark on the continuity between Milton's greatest Latin poems and his greatest English ones. Hale points out that both halves of Milton's *Poems* end with an elegy, 'Lycidas' and the 'Epitaphium Damonis' respectively; that is, he expresses unyielding grief and anger twice within a pastoral landscape, privileging neither English nor Latin. Moreover, not only is the tenor of the two poems alike, but also specific passages within the Latin are reminiscent of his English poetry. For example, his love of twilight imagery, especially of shadows cast by trees at twilight ('The Nimphs in twilight shade of tangled thickets mourn'; 'arched walks of twilight groves, I And shadows brown that Sylvan loves I Of Pine, or monumental Oake'), is not less beautifully expressed in the 'Epitaphium Damonis': 'supra caput imber & Eurus I Triste sonant, fractaeque agitata crepuscula silvae'. More generally, the very greatest Latin poems of English poets, rather than being an opportunity for poets to assume new, Latin-based personae, share the concerns of the author's English œuvre. George Herbert's poem on the death of his mother, the one beginning *Parvam piamque dum lubenter semitam*, has been compared to 'The Collar' in its 'dramatic reversal from acute distress to meek acceptance of God's will at the bidding of an unmistakable *quispiam*'.[62] Filial piety and love find direct expression in Samuel Johnson's 'In Rivum a Mola Stoana Lichfeldiae Diffluentem'. In these poems by Johnson and Herbert, as in Milton's greatest Latin poems, the ancient language did not serve as a mask but was a precondition for their most personal utterances.

For another kind of bilingual work, we might consider literary works in which languages are thoroughly mingled, a hymn like 'In dulci jubilo', or certain medieval sermons and plays, to say nothing of the notorious 'Hisperic' latinity of the *Hisperica Famina* or *Lorica*. Or we might survey the strange genre of macaronic epic which originated in Italy toward the end of the fifteenth century and subsequently spread throughout Europe (Teofilo Folengo's *Baldus*, 'the masterpiece of the genre', was also the most influential example of it).[63] Instead, we will stick to better-known works: Montaigne's *Essaies* and Burton's *Anatomy of Melancholy*. Sentences or verses in Latin are found on almost every page of those works; quotation in Latin is essential to them. Yet the Latin feels very different in the two.

Montaigne's love of books is on easy terms with his contempt of bookishness 'Je ne dis les autres, sinon pour d'autant plus me dire' ('De l'institution des enfans'). It was some lines of Virgil that led him to investigate sexuality in his innovative way ('Sur des vers de Virgile'). Note, however, that the Latin is rarely translated. Latin is not simply an alternate voice in which the bilingual Montaigne expresses himself, but it often is also a *cordon sanitaire* against inappropriate readership.

Robert Burton does not have a consistent method for presenting his Latin quotations. He sometimes quotes in Latin; sometimes follows the Latin with an English translation, interpretation, or paraphrase; sometimes gives the entire quotation only in English; and sometimes gives part of the quotation in English, and part in Latin. Nor is his attitude to his Latin sources and citations consistent. He regrets that his publishers forced him to write in English, but none of his Latin writings are at all memorable. He avows that, while others get their knowledge out of books, he knows his subject through experience, but he makes this avowal in a quotation, and besides his book is made out of quotations. He apologizes for quoting other authors so much, and points to the organization of his material as his own contribution; but elsewhere he continually apologizes for his lack of organization. The book is maddeningly excessive; so is the Latin within it. The play of learned wit is the exuberant tradition of Burton, not Montaigne, despite the centrality of Latin quotation to both authors.

Gibbon's *The History of the Decline and Fall of the Roman Empire* may be adduced as another sort of bilingual work: the text is in English but the notes are in English, French, Greek, and Latin. The footnotes in ancient languages gained a degree of notoriety because of Gibbon's defence of his work in the *Autobiography*: 'My English text is chaste, and all licentious passages are left in the decent obscurity of a learned language'. Latin and Greek are indeed used when sexual matters are discussed, yet the English is not nearly as infrigidative as Gibbon implies. Here is the Empress Faustina, the wife of Marcus Aurelius (vol. i, ch. 4): 'The Cupid of the ancients was, in general, a very sensual deity; and the amours of an empress, as they exact on her side the plainest advances, are seldom susceptible of much sentimental delicacy'. Now the footnote is hardly licentious, even after italicizing *conditiones* ('affairs, liaisons'): 'Faustinam satis constat apud Cayetam, *conditiones* sibi et nauticas et gladiatorias, elegisse'.[64] Of the Empress Theodora, Gibbon writes (vol. iv, ch. 45): 'After exhausting the arts of sensual pleasure, she most ungratefully murmured against the parsimony of Nature; but her murmurs, her pleasures, and her arts, must be veiled in the obscurity of a learned language'. His footnote is bilingual: 'At a memorable supper, thirty slaves waited round the table; ten young men feasted with Theodora. Her charity was *universal*. Et lassata viris, necdum satiata, recessit'.[65] Gibbon's Latin and Greek are present mainly as part of the scholarly apparatus and occasionally to provide an aura of the forbidden.[66] The fact that the quotation is in Latin, even apart from the content of the quotation, is itself suggestive of sexual licence; in the next century Baudelaire knew this perfectly well when he decided to entitle his sonnet 'Sed non satiata'.

The final bilingual works to be discussed include major Anglo-American modernist poems: Ezra Pound's *Cantos*, David Jones's *The Anathémata*, Hugh MacDiarmid's *In Memoriam James Joyce*, and others. No short discussion of the topic or these works is possible, so I will limit my remarks to Pound. The many citations in foreign languages in the *Cantos* are not without precedent. To some extent, Pound's practice is a radicalization of Browning's; both poets quote in foreign languages because they are acting from a principle of historical documentation intended to make the past present. Pound goes further than Browning by giving more quotations (including prose) and by offering them on their own, with fewer guideposts and translations. In addition, Pound turns to Latin and Greek because they have a sacred or mystical status for him, as they did for mystically inclined writers in the nineteenth century. Passages in which he expresses his vision of the sacred often reach an intense pitch through a Greek or Latin utterance: *Aram nemus vult* (c. 74, c. 78), Δρύας (c. 83), χθονός (c. 82, cf. c. 74). Take the last example: the word 'chthonic' had its English origin in nineteenth-century studies of primitive religion, and Pound, like other writers of his generation, was influenced by the new anthropology. He uses the Greek word to present a sacred understanding of the earth, not as the mediated recovery of scholars, but as immediate and direct, by appealing to the earth through the language in which it had once been sanctified.[67] It is also the language the heart cries out in, as Pound's tears are recorded in Greek, δακρύων, in several of the *Pisan Cantos*. In contrast, T. S. Eliot uses ancient languages most often to indicate death or paralysis (as in the epigraph to *The Waste Land*, or 'Mr Eliot's Sunday Morning Service').

Multilingual units within the book are the next topic: a chapter in a novel, a scene in a drama, a poem in a collection. A number of works that incorporate Latin in this way are satirizing the power of Latin, especially among doctors, priests, and lawyers. For example, in two plays Molière makes comedy out of the Latin gibberish which patients want to hear from doctors and which doctors wish to give them. Sganarelle in *Le Medecin malgré lui*, after throwing together some Latin, some words of his own coinage, and a misquotation from a Latin grammar, is applauded and admired by the attendants of a patient. *Le Malade imaginaire* concludes with a burlesque degree-granting ceremony in semi-Latin where the Bachelierus answers all the questions put to him with 'Clysterium donare, Postea seignare, Ensuitta purgare'.

In Thomas Kyd's *The Spanish Tragedy*, Latin plays a crucial role. The drama is concerned with the true status of the nobility, from whom it strips any claim to legitimacy. The very word 'nobility' is emptied of any noble sense and revealed to be simply amoral force in Hieronymo's angry and impotent lines:

> Nor ought auailes it me to menace them,
> Who as a wintrie storme vpon a plaine,
> Will beare me downe with their nobilitie.

(Act 3, scene 13)

Latin is a sign of noble rank, but it is not restricted to noblemen. It is certainly used to flatter the king ('O multum dilecte Deo'), but it is also the language of Hieronymo; Latin, that is, appears at first to be a medium in which Hieronymo and the nobility can meet on mutually respectful (though not equal) terms. The appearance of mutual duties and rights deceived him; his son is killed, and Hieronymo speaks a Latin dirge for him in which the accent of pain is dramatized, not suppressed, by assembling tags from the ancient writers. He plots his revenge by devising one of the most explicit multilingual moments in English literature: his playlet is to be performed by characters each speaking a different language (Latin, Greek, Italian, and French). The immediate point is to create confusion so that Balthazar and Lorenzo can be killed; the larger point is that the meaningless Babel of tongues is the kind of language produced by and suited to an amoral, meaningless social order. When T. S. Eliot quotes from this play in his own multilingual confusion of tongues at the end of of *The Waste Land,* his allusion forcefully recalls Kyd's vision.

In the novel *Tristram Shandy,* much of the humour is created by Sterne's continual interplay between highly stylized Latinate passages (often spoken by Walter Shandy) and no less stylized plain passages (often spoken by Corporal Trim). But Sterne does not confine himself to foreign-sounding English; he gives two chapters with extensive Latin (with *en face* translation into English), and one chapter with French. Perhaps the most famous of the three is the curse of Bishop Ernulphus. We laugh at its absurd excess ('Maledictus sit vivendo, moriendo, manducando, bibendo, esuriendo, sitiendo, jejunando, dormitando, dormiendo, vigilando, ambulando, stando, sedendo, jacendo, operando, quiescendo, mingendo, cacando, flebotomando'), as we do at the absurdity of the Sorbonne doctors who debate (in French) whether it is necessary for birth to precede christening. The humour exposes the emptiness of those pretences of knowledge guarded by erudition. Catholic pretension to authoritative knowledge is a favourite target of Sterne, especially in the earlier books.

Molière uses Latin to go after doctors, Kyd the nobility, and Sterne to mock Catholic authority; Browning uses Latin to depict lawyers unsparingly. Two of the books in *The Ring and the Book* are told from the perspective of lawyers, and both are filled with Latin, generally taken verbatim from Browning's source and usually accompanied by Browning's translation. Since Latin is the medium in which the lawyers work, Browning tries to make poetry out of the jargon of legal Latin. Though he admits to the satisfaction he had in emphasizing both lawyers' buffoonery, Browning is at pains to distinguish the personality and character of Dominus Hyacinthus de Archangelis, the defence lawyer, from that of Juris Doctor Johannes-Baptista Bottinius, the prosecutor. Bottini is vain, ambitious, and greedy, all of which traits are revealed in the main activity of his profession, Latin speechifying. Archangeli may be initially more attractive: he is a family man, more gluttonous than cut-throat. When his young son uses *qui* with the subjunctive, it brings tears to his eyes. We see him at work practising his Latin:

> Count Guido married—or, in Latin due,
> What? *Duxit in uxorem?*—commonplace!
> *Tædas jugales iniit, subiit,*—ha!

He underwent the matrimonial torch?
Connubio stabili sibi junxit,—hum!
In stable bond of marriage bound his own?
That's clear of any modern taint: and yet . . .

Archangeli is less manifestly despicable, but for him the case is largely an opportunity to show off his Latin; he is not very interested in
justice, or human affairs outside his family and circle. His own Latin
words make us aware of the gulf that separates his decent instincts as
a family man from his professional indifference to suffering.

A last example (one of many possible examples) is the Latin poem
that Baudelaire includes in *Les Fleurs du Mal*: 'Franciscæ Meæ
Laudes', subtitled 'vers composé pour une modiste érudite et dévote'
and a parody of hymns like the *Stabat Mater*. He appends a note
justifying his choice of late Latin: 'dans cette merveilleuse langue,
le solécisme et le barbarisme me paraissent rendre les négligences
forcées d'une passion qui s'oublie et se moque des règles'. By choosing Latin, Baudelaire manages at once to be blasphemous, create a
sexual atmosphere, and indicate the class barrier. (Also, the poem
does not scan, a consequence presumably of the French failure to
read Latin accentual poetry metrically.)

Next, let us take examples of multilingualism in smaller units of
literary composition: paragraphs in prose works, lines in verse. The
Latin in Rabelais's *Gargantua et Pantagruel* is put to a variety of
uses, nowhere more effectively than in parodying scholastic disputations. Among the Latin titles in the library of St Victor's, Pantagruel
finds the *Questio subtilissima, utrum Chimera, in vacuo bombinans,
possit comedere secundas intentiones*, a mocking question only
slightly less famous and influential than the question about angels
and the head of a pin.[68] However, the chapter in which multilingualism is most on display is the one where Pantagruel meets Panurge. In
response to Pantagruel's questions, Panurge answers Pantagruel in
thirteen languages (including a couple of invented ones) before
switching to French, his native language, as well as Pantagruel's. The
joke has some of the absurdity of an Irish bull ('if you can't read this,
have it read to you'), and it copiously exemplifies the humanist goal
of *copia*. Most of all, it underlines the physical presence and the fact
of languages, a fascination that recurs in other chapters, where communication takes place by signs or by counterfeiting French. It is
most memorable in the fourth book, when Panurge and Pantagruel
are sailing near the Arctic Ocean and the latter throws handfuls of

frozen words, like candies of variegated colours, to the deck, where they melt and make barbarous sounds. We might note in passing that a multilingualism focused on the physical weight and presence of languages is important for another scatological dealer in absurdities with a penchant for invented languages, Jonathan Swift. For both writers, human language is as much a part of our physical existence as the other ways that our bodies exist in society.

It was the ability to speak French, not Latin, that distinguished the gentry of England, Prussia, and Russia in the nineteenth century, and novels that treat of this class often include French, sometimes for several paragraphs. The first few pages of *War and Peace* include whole paragraphs in French, and the very beginning of the novel is in French. French is the language of Petersburg and embodies the values of Petersburg society, who are contrasted in the course of the novel with a greater Russian value, and French comes to appear as a betrayal of Russia. English novelists do not write in French at the length at which Tolstoy does. Perhaps it is Charlotte Brontë who incorporates the longest French dialogues within English novels, but she does this not to delineate class behaviour but to indicate the presence of francophone foreigners, Adèle Varens in *Jane Eyre*, Robert Moore and his sister in *Shirley*. In the latter novel, the presence of French is far-reaching: the disruptions of industrialization are shown to be international, which accounts for the presence of the Belgian Moore; Yorkshire gentlemen are depicted as stubborn individualists devoted to their own predilections, which accounts for Mr Yorke's impeccable French; and young women learn French, which explains why Caroline Helstone is tutored by Moore's sister. The French is not just a way of driving the plot and motivating characters; it also contributes to the novel's examination of the difference between patriotism and different kinds of parochialism. Moore's sister is parochial, as we see in her unthinking loyalty to the language. The fluent French of Yorke is shown to be essentially a private affair of his own, not an enlargement of sympathies. Moore's first step beyond his self-interested work takes place when he reads *Coriolanus* with Caroline, who would like him to share her love of English literature. After a few long French dialogues, and some quotations from French poetry, Brontë later dispenses with all but a few French phrases—the more usual practice for nineteenth-century novelists.

There is a famous paragraph in French in Joyce's *Finnegans Wake*,

consisting of a single sentence taken from Edgar Quinet and representing Joyce's own view of history:

Aujourd'hui comme aux temps de Pline et de Columelle la jacinthe se plaît
dans les Gaules, la pervenches en Illyrie, la marguérite sur les ruines de
Numance et pendant qu'autour d'elles les villes ont changé de maîtres et de
noms, que plusieurs sont entrées dans le néant, que les civilisations se sont
choquées et brisées, leurs paisibles générations ont traversé les âges et se sont
arrivées jusqu'à nous, fraîches et riantes comme aux jours des batailles.

Joyce admired the beauty of the sentence, and had memorized it; it
runs through the *Wake* in a number of parodies and allusions. When
the unparodied, untranslated French appears in that semantic play-
ground, its clarity gives Joyce's major concerns a uniquely concentrated brief expression. As a result, it reverses the usual relation
between foreign and native, since in that context the French appears
transparent and the English foreign.[69] (The two Latin passages in the
book, in contrast, are local affairs, without the echoes and parodies
which Quinet's French set into motion throughout Joyce's novel.)

Turning next to verse, recall how often Dante incorporates Latin
into the *Commedia*: from the Satanic parody of the *Vexilla regis*
in the *Inferno*, to the cluster of passages from the Vulgate that are
quoted towards the end of the *Purgatorio* (joined, in canto 30, to a
farewell verse to Virgil quoted from his own Latin), to the hymns and
scriptures quoted in the *Paradiso*, including the time when the spirits
of the just assume a shape that spells out a text from the Vulgate in
Gothic letters (canto 18). However, the most striking multilingual
moment in Dante's *Commedia* occurs in canto 26 of the *Purgatorio*,
where Arnaut Daniel answers Dante's question in eight lines of
Provençal, an indication of the extraordinarily high prestige that
language held for Italians and itself a moving tribute to Daniel.

Latin is used freely in English medieval and Renaissance poetry. In
poems by Langland and Skelton, entire lines of Latin are included,
sometimes constituting a refrain, where the skill is in adapting the
repeated line to new contexts and pressures in each stanza. In
William Dunbar's most famous poem, traditionally known as the
'Lament for the Makaris', the refrain is taken from the Office for
the Dead, *timor mortis conturbat me*. He uses Latin refrains in
other poems, and this particular refrain had been used in a fifteenth-
century carol and in a poem by John Lydgate. None the less, the
liturgical, communal import of the refrain has a new intensity in this

lyric as Dunbar imaginatively rethinks the *danse macabre* tradition and gives a dramatic shape to a catalogue which he extends to include his own poetic forebears. But he had few successors; subsequently perhaps only Wyatt writes a Latin refrain with equal power. In 'Who lyst his welthe and ease retayne', Wyatt, taking a phrase from Seneca, positions the refrain in the second half of the final line in each stanza: 'circa Regna tonat'. The poem is said to have been written when Wyatt, from the Tower, watched the execution of Anne Boleyn. Seneca's Latin, in the words of Geoffrey Hill, 'rounds off each of the five stanzas—a death-blow and a death-bell'.[70] After Wyatt, poems containing individual lines in another language are rare. Such lines occur in the comedy of Pope and Byron, and in Browning for historical scene-setting, but in all three poets the most significant multilingual effects occur in phrases, not lines (and also, in the case of Browning's *The Ring and the Book*, in longer passages).

There is a shift in the practice of modernist poets. Pound in the *Cantos* enlarged the scope of multilingualism in poetry by including entire passages in foreign languages, and Eliot extended it in *The Waste Land* in many individual lines. Yet the reasons for Pound's and Eliot's foreign quotations are different. Pound is most interested in making the past live, so that the words of Malatesta or Confucius, for example, appear contemporary with our words and world. Eliot wants to make the most of the foreign as foreign. 'One marked feature of the foreign eruptions within *The Waste Land*', Christopher Ricks observes, 'is their initiating themselves as not only foreign but about foreignness: first a Lithuanian speaking German about not being Russian, and then, twenty lines later, someone singing in German about his Irish girl, "Mein Irisch Kind"'.[71] Moreover, the Sanskrit at the end has its point in the fact that it is foreign, something no longer available within a post-Christian culture, that is, something not less strange to us than 'our equivalent' to *shantih*, 'the peace which passeth understanding', now is.

What about works with a title in a foreign language? One of the most famous examples is perplexing. Why did Milton choose the Italian titles 'L'Allegro' and 'Il Penseroso'? The poems draw primarily on Shakespeare, secondarily on Spenser. Perhaps the metrical form of the ten-line prelude to each poem owes something to the Italian canzone (the preludes alternate lines of six and ten syllables, and canzoni alternate lines of seven and eleven syllables), but after the preludes, the poems owe nothing more to Italian. The language of the titles ought to be seen as an expression of Milton's proclivity toward Italy, his orientation and allegiance towards Italian humanism, and as a promise to be redeemed in future work. In contrast, the Italian of Donne's *La Corona* makes explicit its debt to Italian practice (for example, Annibal Caro's 'Corona'),[72] perhaps suggesting a continuity with traditional and popular worship while adapting that worship to Anglican norms.

Latin titles are particularly common, as we might expect, in religious works: Dryden's *Religio Laici*, Browne's *Religio Medici*, Smart's *Jubilate Agno*, Newman's *Apologia pro vita sua*, and perhaps Wilde's *De Profundis*. Smart's title is notably inventive: he combines the Old Testament God (the opening of Psalm 100, *Jubilate Deo*) with the New Testament Christ, *Agnus Dei*. He suggests here in miniature what he does at length in his translation of the Psalms, namely work out his own harmony between the Testaments. In Victor Hugo, the Latin titles frequently have a mystical aura, spiritual rather than doctrinal. In the *Châtiments*, they offer themselves as sacred words freed from or struggling against priestly and kingly perversion: 'Nox', 'Sacer Esto', 'Ultima Verba', 'Lux'. The mystical associations of Latin also motivated the title of a famous Russian Romantic lyric, 'Silentium' by Fedor Tiutchev, an appropriate choice since in addition to aggrandizing silence, Latin in some sense embodies it, as a language hardly spoken in Orthodox lands. Mandelstam's 'Silentium' not only alludes to Tiutchev's, but the Latin title, like his French title 'Notre Dame' (also in *Stone*) expresses his allegiance to European culture, his 'nostalgia for world culture'. In Baudelaire, the Latin titles have mystical, sexual, and blasphemous connotations: 'Mæsta et errabunda', 'Sed non satiata', 'Semper eadem', 'De profundis clamavi'. In *Poems and Ballads*, Swinburne followed Baudelaire's example with 'Anima Anceps', 'Ilicet', and 'Satia te Sanguine'. Swinburne's Latin, like Baudelaire's, creates an atmosphere; if they allude to antiquity or the Middle Ages, the allusion is remote.[73] Another use for Latin titles is to enlarge the distance between the speakers of the poems and the author of the book; the Latin titles of Browning's *Dramatis Personae* and Pound's *Personae* both insist on the author as artificer, as distinct from the voices to be heard in the lyrics.

Greek has rarely been chosen for titles. There is Pope's Περὶ Βαθοῦς, where the allusion to Longinus was chosen to mock the pretence of the high-flying deep-sinkers in poetry. The five Greek words that serve as titles to Goethe's 'Urworte. Orphisch' outdo, or at least equal, the expansive mysticism of Hugo's Latin titles. Of English works, perhaps Hardy's ΑΓΝΩΣΤΩΙ ΘΕΩΙ ('To the Unknown God', from Acts 17: 23) is the weightiest; it is the poem with which he concludes *Poems of the Past and Present*. The three Greek titles in Pound's *Personae* (1926) are straightforward allusions to antiquity.

French, in contrast, has often been a popular language for titles. Let us take three contrasting examples, starting with Keats. Though the title 'La Belle Dame sans Merci' is taken from a poem by Alain Chartier, it is not being offered as a literary allusion. The title is French because the *femme fatale* is French. The language implies that such behaviour, and such opportunity, is not English; the French, as often, both forbids and attracts. In contrast, Whitman's 'Salut au monde!' reverses the usual associations of the French language in England and America. A language notorious for its snobbery and social exclusion is here made to create an indiscriminate, democratic embrace. Lastly, Wallace Stevens's greatest poem with a French title is the *Esthétique du mal*. An *Aesthetics of Evil* would not have an equivalent impact, nor would an *Aesthetica Mali*; it would be too ponderous in English, and worse in Latin; too much like a serious theological tome, that is, too much on religion's own terms. To choose French is to play, and to play is to defeat the ponderousness of Christianity, to correct its crucial misjudgements of life and death.

It is hard to make generalizations about epigraphs in foreign languages. Gérard Genette has argued that the first epigraph in the modern sense appeared in La Bruyère's *Caractères* (1688), a quotation in Latin from Erasmus' famous letter to Dorp. Genette argues that epigraphs proliferate in fiction only with the Gothic novel in England.[74] Each chapter of Radcliffe's *Mysteries of Udolpho* and Lewis's *Monk* has an epigraph, but almost all of them are in English, and the same is the case with the vastly more influential novels of Sir Walter Scott. For foreign-language epigraphs, we should turn to a different genre. Joseph Addison's mottos in *The Spectator* encouraged the reading public to expect specifically Latin or Greek quotations; in no. 221, he defends his practice on the grounds that the common people have a natural love of Latin, that even ladies have complimented him on his Greek mottos, and that he takes care to make provision in the body of his paper for unlearned friends who cannot relish the motto. Samuel Johnson makes sure that the Greek and Latin epigraphs in *The Rambler* and *The Adventurer* also appear in translation. Epigraphs, however, whether in English or a foreign language or both, mostly have an oblique, at times even whimsical, relation to the text.

Novels with multilingual epigraphs at the head of chapters become common only in the nineteenth century. They then appear in Gothic fiction, in Poe's stories and Marturin's *Melmoth the Wanderer* for example, but they are not limited to that subgenre. In fact, they do not form a coherent class of books at all; perhaps the most famous such works are Pushkin's *Eugene Onegin* ('a novel in verse'), Stendhal's *Le Rouge et le Noir*, and *Middlemarch*. I would emphasize the playful character of many of these mottoes, as when Pushkin quotes Horace's 'O rus' to make a multilingual pun. Sometimes, however, and especially among poets, a foreign-language epigraph acquired a peculiar intensity. When Samuel Taylor Coleridge was seeing 'Ode on the Departing Year' through the press, he wished to have a Greek quotation from Aeschylus' *Agamemnon* printed on the fly-title. He told the printer: 'The Motto! where is the Motto! I would not have lost the *motto* for a kingdom twas the best part of the Ode.' When the motto still failed to appear, he pleaded with the printer: 'Motto I beseech you, let the Motto be printed; and printed accurately.'[75]

The last unit of multilingualism under consideration is that of the word and phrase, and in genres like the novel (at least, outside of France) it is virtually omnipresent. Since French was spoken by the Prussian, Russian, and English nobility, and in England especially by women, novels concerned with those groups could hardly avoid it; on the other hand, few novelists quote as much French as Tolstoy or Charlotte Brontë. Most confine themselves to phrases and very occasional sentences. Other languages are rarer, serving to set a scene in a foreign land, like the Javanese in Multatuli's *Max Havelaar* or, say, the Urdu in Kipling's 'In the Presence' or, controversially, the Spanish in Hemingway's *For Whom the Bell Tolls*;[76] or conversely to reflect the presence of foreign speakers in one's own country, like the Polish and German in Dostoevsky's novels and stories with an urban setting. Dickens's attitude to foreign languages is remarkable by contrast: he often shows an active antipathy to them. French, German, Latin, and Greek are found 'murdering the innocents' in *Hard Times*; in *Bleak House*, Latin is the language of the villian Tulkinghorne as well as being responsible for the deformation of

Richard Carstone's character; and Greek and Latin together have dessicated Miss Blimber in *Dombey and Son*: 'She was dry and sandy with working in the graves of deceased languages. None of your live languages for Miss Blimber. They must be dead—stone dead—and then Miss Blimber dug them up like a Ghoul.'[77]

Suspicions about the evils of those who mix foreign phrases into their conversation have been evident in literature long before the novel came into being. Chaucer put foreign phrases into the mouth of the summoner in order to make his nasty inclinations evident. As Geoffrey Hughes puts it, the summoner's speech is 'liberally spiced with biblical tags, Latin and French phrases and plenty of persuasive cant to appeal to his prosperous target market'.[78] In *Love's Labour's Lost*, 5. 1, Holofernes' Latin pedantry is effectively stymied by Custard's *reductio ad absurdum*: *honorificabilitudinitatibus*.

Latin phrases are rarer in novels but on occasion assume central importance, as in *Moby-Dick*, when Captain Ahab at his most diabolical baptizes the harpoon with blood in the name of Satan: 'Ego non baptizo te in nomine patris, sed in nomine diaboli.' The language of the church was still available as the language of blasphemy. In contrast, there is one novelist, at least, for whom Latin is present as part of the normal order of social exchanges: Walter Scott, who not only makes his characters speak bits of Latin more often than other novelists, but includes it in the speech of a variety of characters. Antiquaries, unsurprisingly, are given to it, but it is not only the language of pedants, and it is not quoted only in *The Antiquary*. In *Redgauntlet*, Darsie Latimer's Latin is both gentlemanly, as in his quotations from Horace and Virgil, and professional, since he is a student of law and uses legal jargon. In addition, Latin is also the language of the Jacobite cause: 'Haud obliviscendum' is the motto Redgauntlet attaches to the relic of his brother he wears constantly around his neck, the Latin meant to be a guarantee that the recollection of injury will be perpetual. In that Jacobite context, however, the Latin is expressive not only of classic perpetuity but also of Romantic futility. However, the reason Scott could use Latin to illustrate diverse characters is that the novel is set in the eighteenth century. Novels concerned with later periods cannot turn to Latin except under more limited circumstances since the domain in which Latin was present had shrunk.

Greek is rarer in novels. The Reverend Dr Folliott is always quoting Greek in Peacock's *Crotchet Castle* (including some of Nonnus' best lines), but he is not a pedant: 'even in these tight-laced days, the obscurity of a learned language allows a little pleasantry'. There were such people in the nineteenth century for whom the apposite quotation always happened to be Greek; in Peacock's letters, the more informal his tone, the more he quotes Greek. Nothing could be further from the deadly seriousness of the Greek in *Jude the Obscure*. Greek is not just pleasant for Jude, it is a sensuous reality: the sight of the Greek words meaning 'The New Testament' in chapter 7 of book i and the sound of some verses from 1 Corinthians in chapter 3 of book ii have an inexplicable and enchanting power over him.

In drama Greek is even rarer. Faustus dismisses Aristotelian metaphysics in the first scene of Marlowe's drama: 'Bid *on kai me on* farewell'. But the Greek (ὄν καὶ μὴ ὄν) was so unfamiliar to audiences that it was printed as either *Oncaymæon* or *Oeconomy* until Bullen emended the text in 1885.

With some foreign phrases in Pope, Byron, and Browning our survey of literary multilingualism will be complete. When Pope retells the story of the city mouse and the country mouse (in his imitation of that part of Horace, *Satires* 2. 6), the French is a sign of civilized good manners in both. The country mouse is determined to prepare the best possible meal for his town friend, *coute qui coute*, and the city mouse, trying not to show his contempt too much, invites him in return to dine with him in town. They sit down after a banquet, *tête à tête*, and the town mouse elegantly attends to his friend, advising him about the dishes, 'Que ça est bon! Ah goutez ça!' before the cat chases them away. The language of social comedy is not surpassed by Pope anywhere else, and because of the comedy the story is not felt to have been moralized. In fact, to talk about a moral at all is too coarse for the poem. One critic has called this imitation 'a poetry of self-delighting self-parody'; through Pope's language, we are amused by the virtues he admires, since he gives a playful parody of the virtues of the country life, friendship, and hospitality, and at the same time we are charmed 'with what he characteristically condemns', dependence at court.[79] The poetry is too civilized for preaching, which (we may understand) the use of French precludes.

Byron's multilingual comedy is quite different. In *Don Juan*, French may be the language of love, but it is also the language to expose deceptions about love. Whether or not the Duchess of Fitz-Fulke would call herself an *intrigante*, indeed somewhat *méchante* in the amorous sphere, Byron does, and he makes his readers aware that her flirting rhymes with her plaguesomeness, thanks to French: 'The Duchess of Fitz-Fulke, who loved *tracasserie*, I Began to treat him with some small *agacerie*' (canto xiv, stanza 41). The OED credits Byron with extending the sense of *liaison* to include 'an illicit intimacy between a man and a woman'; the two references to a 'chaste *liaison*' in Don Juan promote our suspiciousness about liaisons. With Latin, Byron skirts even closer to violating sexual taboos. 'But Virgil's songs are pure, except for that horrid one I Beginning with "*Formosum Pastor Corydon*"' (canto i, stanza 42). Virgil was in the awkward position of being celebrated for his purity while having written pederastic poetry. The awkwardness would not matter very much if everyone would simply agree not to mention that slip, but 'Byron was born to say'—all but say—'the things one must not say'. In canto ix, when Don Juan attracts the attention of the Empress Catherine, Byron meditates on 'thou "teterrima Causa" of all "belli,"' translated in the next stanza as 'the worst Cause of war' and then corrected to the *best*. Though Byron does not go on to quote the particular word Horace uses, he does suggest it phonetically, and Christopher Ricks has cunningly hunted down the displaced occurrences of the word in the subsequent stanza.[80]

No one would call Browning's Latin ribald, but it is not less energetic, particularly when the subject is the deformation of character caused by or revealed through Latin. In 'The Bishop Orders His Tomb at Saint Praxed's Church', we overhear a bishop on his deathbed. He has little interest in spiritual matters; instead, he reveals the spirit of the Renaissance in 'worldliness, inconsistency, pride, hypocrisy, ignorance of itself, love of art, of luxury, and of good Latin' (Ruskin's description of the poem). Perhaps especially in love of good Latin; the bishop is a typical sixteenth-century Roman in his insistence on using only Cicero's words (Erasmus would have called him a 'Ciceronian monkey'). He is exultantly contemptuous that a rival's epitaph includes a late Latin word ('elucescebat'), unlike the pure Ciceronian epigraph he has devised for his own tomb. As with *The Ring and the Book*, Latin is the medium of the *déformation professionelle*.

In short, to know why writers switch to another language in their works we need to know something of the political, cultural, social, economic, and religious status of the languages at a particular time. Latin, for example, may be used to lay a claim to religious orthodoxy, but also to suggest blasphemy or mysticism; it may announce stylistic correctness, but also sterile pedantry; it may reflect chaste censorship, but also excite prurience; it may be the professional language of the doctor, lawyer, or scholar, but also the amateur language of the gentleman. It may intimate, as it may embody, both proper authority and authoritarian fraud.

We might look at multilingualism in literature in units even smaller than a word or phrase. At the border between languages, it is not always evident what is foreign and what is not. Is 'elite' an English word, or is it 'élite'? Should it be '*élite*'? Under 'foreignism', *The Oxford Companion to the English Language* remarks that 'there tends to be a gradation in English from less to more foreign' and that 'it is difficult to specify where the "properly" foreign begins'. Moreover, some foreignisms are 'more foreign than others, and more foreign for some than for others'. Under 'loanword', the authors distinguish borrowings that have not been assimilated (usually 'the terminology of specialists and italicized and glossed when used'), borrowings that have been adapted to some extent into the native system ('with a stable spelling and pronunciation'), and borrowings indistinguishable from the rest of the lexicon (that is, 'open to normal rules of word use and word formation'). They also add a caveat: 'It is seldom possible, however, to separate the stages of assimilation so neatly.' Some words may be assimilated practically at once; others may exist for a long time at a local level before being assimilated nationally or internationally.[81]

Latin foreignisms have been adapted into English both by those who know and by those who are ignorant of Latin. Though Byron, for example, takes care to use a verb of motion with 'in medias res' ('Most epic poets plunge in "medias res,"' *Don Juan*, i. 6), the phrase is now often used without regard to Latin syntax, occurring in expressions like 'to begin in medias res'. The *Oxford English Dictionary* lists the form 'strictu sensu' in addition to the correct Latin, 'stricto sensu'. Those usages reflect the extent to which Latin has been assimilated into normal English usage, with its simpler case system and uninflected adjectives. Speakers with little Latin and no Greek perpetuate hypercorrected English plurals like *octopi* (and not *octopuses* or *octopodes*). Other writers have consciously assimilated Greek or Latin to English usage. In *Tristram Shandy*, the effort to record the labour of slogging through Greek and Latin leads Walter Shandy to conjugate a Greek equivalent for slogging as though it were an English one: 'Seven long years and more τυπτω-ing it, at

Greek and Latin'.[82] This also has the advantage of suggesting, phonetically, that the slogging may have been accomplished rather gingerly, on tiptoe. Browning, in order to show an English reader just how much Latin is a native idiom for Archangeli in *The Ring and the Book*, makes the defence lawyer use Latin like English. As his young son masters the Latin idiom in which 'qui' is used with the subjunctive, that is, when his son '*Qui*es [him] *cum subjunctivo*', Archangeli announces that he could cry.[83] In this line, 'qui' is used in a very English way, like the 'but' of 'but me no buts' or like Shakespeare's 'Grace me no Grace, nor Vncle me'.

The assimilation works in the other direction as well, where English is adapted to Latin (or another language). Expressions and syntax that deviate from the norms of a language because they are modelled on the norms of another language are examples of what linguists call interference. In English literature, examples of interference range from the broken English of Queequeg and Friday to the ornate English of Milton at his most sublime. However, this is to get ahead of ourselves, since language interference is the topic of Chapter 3, and before essaying that topic, we will look at the contrary ambition, the desire to make English pure.

CHAPTER TWO

Varieties of Language Purism

SOME ENGLISH WORDS advertise their provenance. In literary contexts, *irremeable* and *irriguous* announce something about Latin and Latin's relation to English, as *ugh* and *bug* do about the Saxon nature of English. What they announce, and the force they have gained because of their perceived etymology, have been influenced by movements to purify English. These movements have differed in their targets and in their ambitions; targets have included dialects, taboo words, the language of a particular social class, low words, and foreignisms, and the ambitions have ranged from purifying the entirety of the language to reforming some part of it, such as the language of verse, or of polite literature in general, or the written word. In England since the Renaissance, the two most influential forms of language purism have been directed at opposite targets. Sometimes low words have been the chief cause of anxiety and offence, and many Saxon words, guilty by association with low words, underwent a process of purification or even purgation. At other times, latinized English was the major source of offence, and latinate vocabulary was rejected as foreign to the native genius of English. The first sort of purism was mainly derived from French neo-classicism, and aimed to reform literature, especially poetry in the high style. The second purism was perhaps most significant in English literature during two periods: the Renaissance and the nineteenth century (when it was influenced by German Romanticism); in its extreme forms it envisaged recasting the entire vocabulary of English. Having studied these purist impulses in their several forms, I will then consider the specific case of the monosyllable in English literature, a linguistic entity to which uniquely native English virtues have been imputed.

English, like other languages, borrows words on an *ad hoc* basis: *bamboo* (possibly Canarese, transmitted through Dutch), *canoe* (native Haitian, through Spanish), *kangaroo* (native Australian), *kuru* (Fore), *shampoo* (Hindi). However, beyond such incidental borrowings, the English vocabulary draws on three foreign sources, adding to its Anglo-Saxon base French, Latin, and Greek. These four vocabularies make up most of the English language: fire, flame, conflagration, holocaust; sickness, malady, infection, epidemic.[1] Though fewer words are derived from it, Old Norse gave English many of its most common words: are, cut, want, wrong, ill, ugly, law, root, anger, they.[2] As a result of its extensive borrowings, the English vocabulary is rich in pairs and triplets that have similar meanings but different associations: freedom/liberty, hearty/cordial, go up/ascend, new/innovative/neophyte, oversensitive/supersensitive/hypersensitive, fellow feeling/compassion/sympathy, anthill/formicary/myrmecology, kingly/royal/regal.[3] Exploring among these pairs is a favourite Elizabethan activity.[4] 'Apparently the Elizabethans discovered the possibilities of etymological dissociation in language: *amatory* and *love*, *audition* and *hearing*, *hearty welcome* and *cordial reception*: these quasisynonyms offer new opportunities for semantic differentiation. Two terms for the same *denotatum*: new *connotations* can arise, stylistic, poetic possibilities are offered . . .' Sylvia Adamson notes how often Elizabethan styles interweave latinate and Saxon English: Bacon's *find talk and discourse*; Donne's *contignation and knitting*; Browne's *breach or dichotomy*; *fire and scintillation*. In contrast, couplings of latinate words or phrases with other latinate words or phrases often mark a parodic style, indicating an affected or pedantic speaker.[5] Shakespeare is the great master at moving between different sources of the English vocabulary:

> Will all great Neptunes Ocean wash this blood
> Cleane from my Hand? no: this my Hand will rather
> The multitudinous Seas incarnardine,
> Making the Greene one, Red.
>
> (*Macbeth*, 2. 2)

Or:

> Absent thee from felicitie a while,
> And in this harsh world draw thy breath in paine
>
> (*Hamlet*, 5. 2)

In the lines from *Macbeth*, there is little semantic difference between 'The multitudinous seas incarnadine' and 'Making the green one red'. Yet the lines are not redundant. Either line alone would be insufficient, either pretentiously hyperbolic or unrealistically exaggerated. Together they enact Macbeth's recognition of the magnitude of his guilt in reciprocal registers. In the lines from *Hamlet*, the latinate first line with its greater formality gives Hamlet a barely won stoic distance from his words, while the monosyllables of the next withdraw the reserve and convey immediate pain.[6]

Because a number of paired synonyms in English derive from Anglo-Saxon (or sometimes French) on the one hand and Latin (or Greek) on the other, a link between etymology and register has often been perceived. High terms, such as *multitudinous* and *incarnadine*, are often latinate, and low or neutral terms are often Anglo-Saxon. This is a matter of perception as well as of etymology. The 'four-letter words' in English are frequently described as Anglo-Saxon, even quintessentially Anglo-Saxon, but from the point of view of strict etymology, this is the case only with 'the main anal terms'.[7] In this chapter, the term 'Anglo-Saxon' will be reserved for etymology and 'Saxon' will be adopted for matters of perception; similarly, 'Latin' will be used in etymological descriptions, but 'latinate' will refer to words, phrases, and syntax which are perceived to be derived from a Latin source (though some of these instances are actually derived from Greek).[8]

A purism directed against low words in English will often be hostile to the Saxon vocabulary; a purism directed against latinisms in English will favour it. The former was modelled on French classicism. Before Malherbe came, the French language, far from showing itself hostile to foreign languages, enriched itself with Italian, Latin, and Greek vocabulary. Hundreds of Italian words were borrowed, many still in use, especially technical terms related to finance, art, the army, and the navy.[9] Henri Estienne mocked French courtiers for their Italianized speech. The literary language of the Pléiade as well as of Rabelais borrowed heavily from Latin and Greek. In *La Deffence et illustration de la langue françoyse*, Du Bellay urged the future poet to be fearless in introducing neologisms, especially in a long poem, though 'avec modestie toutesfois, analogie & jugement de l'oreille'. Ronsard was less discriminatingly acquisitive: 'Plus nous aurons de mots en notre langue, plus elle sera parfaicte.' *Richesse—copia*—was to be attained by imitating antiquity in neologisms and also constructions based on classical examples.[10] In his elegy to Marguerite de France, duchess of Savoy,

Ronsard regretted the inability of his muse to speak Greek more extensively:

> Ah! que je suis marry que la Muse Françoise
> Ne peult dire ces mots comme faict la Gregeoise,
> Ocymore, dyspotme, oligochronien:

ὠκύμορος: dying early; δυσπότμος, ill-starred; ὀλιγοχρόνιος, short-lived. In his note to this line, he is more hopeful about the potential French status of those words: 'Ces mots grecs seront trouvez fort nouveaux: mais d'autant que nostre langue ne pouvoit exprimer ma conception, j'ay esté forcé d'en user, qui signifient une vie de petite durée. *Filosofie* & *mathematique* ont esté aussy estranges au commencement: mais l'usage les a par traict de temps adoulcis & rendus nostres.' This is the kind of writing which led Boileau to regret that Ronsard's Muse spoke Greek and Latin. Although a few of the neologisms of the sixteenth century were to become a standard part of the language (*patrie*, for example, the use of which provoked an attack on Du Bellay, who was wrongly blamed for inventing it), the desire to expand the limits of French by recourse to other languages did not outlast Ronsard's century. In the words of Mark Pattison, an acute, francophobic Victorian scholar and essayist, 'The occupation of enriching the language with new terms gave way in the next century to the opposite one of selecting and rejecting . . . To repel foreign elements, to weed, to exclude, to eliminate, such is the constant tendency of their taste in language.'[11]

The proposed elimination of Latinized vocabulary was only one aspect of French neo-classicism. Low words, too, were banned from the language of verse, with partial exceptions made for comedy. A number of reasons motivated the reform: the desire for order and for uniform standards, and with it an insistence that there is only one correct form of expression; snobbery at court and in the salons; aspirations towards elegance and anxieties about giving offence or shocking.[12] With Malherbe came the emphasis on accessibility, on unimpeded intelligibility, an emphasis deepened by Vaugelas in the mid-seventeenth century and later, with Rivarol in the second half of the eighteenth century, made to appear synonymous with French itself ('Ce qui n'est pas clair n'est pas français').[13] Neologisms, archaisms, and classical borrowings were to be removed from the literary language; at the same time, words of everyday, practical use were also to be eliminated in verse, and in literary contexts generalizations and periphrasis were to take the place of ordinary expressions.

English neo-classicism followed the French example. Ready intelligibility—*perspicuity* was the contemporary term—was to be gained by insisting on natural word order; avoiding puns, quibbles, and conceits; regularizing prosody; and excluding the 'common, vulgar, domestic, and ordinary' from the poetic vocabulary.[14] However, there was a crucial difference between English and French practice: while Ronsard and his peers could be regarded as obsolete until their merit was rediscovered by Sainte-Beuve in the nineteenth century, Milton and Shakespeare could not be so overlooked. Some of their hard words, rather than being rejected as uncouth, became a standard part of poetic diction. Adamson, in her study of the literary language of the period, observes that 'of the renaissance latinisms that Addison (incorrectly) attributed to Milton, *embryon* (as adjective) was taken up by Brooke, Harte and Wesley, *miscreated* by Cobb, Croxall and Fawkes, and *Cerberean* by Blackmore, Pitt and Pope'.[15] The second edition of the *OED* credits Milton's *Paradise Lost* with 137 coinages (an overestimate, as always with famous authors in the *OED*); two-thirds of them are adjectives, many of which became part of the poetic diction of subsequent ages: *amaranthine, horrent, impassive, loquacious, obtrusive*. Often Shakespeare's neologisms (there are perhaps as many as 1,700 of them) became part not just of the language of subsequent poetry, but of the language itself. Two-thirds of Shakespeare's latinate coinages continued in use; many have survived to this day.[16] Nor is the continuity of the later language with the latinate coinages in Renaissance literature limited to Shakespeare and Milton; Sir Thomas Browne was particularly successful at coining enduring neologisms.[17]

While Shakespeare's quibbles were deprecated, Milton's laborious harshness regretted, and the profuse literature of the Renaissance felt to be in need of discipline, no general attack on latinate vocabulary was launched from the Restoration to the end of the eighteenth century.[18] In other respects, however, the Latin influence on English style was vehemently rejected. With few exceptions (one of which will be studied in the next chapter), the imitation of latinate syntax, word order, period length, and so on, was discouraged, and more transparent English renderings were favoured. Adamson notes that, in contrast to the English writers of the Renaissance, later authors sought not to reproduce various latinate effects but to find equivalents to them: 'By the end of the seventeenth century there was a widespread belief that each language had its own particular "genius"; it followed that instead of remodeling English in the form of Latin, writers should seek native means for achieving classical effects.'[19] Latin retained its presence within English poetry, and Milton began to cast his long shadow; but they were remade to satisfy demands for clarity and even a sort of gentlemanly ease; there arrived that easy Ciceronian style, so Latin yet so English all the while.

This refashioning led to the acceptance and even relish of latinate English so long as such language was limited to diction; such diction was perhaps most acceptable when it was manifested in adjectives. One reason that the eighteenth century was the 'century of the adjective', a period when 'adjectival use increased out of all proportion to preceding or following uses', was that adjectives do not distract attention away from the basic noun–verb structure of the line.[20] Most of the time, the adjectives continue to be taken from the Saxon register. In Dryden's poetry, the ones most frequent are *bad, good, high, long, old, public, true, wise*; in Pope's, *bright, fair, new, sad, silver, soft, various*; in Johnson's, *gay, general, great, new, vain*.[21] However, frequency is not the only kind of importance, nor is it a measure of significance; even a single highly latinate epithet may go far to colouring a passage, and if it fails to do so, the failure tends to be striking. Let us examine, then, a handful of these latinate epithets, bearing in mind the triple set of relations in which they need to be read: in respect to Latin, in respect to English poetic tradition, and in respect to the plainer English words they have replaced.

Take *irriguous*. The word entered English poetry with Milton: 'the flourie lap | Of som irriguous Valley', *Paradise Lost*, 4. 254–5. The valley is well-watered, irrigated, moist; why turn to a latinate word? Though Latin *irriguus* is used in both the poetry and prose of classical literature, it may have been associations with the Vulgate that drew Milton to the word: Isaiah 58: 11 promises that 'thou shalt be like a watered garden', and Jeremiah 31: 12, that 'their soule shall be as a watered garden'. Though theses phrases are not close enough to Milton's English for us to conclude that he must have had them in mind, the powerful images of redeemed happiness, with explicit reference to a garden, bear appropriately on the description of Eden. Whatever we conclude about its allusive force, *irriguous* was still a new word when Milton used it (coined, according to the *OED*, by

1653), and not only new but remote from ordinary English; its strangeness underlines the magnitude of the loss of paradise.

The epithet became a standard poeticism in the eighteenth century. Irriguous lawns, vales, dales, and meads may be found in Fenton, Thomson, Akenside, and Somervile during the first half of the century, and Dyer, Fawkes, and Erasmus Darwin during the second half. *Irriguous* persisted into the next century: Coleridge, Wordsworth, and Clough employed it. These poets are mostly either consciously echoing Milton or writing conventionally. Occasionally, however, the word is extended by imitating its other Latin usages, as when it is used in an active sense, or as when an ancient metaphor is renewed by John Philips's *irriguous sleep* (*Cyder*, 1708). A well-judged recreative use of the epithet occurs in Joseph Thurston's mock-heroic *The Fall*, a poem that has fallen almost totally into oblivion despite the fact that it is far more skilful in its choice of epithets than most eighteenth-century poems after Pope. Thurston returns to the word its original physical sense, and he maintains decorum by means of the abstracting Latin, when he writes of Danaë that 'She lay irriguous with descending *Jove*' (*The Fall*, 1. 129, 1732). Thurston combines the active and passive senses of the word, Zeus's descent and her response; it suggests lubricity without crudity. Modern critics who have thought that Milton's combination of *lap* and *irriguous* introduced a sense of sexual fertility in his description of Eden are not being parochially modern; the connection could be made in the eighteenth century. In good writers, latinate English has always been able to express physical reality directly; think of Herrick's 'liquefaction', Yeats's 'dark declivities'.

Take *irremeable* next. There is a close connection—one that is not exclusively etymological—between the English and the Latin word. In book 6 of the *Aeneid*, with the Sibyl as guide, Aeneas penetrates into the underworld. Once Cerberus has been given his sop, Aeneas gets clear of the *ripam irremeabilis undae* (6. 425), the bank of the Styx, across which Charon had just conveyed him. In Dryden's translation, Aeneas 'took th' irremeable way'. The English word persists in eighteenth-century translations: in Trapp, Aeneas 'behind him leaves The Border of th'irremeable Lake' (1718), and in Pitt, he 'left behind th' irremeable flood' (1740). No one, to my knowledge, translates Virgil's other use of *irremeabilis* (*Aeneid*, 5. 591) as 'irremeable', and after Dryden, the English word became closely connected with the passage in book 6.[22] For more than a century in its evolution, the English word does not develop independently of the Latin; it is not only latinate, it should probably be seen as a latinism. Pope twice introduces it into his *Iliad* (19. 312; 23. 92); on neither occasion is there a Greek equivalent in the text, but Pope saw the *Iliad* through Virgilian lenses, and he extended the passages in a natural, Virgilian way: 'All trod the dark, irremeable Way' (19. 312) and 'Forbid to cross th' irremeable Flood' (23. 92, of Patroclus, denied entry into Hades). Even when the word occurs in poetry that is not a translation from a classical language, it often introduces or reinforces a classical reference; so in Swinburne's *Atalanta in Calydon*, Meleager recounts his adventures with the Argonauts: 'we shot after and sped | Clear through the irremeable Symplegades'. After Dryden, uses of the word explicitly point to Latin and often to the specific passage in Virgil. Sceptics might see particular occurrences of the word as an exotic trinket, antique stage-dressing; defenders would want to make the case that since there is no English, no Christian, equivalent to the classical notion of fate, the Latin term is thrust upon us in such contexts.

In his letters Johnson requires *irremeable* on two occasions. On 3 October 1767, he tells Hester Thrale that he feels 'something like the shackles of destiny' in Lichfield, and that when he leaves, he will not easily be persuaded to take the 'irremeable road' back to the other side of the Styx. Here the Virgilian allusion designates Lichfield hell, the land of the dead. In general, references to Roman antiquity permit Johnson to give utterance to views to which he emotionally inclines but which it is understood that he, as a Christian, does not finally accept; they allow him to acknowledge an emotional state while maintaining distance from it. Perhaps for this reason he translates, a few months before his own death, an ode by Horace about death's finality. In his final letter to Hester Thrale (8 July 1784), *irremeable* is highly charged:

When Queen Mary took the resolution of sheltering herself in England, the Archbishop of St. Andrew's attempting to dissuade her, attended on her journey and when they came to the irremeable Stream that separated the two kingdoms, walked by her side into the water, in the middle of which he seized her bridle and with earnestness proportioned to her danger and his own affection, pressed her to return. The Queen went forward.—If the parallel reaches thus far; may it go no further. The tears stand in my eyes.

The apprehension of fate—destructive, imminent, and irrevocable—

is made present by the Virgilian allusion, as by the (fictional) history of Queen Mary's equivalent to crossing the Rubicon, and the letter is correspondingly a letter of 'lamentation, warning, and farewell'.[23]

Or consider words like *acrimonious* and *volatile*, which gained their moral significations through metaphoric extensions from the language of science. It has been argued that readers for whom the scientific metaphors of Johnson's day are no longer evident have wrongly supposed eighteenth-century literature to be abstract and devoid of imagery. W. K. Wimsatt sought to redeem Johnson's *Rambler* essays from the charge of lifeless, abstract writing by insisting that his language was frequently metaphoric in its adapting the vocabulary of natural philosophy to moral themes.[24] The subsequent success of the metaphors has prevented later readers from recognizing their vividness. Like neologisms, metaphors often suffer the fate either of becoming obsolete, and so seeming capricious, or becoming conventional, and so appearing dull.

None the less, when Donald Davie writes of *acrimonious* that 'it is for us a dead metaphor, whereas for Johnson and his predecessors it was a very lively metaphor indeed, daringly far-fetched', he overstates the case.[25] The *OED* credits Johnson in 1775 with extending the meaning of *acrimonious* to include 'bitter and irritating in disposition or manner', and although Davie was correct to point to the deficiency of the *OED*'s documentation, he did not himself repair it. The word in the metaphoric sense, according to Chadwyck-Healey, first appeared in 1659; it became common after about 1750 (Tobias Smollett favoured it in his novels).[26] There is no reason to see it as 'daringly far-fetched' or even as '*very* lively'. *Volatile*, which Davie adduces along with *acrimonious* as exemplifying the eighteenth-century naturalization of scientific terms, presents a similar case. The first usage in the *OED* in this sense comes from Clarendon (1647: 'the Volatile, and Unquiet Spirit of the Lord Digby'), and it is regularly so used for a century before Johnson. It is a live metaphor, in that both the scientific and the moral sense are extant in the eighteenth century, but there is no evidence to suggest that it is a very lively one.

To summarize: it is crucial, in close reading, to attend to the triple set of historical relations in which such latinate epithets are enmeshed. In our examples, the relation to Latin was grounded in a biblical promise, in a description of fate in Latin literature, and in chemistry. Not all Latin-based adjectives can be tied to such specific sources; more common ones—*horrid, instructed, obscene, purple,* etc.—have vaguer connotations of antiquity. The thing is to be aware of the range of possible Latin sources informing the words, whether literary, theological, scientific, or general. The second relation, how particular words are placed within the English poetic tradition, must be investigated in order to hear the strangeness of the terms, to see how far- (or near-) fetched they are, and to make sense of how they stand in relation to a convention. *Irriguous* is an unusual term when Milton uses it, a signal that in a fallen state to imagine paradise requires unusual effort; when Thurston uses it, he appeals to the conventional poetic sense (in which meaning has been largely bleached out of it) for decorum's sake while restoring its direct, physical connotations. Similarly, to determine whether *volatile, horrid,* or *acrimonious* is a vivid term in a particular instance, it is necessary first to locate their written histories, for which purpose the *OED* is at once indispensable and inadequate.

The final relation—that of the latinate epithet to the plainer English word it replaced—returns us to the question of Saxon and native English. Both *irremeable* and *volatile,* it could be argued, as words that were taken from domains in which Latin dominated, have no plain English equivalents. It is not an argument that has satisfied nativists, who have sought to find Saxon English equivalents to such words; historically, however, an even stronger animus was directed against words like *irriguous,* used to avoid *wet* or *moist* for the sake of poetic diction. If we adopt Donald Davie's distinction, we say diction rather than language:

'Diction' is a selection from the language of men . . . One feels that Hopkins could have found a place for every word in the language if only he could have written enough poems. One feels the same about Shakespeare. But there are poets, I find, with whom I feel the other thing, that a selection has been made and is being continually made, that words are thrusting at the poem and being fended off from it.[27]

The verbs *thrusting* and *being fended off* suggest too emphatically that the registers are antagonistic; they preclude the possibility of cooperation and mutual support. All the same, it is true that in the high style from Dryden to Johnson, the major impetus at work in diction was the avoidance of low terms, which are almost always Saxon. Of course, neutral Saxon words appeared continuously in the poetry of the period because basic articles, prepositions, verbs, and nouns could hardly have been avoided; moreover, some Saxon words were elevated in dignity: *mead, vale, dale, hind, glebe*. None the less, the possibility of a lapse in decorum through the appearance of low terms created both anxiety and the pressure which Davie describes as obtaining when words thrust at and are fended off from poems.

It is often difficult for us to determine why certain words created such uneasiness in the past. In the dedication to his translation of the *Aeneid*, Dryden writes that he cannot translate *mollis amaracus* as sweet marjoram, since such 'village words' give the reader 'a mean idea of the thing'. So Ascanius is laid down on a 'flowery bed' rather than on soft marjoram. This contrasts sharply with Shakespeare's 'marjoram', employed on four occasions, once in the beautiful list of flowers in *The Winter's Tale*. Shakespeare not only includes low words, he does not hesitate to put low and high words in tight proximity. Lear appeals to 'the great Goddes | That keepe this dread-full pudder [pother] o're our heads'. Dryden hesitates to include risky words—as Virgil does, though the words Dryden avoids (like *marjoram*) are not the words that Virgil excludes (for example, *sterto*).

Shakespeare's use of language continually alarmed readers in the eighteenth century. Pope expunges the word 'hats' from *Julius Caesar* (Pope and Sewell print a dash for it in *Julius Caesar*, 2. 1, though they leave it untouched the four other times it occurs). One of the most perplexing examples is Dr Johnson's discussion of Lady Macbeth's speech in Act 1, scene 5:

> Come thick Night,
> And pall thee in the dunnest smoake of Hell,
> That my keene Knife see not the Wound it makes,
> Nor Heauen peepe through the Blanket of the darke,
> To cry, hold, hold.

Johnson writes that all the force of poetry is exerted in this passage: 'the force which calls new powers into being, which embodies senti-ment, and animates matter'. The speech so disturbs Johnson that he mentally revises it by attributing it to Macbeth himself. It is not only Lady Macbeth that disturbs him; the disparity between the words and the ideas is his chief objection. 'Dunnest' is an epithet 'now seldom heard but in the stable'. Worse, the sentiment 'is weakened by the name of an instrument used by butchers and cooks in the meanest employment; we do not immediately conceive that any crime of importance is to be committed with a *knife*'. Moreover, 'peep' and 'blanket' so debase the passage that Johnson finds it nearly comical: 'for who, without some relaxation of his gravity, can hear of the avengers of guilt "peeping through a blanket"?'[28]

What is wrong with marjoram, hats, and blankets? Are they the innocent Saxon victims of a ruthless latinizing ambition? Before essaying an answer, let us consider a more accessible example. In his translation of the *Iliad*, Pope justifies his refusal to translate the word *ass* on the grounds that 'upon the whole, a Translator owes so much to the Taste of the Age in which he lives, as not to make too great a Complement to the former'.[29] An ass in Pope's day (as in ours) was not (as it had been in Homer's time) a good comparison for the unwillingness to retreat, since its English associations include 'clumsiness, ignorance, stupidity' (*OED*). Besides, there is the uncomfortable phonetic likeness to *arse*, which worried the eighteenth century and which ultimately resulted in the obscure creation of *donkey* (1785).[30] Phonetic proximity to taboo words is a recurrent anxiety in languages, although the particular taboos, and their intensity, keep changing. For centuries, this has brought about linguistic innovations in English: *earl* rather than *count*; *donkey* rather than *ass*; *rooster* rather than *cock*. *Pissabed* and *windfucker* did not serve as alternatives to *dandelion* and *windhover* for very long.[31] In the 'palmy days' of Victorian euphemism in America, *bull*, *chair*, *shirt* could not be said aloud in polite company.[32] In America at the end of the twentieth century, *niggardly* seems to have similarly acquired guilt by association.

The risk of being embarrassed by taboo words—usually related to the envelope which surrounds the body in society, but also, critically, a matter of naming and name-calling—increases in elevated poetry after the seventeenth century. Chaucer, untroubled, includes *fart*, *shit*, *queynte*, and *swyve*. Shakespeare is prevented from doing so by the 'ill-named' Master of the Revels, but far from writing a language that precludes any suggestion of taboo words, he playful alludes to them and skirts round the prohibitions.[33] With the Restoration, elevated poetry is far more chary, and more formal; none the less, this does not necessarily exclude humour and the life of the body. Thurston's choice of the word *irriguous* includes both humour and a physical state of the body, while the high latinate style maintains decorum. Dryden, who in the nineteenth century was condemned for the filth he interpolated in his translation of the *Georgics*, creates a complex interplay of levels of diction, allowing the sublime and majestic both to interpret and be interpreted in the light of the quotidian and the bodily.[34] The intense and divergent responses to Dryden—Hopkins thought he laid the strongest stress in all English literature on the 'naked thew and sinew' of the English language while Housman believed that his insistence on correctness and splendour ruined his poems[35]—result from attending to very partial selections from his vocabulary.

Still, *marjoram* and *knife* do not sound like taboo words, and they were resisted by forces different from those that decried the use of *ass*. Both Dryden and Johnson reject the words because of their meanness, their association with the lower classes. Dryden rejects *marjoram* because it gives readers 'a mean idea of the thing'. Johnson associates *dun* with the language of the stable and *knife* with the language of butchers and cooks 'in the meanest condition'. That such an association is perfectly appropriate for Macbeth ('this dead Butcher, and his Fiend-like Queene') is lost on Johnson.

However, Johnson, though oblivious, is hardly stupid. In the *Rambler* discussion, he astutely outlines the difficulties involved in censuring words as low: no word is intrinsically mean; we do not agree on which terms are low; ideas of dignity in one age imply indignity in another. Moreover, the 'imperfections of diction' which he finds in the speech will be 'wholly imperceptible to a foreigner, who learns our language from books, and will strike a solitary academick less forcibly than a modish lady'. Johnson is far from wishing to make modish ladies the arbiters of acceptable writing; he is acknowledging a problem. In the preface to his edition of Shakespeare, he readily dismisses as irrelevant neo-classical dogmas of the unities and certain neo-classical scruples of decorum; the problem of diction, however, is more obdurate. We speak a language which we did not make; words come with a network of associations whether we want the associations or not. If we do not wish to provoke sniggering, words that invite sniggering should be avoided, or else we are at best writing in a high-minded vacuum in which we expect words to be stripped of their normal connotations. It is doubtful that even solitary academics can resist laughing when Robert Browning writes *twats* in *Pippa Passes* 'under the impression that it denoted some part of a nun's attire' (*OED*). On the other hand, to use a diction that never risks the laughter of modish auditors would amount to an anaemic impoverishment of literature—as would be the case if Shakespeare were prevented from conceiving of Macbeth as a butcher, or if Milton eschewed his occasional homely phrases, as Addison would have had him do.[36]

Apprehensions concerning low, mean, common, and vulgar terms are particularly forceful in the eighteenth century, and so is an uneasiness about using specific terms instead of more general ones. Adamson substantiates her observation that in 'neo-classical writing, specialist varieties [of vocabulary] are almost invariably purveyors of limited or perverted perspectives' by quoting from the criticism of Johnson, Addison, and others; moreover, she adds that it is not until the modern period that such varieties are 'seen as sources of fresh aesthetic or moral insights'.[37] (Perhaps that is another reason for avoiding *marjoram*, shunned not only by Dryden but by many of his successors, from Christopher Pitt to Wordsworth and Tennyson.) In this respect, neo-classical diction is at the furthest remove from English writing in other periods. While Racine is content with the word *fleur*, Shakespeare has hundreds of flowers in his works.[38] Dryden, Pope, and Johnson are in comparison impoverished in their poetic floriculture, but in the next century Wordsworth, Keats, Clare, and Tennyson fully revived the practice.[39]

The aesthetic that favoured generalization was not directed specifically against Saxon terms, since latinate ones, too, may be found too exact. Still, one result was that yet another danger was perceived in the use of plain English terms. The problem, moreover, did not disappear when that aesthetic was replaced by its opposite, by versions of Blake's famous marginal note in Reynolds's *Discourses*, 'to generalize is to be an idiot'. The twentieth-century poet R. S. Thomas, a lover of exact natural description, none the less has doubts about its value in poetry: 'But there is a problem bound up with the question of the exact word. Significant poems seem not to be written about Stone Curlews, Dartford Warblers, and Lesser Spotted Woodpeckers, nor about military orchids, water lobelia and antirrhinums, but rather about birds and flowers'. He continues, 'It is as though, for poetry, general words will do'.[40] Perhaps Thomas is half right: there is no reason to value particular terms, particular birds and flowers, unless the poem ties the particular to something more general; this is not, however, to prefer the general to the particular, as Thomas reluctantly concludes, but to doubt whether preferring one or the other even makes sense. When Wordsworth writes, 'But there's a tree, of many, one, | A single field which I have look'd upon', he is at once utterly specific and exceedingly general. But rather than pursue a metaphysical question of the one and the many, let us return to the question of diction. Even among some writers of the twentieth century, lesser spotted woodpeckers and antirrhinums have been avoided for the same reasons that Dryden avoided marjoram: the expectation that readers would find the words risible. The 'blue tit' in poems by Vernon Watkins and T. Sturge Moore, the botanical Latin in the poetry of Hugh MacDiarmid, have challenged and perhaps weakened this expectation.

For a variety of reasons, then, eighteenth-century poetic diction held ordinary Saxon English at arm's length. Low, taboo, and specific words embarrassed poetry, and such words are pre-eminently represented by Saxon terms. Suppressing such terms was a way to acknowledge and even to enhance their weight, and so prepared the ground for the Romantic revaluing of plain English. Moreover, the dual contradiction within the way that the aesthetics of perspicuity was practised—favouring latinate terms which were not perspicuous but shunning Saxon terms which were—led to an angry and moralizing subsequent revaluation. Before continuing to that part of the story, however, let us look at some prose works of the period, where the latinate and Saxon registers coexisted sometimes as happily as in Shakespeare, and at one poet in whose work the equipollence of both these kinds of English was central.

Much of the comedy in both *Tom Jones* and *Tristram Shandy* comes from the collision of latinate and Saxon English. Sometimes this takes the perennially popular form of opposing inflated and pretentious language to plain speaking. In chapter 15 of volume i of his life and opinions, Tristram Shandy spends several pages quoting an article in his mother's marriage settlement written in turgid and latinate legalese ('And that the said Elizabeth Mollineux shall and may, from time to time, and at all such time and times as are here covenanted and agreed upon,—peaceably and quietly hire the said coach and horses, and have free ingress, egress, and regress throughout her journey . . .'); he then concludes, 'In three words,—"My mother was to lay in, (if she chose it) in London."'

More often, Sterne finds comedy in both registers. The plain speaking of Corporal Trim is as stylized and funny as wayward latinate elaboration from Walter Shandy. In one episode (chapter 27 of volume iv), Phutatorius's 'desperate monosyllable Z—ds' is pro-

voked when a roasted chestnut passes through a sufficiently wide
hiatus in his breeches: 'But the heat gradually increasing, and in a few
seconds more getting beyond the point of all sober pleasure and then
advancing with all speed into the regions of pain . . .' *Zounds*, as both
an interjection, cry of pain, and a monosyllable, belongs eminently to
the Saxon register; the narrative is none the less heavily latinate and
abstract. This incongruity is matched by other disparities: between
the name *Phutatorius* and its meaning ('copulator'); between the
genial mask of the social occasion and its ruthless politics; and by the
participants' different misprisions of the event. Sterne is at his best
when the absurdities are multiple.

The narrative style of *Tom Jones* capitalizes on changes of register
and tone. Chapter 11 of book v opens with a long Homeric simile in
which a Saxon word is followed by a poetical periphrasis, including
a latinate epithet: 'As in the Season of RUTTING (an uncouth phrase,
by which the Vulgar denote that gentle Dalliance, which in the well-
wooded Forest of *Hampshire*, passes between Lovers of the Ferine
Kind) . . .' Had Fielding reversed the order of his sentence, ending
rather than beginning with 'rutting', he would have offered an amus-
ing irony at the expense of poetic description, analogous to Sterne's
undercutting of legalistic jargon. But by beginning with 'rutting',
Fielding suggests something more subtle, the intrinsic partiality of
both plain speaking and poetical expression, the necessity for both
kinds of language. The other order—latinate English followed and
often deflated by Saxon English—is a recurrent joke in both Sterne
and Fielding; Sterne often turns it with the phrase 'in a word', 'in
three words', etc., and Fielding with a variety of phrases, 'anglicê', 'in
the vulgar tongue Translated', 'in simple phrase', 'in short', etc.

Central to Fielding's moral sense is the capacity to present,
through humour, a mixture of partiality and impartiality in his
characters.[41] After discovering Sophia's love for Jones, Mr Western
confronts him (chapter 9, book vi):

He then bespattered the Youth with Abundance of that Language, which
passes between Country Gentlemen who embrace opposite Sides of the
Question; with frequent Applications to him to salute that Part which is
generally introduced into all Controversies, that arise among the lower
Orders of the *English* Gentry, at Horse-races, Cock-matches, and other
public Places. Allusions to this Part are likewise often made for the Sake of
the Jest. And here, I believe, the Wit is generally misunderstood. In Reality,
it lies in desiring another to kiss your A— for having just before threatened

to kick his: For I have observed very accurately, that no one else ever desires you to kick that which belongs to himself, nor offers to kiss this Part in another.

The measured tone of the narrator gently caricatures the rough, unmeasured behaviour of Western and of English squires by explaining a phrase that needs no explanation, by denying that plain speaking is plain. The narrator is neither scandalized nor perturbed, but plays the part of a helpful cicerone to readers unfamiliar with country ways. By taking the semantics of the curse seriously while ignoring its social aggression, Fielding makes it seem quaintly barbarous. He does not, however, thereby condescend to the want of politeness in the country. He directly contrasts Western with the fine gentleman of the town and the squire's own parson, neither of whom curse; rather than descend to a blunt Saxon level, the courtiers speak politicly and the parson quotes Seneca. But courtly hypocrisy and feeble moralism are by no means offered as the desirable alternatives to Western's bluntness. Fielding's moral vision includes all the characters, and their characteristic ways of speaking, rather than being located in a single character or kind of speech. (Even Allworthy is too easily deceived by hypocrisy.)

The eighteenth-century novel delights in the range of language which its characters employ. According to the second edition of the *OED*, Richardson's *Clarissa* (1748) coined not only *circumjacency*, *concedence*, *disavowal*, *execratious*, and *prescriptive*, but also *asquat*, *chuffily*, *farmyard*, *flightiness*, *out-door*, and *pimply*. The first edition introduced *ugh* into the English novel, the third introduced *um*.[42] Both sounds had to wait another century before appearing in serious poetry (in Browning).

In the hymns of Charles Wesley, Saxon and Latinate English are of equal importance, sometimes cooperating with each other and sometimes opposing their complementary forces. Donald Davie has emphasized the cooperative aspect, and writes that Wesley's latinisms are 'not threaded on the staple Anglo-Saxon of his diction in order merely to give a pleasing variety in sound and pace' but 'so that Saxon and classical elements can criss-cross and light up each other's meaning'. Davie quotes from the hymns beginning 'Sinners, your Savior see!' and 'Author of Faith, Eternal Word':

> Author of Faith, appear!
> Be Thou its Finisher.

> Author of Faith, Eternal Word,
>   Whose Spirit breathes the active flame;
> Faith, like its Finisher and Lord,
>   To-day as yesterday the same:

He comments 'the ungainly "finisher" is there to remind us that "Author" means "originator".' Wesley's appeal to the exactness of Latin etymology, however, is not the only reason why he chooses a latinate word. In 'Christ the Friend to Sinners', Wesley writes:

> That I, a child of wrath and hell,
>   I should be call'd a child of God!
> Should know, should feel my sins forgiven,
>   Blest with this antepast of heaven!

Geoffrey Hill has emphasized how the latinate word 'antepast', a narrow almost intellectually mannered word, resists the effusive enthusiasm of 'feel', so characteristic of early Methodism with its open, broad spectrum of meanings.[43] Wesley's best hymns release fervent enthusiasm and energy of feeling, but they also try to the check the danger represented by uncontrolled feeling through the introduction of an erudite term, or a tightly controlled phrase that will not allow enthusiasm to boil over.

Besides the hymns of Wesley, one genre of poetry in this period made as much of Saxon terms as did the novel: satire, including invective. *Pox*, as a verb, is 'only in vulgar use', according to the *OED*, which credits Dryden with the first citation:

> Religion thou hast none: thy *Mercury*
> Has pass'd through every Sect, or theirs through Thee.
> But what thou givs't, that Venom still remains;
> And the pox'd Nation feels thee in their Brains.

> (*The Medall*, ll. 263–6; 1682)

Pox is better suited to the invective of *The Medall* than to the heroic satire of *Absalom and Achitophel*. In it, Dryden offers a concentrated and double insult: Shaftesbury is a mercurial time-server, but his mercury is not efficacious on the venom with which he poxed the nation.

Pope, too, uses this verb in what are perhaps his most vicious lines:

> From furious *Sappho* scarce a milder Fate,
> P—x'd by her Love, or libell'd by her Hate:

> (*Imitation of Horace*, sat. 2. 1. 83–4; 1733)

This couplet was Pope's first attack on Lady Mary Wortley Montagu ('He could never quite dismiss her from his mind'[44]), and it was his most cruelly unjust. (Her brother had died of smallpox, and though she recovered from it, her face was scarred and she lost her eyelashes; moreover, she showed considerable heroism in variolating her own children against it.) The conventions of satire allowed decorum to be breached in expressing rage at depraved vice. Such rage is not only expressed in vulgar terms like *pox*; Pope uses low Saxon mono-syllables like *bug, dirt, stink* just as effectively:

> Yet let me flap this Bug with gilded Wings,
> This painted Child of Dirt that stinks and stings;
>
> (*Epistle to Dr Arbuthnot*, ll. 310–11; 1734)

Rochester and Swift break decorum, or break with decorum, even more markedly, when they find a place for taboo words in their poems. Strephon observes Celia's dressing room in Swift's 'The Lady's Dressing Room', a poem which describes physical evidence of her bodily functions rather than the beauty of her body. Pope and Milton are echoed as Strephon is increasingly disabused, a process which culminates in his realization: 'Oh! Celia, Celia, Celia, shits!' Swift is impatient with squeamishness and false delicacy, with a literary decorum that fundamentally misrepresents the human ani-mal's way of being in the world, and he chooses to break literary decorum by turning to a word not in decent use as a way to break the conspiracy of polite silence, as he saw it, about the body. Still, though the word is perfectly accurate, the sentence derives most of its force from the use of a forbidden word, not from ingenuity in choosing or arranging the words. It is the final word of both a line and a verse paragraph, and it is effective as a climax because a taboo is being vio-lated. Contrast this couplet from 'Strephon and Chloe':

> And as he fill'd the reeking Vase
> Let fly a Rouzer in her Face.

The force of those lines depends not only on the scatology but also on the surprising word 'Rouzer'; Geoffrey Hill has observed, 'It would be difficult to find a word that blends the outrageous and the festive more effectively than this.'[45]

Rochester is interested in sex, not scatology, and he is particularly interested in sexual politics. In his 'Satyr on Charles II', he writes:

Peace is his Aime, his Gentlenesse is such
And Love, he loves, for he loves fucking much.
Nor are his high Desires above his Strength,
His Sceptter and his Prick are of a Length,
And she may sway the one, who plays with th'other
And make him little wiser than his Brother.

The emphasis is equally on sex and politics. Elsewhere, Rochester delights in flaunting his freedom from sexual taboos; in this poem, the similar freedom which Charles enjoys is not flaunted but examined in its political implications. It is not sex that matters in this case, but politics corrupted by sex, the indulgence of private pleasure at the expense of wise government. So Rochester has no need to underline the word, or place it in an emphatic position and thereby acknowledge the power of decorum by breaching it. When *fuck* openly returns to English poetry in the twentieth century, it is used very differently. Ezra Pound tries to give it a neutral or even sacral meaning (in his description of Circe's house in canto 39), but he is not successful in changing the timbre of the word and does not repeat the attempt. With E. E. Cummings, the word has become expletive ('I will not kiss your fucking flag') and reflects the dominant usage whereby it has little semantic meaning and can be used indiscriminately and in various parts of speech (including the infix, absofuckinglutely). Such usage (sometimes called 'verbicidal') drains the word of meaning and is far from Rochester's own use.

To summarize: from the Restoration to the end of the eighteenth century, Saxon and latinate expressions in English writing separated, and in poetry they formed segregated registers. Neo-classical purism led to an uneasiness about low and vulgar terms that was mostly concerned with Saxon words, whereas anxieties about pedantry focused on complexities of word order and syntax, especially, rather than on latinate vocabulary. In the novels of Fielding and Sterne, this distinction between Saxon and latinate was acknowledged, but one was not given a preference over the other. When low Saxon words were deployed in verse, they often had an aggressive force, as in satire, and sometimes even a transgressive force, as with Swift's assault on decorum. The result was to charge the Saxon register with a moral force: it was to be the language of unpremeditated sincerity. When sincerity became valued more highly, so did this kind of language.

Another kind of purism is directed against foreign elements in a language. In contrast to neo-classical purism which derived from

France, this purism was most influentially expounded in Germany, and most discussions of it take their point of departure in the German Romantic combination of language purism and nationalism. However, purist lexeis instrumental in the self-identity of social and ethnic groups, and even of nations, were evident long before then. In the first chapter, we looked briefly at Greek purism at the time of the Roman Empire, and also at Estienne's proposal to free French from the sway of Italian. The prestige and influence of Italian during the Renaissance also worried English writers, like Thomas Wilson. One of the most famous examples in literature is Ferdowsi's *Shahname*, completed in 1010 and written in a Persian almost free of Arabic loan words; however, this is an example of literary purism since it was the language of poetry, not the language generally, that was purged of Arabic vocabulary.

In England since the Renaissance, anti-foreign purist movements have recurrently sought to reshape the whole language. In the sixteenth century, Ralph Lever's *The Arte of Reason* (1573) offers the most uncompromising attempt to find native English equivalents to the technical philosophical vocabulary derived from Latin. He replaces *reason* with *witcrafte*, *preface* with *forespeach*, and in a list at the end, he translates *conclusio* by *endsay*, *animal* by *wight*, etc. In *The Arte of English Poesie* (1588), Puttenham gives rhetorical terms as marginal headings, and they appear as both classical jargon and Saxon English: '*zeugma* or the Single supply', '*Prozeugma* or the ringleader', '*Sillepsis*, or the double supply', etc. (Peacham, in contrast, had given only the Greek terms as headings in *The Garden of Eloquence*, 1577.) None the less, one scholar insists on the relative paucity of such nativizing attempts, and points out that even Cheke, who was 'of the opinion that our own tung shold be written cleane and pure, unmixt and unmangeled with borrowing of other tunges', did not follow this opinion in his own writing, except for the biblical translation first published in 1843.

However, the case is overstated when this scholar concludes that 'there was little of such [purist] feeling in the sixteenth century'.[46] It is true that William Camden and Richard Carew both praised the English language because its vocabulary is a mixture of words from other languages, but even they insisted on the particular Saxon qualities of the language. Anglo-Saxon was praised in the period, and latinate English sometimes denounced. Thomas Phaire attacked the authors of medical treatises: 'how long would they haue the people ignorant? Why grutche they physicke to come forth in Englyshe? Would they haue no man to know but onely they?'[47] Scholars who have studied the 'Saxonists' of the Renaissance point to the long-lasting association they made between Saxon English and particular virtues: 'plain forthrightness as over rhetoric or polish', 'manly honesty as against a suspect elegance', 'native English strength as against borrowed foreign foppery'.[48] In the next century, Ben Jonson wrote in *Timber* that Spenser 'in affecting the Ancients, writ no Language'. To subject English to Latin admixtures could be perceived as a betrayal of England; it could unleash hatred (a theme of the next chapter).

Though complaints about latinate English continued after the Restoration, and though the latinate English of Milton and Browne, especially, was sometimes censured, it did not provoke the same hostility that low Saxon words inspired. The purist impulse had found a new enemy: the French language.[49] Addison begins one of his *Spectator* essays with the wish that 'certain Men might be set apart as Superintendants of our Language, to hinder any Words of a Foreign Coin from passing among us; and in particular to prohibit any French Phrases from becoming Current in this Kingdom, when those of our own Stamp are altogether as valuable'.[50] Johnson expressed anti-French sentiments vigorously. In the preface to the *Dictionary*, he worries that Englishmen will be reduced 'to babble a dialect of France'. He censures Dryden, Pope, and Hume for their gallicisms, and Hume in particular irritates him—for Johnson, Hume represents the double betrayal of Britain and English.[51] Johnson was uneasy at any prospect of language being made impure;[52] and he often connected it with an act of betrayal. Milton, Johnson complains, warped by his allegiance to 'a perverse and pedantic principle', wrote in ' "a Babylonish dialect," in itself harsh and barbarous'.[53]

So it is keenly ironic that Johnson's dictionary and literary style would come to be represented as barbarously mixed, pedantically impure. Grossly exaggerated descriptions of Johnson's language became current. Horne Tooke, *The Diversions of Purley* (1786): 'Nearly one third of this Dictionary is as much the language of the Hottentots as of the English.' Noah Webster, in a letter of 1807, objects to the 'two thousand or more' fictitious latinisms of the *Dictionary*, handed down from previous dictionaries but never actually used: 'They no more belong to the English language than the same number of Patagonian words.'[54] In his preface to the *Specimens of the Later English Poets* (1807), Southey condemns the sixteenth-century poet Stephen Hawes because his verses are 'as full of barbarous sesquipedalian Latinisms, as the prose of the Rambler'. Macaulay complains of Johnson in 1831 that

> it is well known that he made less use than any other eminent writer of those strong plain words, Anglo-Saxon or Norman-French, of which the roots lie in the inmost depths of our language; and that he felt a vicious partiality for terms which, long after our own speech had been fixed, were borrowed from the Greek and Latin.[55]

The pejorative *Johnsonese* came into use because of Macaulay (who coined it in that essay of 1831, and not, as the *OED* claims, in an essay on Madame D'Arblay in 1843). Certain definitions, selectively chosen in order to misrepresent the tenor of the dictionary, gained notoriety (*dross*: 'the recrement or despumation of metals'; *network*: 'anything reticulated or decussated, at equal distances, with interstices between the intersections'); other definitions, straightforward and Saxon, were overlooked (*piss*: 'to make water'; *squirrel*: 'a small animal that lives in woods, remarkable for leaping from tree to tree').

Johnson was a particularly attractive target in the nineteenth century, though similar criticism was aimed at other eighteenth-century writers. These are enough, however, to document the new intensity of the anti-latinate feeling in the nineteenth century. Sometimes this feeling amounted to a full-scale programme for purifying the vernacular of words that are derived from foreign sources. In Germany, the most influential figure was Joachim Heinrich Campe, who produced the *Wörterbuch zur Erklärung und Verdeutschung der unserer Sprache aufgedrungenen fremden Ausdrücke* in 1801; he subsequently co-edited a five-volume dictionary of the German language in 1807–11. *Verdeutschung* was opposed to *Eindeutschung*: foreign words were to be replaced by native ones, rather than assimilated to the native spelling and pronunciation. It has been calculated that Campe's dictionaries, in addition to including purist innovations from other sources, contain 3,500 of his own purist neologisms, 'of which some 250 (a large number) gained a measure of acceptance'.[56] Goethe, Schiller, and Wieland mocked Campe, but his influence was wide and virtually inescapable. In England, a systematic attempt to saxonize English came later and was less successful. Few, if any, of the alternatives to latinate words which William Barnes listed in *An Outline of English Speech-Craft* (1878) became current; however, some new terms coined by those sympathetic to the movement did catch on: *foreword* began to be used in place of *preface*, and for a few decades *sun-print* and *sun-printing* could be used as alternatives to *photograph* and *photography*. A new philological awareness of the Saxon nature of English was publicized by Furnivall, Murray, and Trench.[57] Patriotic advice such as John Hookham Frere's became commonplace: 'And don't confound the language of the nation | With long-tailed words in *osity* and *ation*.'[58] By the end of the nineteenth century, it has been claimed, the 'strenuous campaign' to promote Saxon English had 'largely succeeded in driving latinate vocabulary out of the literary lexicon'.[59]

This is an overstatement, even with the qualifier 'largely'. For one thing, it applies more directly to prose writers than to poets. Wordsworth and Coleridge both praised the heterogeneity of the English vocabulary and believed that for this reason English was more expressive than German.[60] Poetic diction proved enduring, even after ordinary speech was revalued and found fit for poetry. *Irriguous* found its way into the poetry of Wordsworth, Coleridge, and Clough, and *irremeable* into Swinburne. In a brief lyric like 'A slumber did my spirit seal', dominated by monosyllables and with a few disyllables, Wordsworth chooses *diurnal*, the sole trisyllabic and latinate word in the poem, for dignity and sublimity; his innovation is to derive dignity not only from the latinate word but also from the Saxon 'rocks, and stones, and trees'.

In prose, even in Dickens, latinate English continued to be used effectively and surprisingly. In *David Copperfield*, Mr Micawber is a gentle character whose comedy (like that of characters in Sterne and Fielding) is in his sesquipedalianism:

'Under the impression,' said Mr. Micawber, 'that your peregrinations in this metropolis have not as yet been extensive, and that you might have some difficulty in penetrating the arcana of the Modern Babylon in the direction of the City Road—in short,' said Mr. Micawber, in another burst of confidence, 'that you might lose yourself—I shall be happy to call this evening, and install you in the knowledge of the nearest way.'

All levels of style are available to Dickens. For the death of Mrs Gradgrind (in *Hard Times*) he adapts latinate, archaic, poetical, and biblical diction, to create an apparent oxymoron, the Dickensian high style:

She fancied, however, that her request had been complied with, and that the pen she could not have held was in her hand. It matters little what figures of wonderful nomeaning she began to trace upon her wrappers. The hand soon stopped in the midst of them; the light that had always been feeble and dim behind the weak transparency, went out; and even Mrs. Gradgrind, emerged from the shadow in which man walketh and disquieteth himself in vain, took upon her the dread solemnity of the sages and patriarchs.

None the less, it is not an overstatement, it is not even controversial, to point out that of the two sources of vocabulary, it was the Saxon that more often inspired creative responses in the nineteenth century. Dickens's genius operates prodigiously with it, on it: from names (Gamp, Podsnap, Pecksniff, etc.) to neologisms (*butterfingers, the creeps, in the same boat, round the corner*, etc.).[61] In the nineteenth century, ordinary speech became a stimulus, not an obstacle, to poetry: from the 'language really used by men', selected, purified, and adopted by Wordsworth in the *Lyrical Ballads*; to the impromptu, improvisational conversation of Bishop Blougram in Browning's monologue; to the ordinary talk set to hexameters in Clough's *Amours de Voyage* or *The Bothie of Tober-na-Vuolich*. In the eighteenth century, latinate poetic diction sometimes self-consciously advertised its latinity, for a variety of reasons; now Saxon diction likewise made self-conscious displays of Saxonness at times, pre-eminently in the cries, groans, outbursts, and interjections which must appear Saxon in order to appear sincere.

In comparison with other literatures, English poetry has few interjections, being largely limited to *ah, alack, alas, eh, oh*, and *woe*. Greek, in contrast, is rich in them: in a single play of Sophocles, Electra cries out *o, io, pheu, aiai, talaina, oimoi moi, io moi moi, ee io, ee aiai, io gonai, oimoi talaina, oi 'go talaina, otototoi to toi, io moi moi dystenos.*[62] *Oh* and *ah*, sometimes *o* and *a*, are constants of English drama. They sometimes touch the height of Charmian in *Antony and Cleopatra*: [63]

> It is well done, and fitting for a Princesse
> Descended of so many Royall Kings.
> Ah Souldier!

And sometimes sink into the bathos of James Thomson:[64]

> O Sophonisba, Sophonisba, O!

In the nineteenth century, the variety of interjections that appear in verse increases markedly. As satire, the interjections of Byron's *Don Juan* did not mark a distinctive break with literary tradition; on the other hand, Wordsworth's poems caused offence by introducing into literature speech and sounds which had previously been removed from it. The burr of the idiot boy was not the sound with which to gratify the audience's known habits of association. By the time Browning introduced *hmm* and *ugh* into non-dramatic verse (in *The Ring and the Book*) and *grrr* into literature ('Soliloquy in a Spanish Cloister'), poetry was far less resistant to quotidian speech; a few more human noises could be accommodated in verse. The point to emphasize is the new value found in words that are sincere and non-selfconscious, that signal immediate or naked being in the world. In *The Philosophy of Style*, Herbert Spencer writes that 'when oral language is employed, the strongest effects are produced by interjections, which condense entire sentences into syllables'.[65] The extreme significance placed in one strain of modernism on the inarticulate cry of pain, or on the tabooed words and grunts of sexual ecstasy, continue a Romantic priority. Hopkins exploits and redirects that priority. In the last line of 'Carrion Comfort', he combines sacred and profane, the theological and the colloquial: 'I wretch lay wrestling with (my God!) my God.' The parenthesis '(my God!)' is both an idiomatic vernacular shout of surprised recognition and an abrupt prayer wrenched out of him; it also echoes Christ's words on the cross.

One reason why the Saxon register of language had a new importance in the period was that plain Saxon language had become associated with forms of speech that now had a new significance in poetry: cries, swearing, interjections, and other outbursts of strong feeling. These have another distinctive feature: they are usually monosyllables. The association of monosyllables with the sincere utterance of an authentic self was by no means first made by the Romantics. Several chapters of the fourteenth-century mystical treatise *Þe Clowde of Vnknowyng* (7, 37–9) are devoted to the power of such words; one of the chapters is devoted to the question, '& whi peersiþ it heuen, þis lityl schort preier of o litil silable?' The *OED* devotes a sub-entry in its first definition of *syllable* to those times the word is used 'pregnantly of a word of one syllable'; examples in poetry range from Gower ('That o sillable hath overthrowe | A thousand wordes') to Cowper ('Those awful syllables, hell, death, and sin'), and the prose examples run from the Lutheran Reformation to the French Revolution.

For centuries, monosyllables were associated with authentic speech and natural English. Since the purist attitudes towards authentic speech and natural English have varied, and have often been contradictory (sometimes within a single writer), a literary history of monosyllables will recapitulate English language purism. With the growth of linguistic self-consciousness in the Renaissance, questions about monosyllables, their relation to the English language, and their place in English literature were frequently raised. These disputes—the fitness of monosyllables in verse, advantages of the monosyllable in expressing concepts or feelings, whether monosyllables lack dignity, and whether monosyllables represent and polysyllables misrepresent the true nature of English—continued unabated, renewed by being cast in the vocabulary of each literary period. So long as latinate English and Saxon English are associated with different power interests, for example of class, profession, media, and government, the disputes will continue.

Theories and opinions about the prosody of monosyllables were systematically elaborated in the Renaissance.[66] Both Gascoigne and Puttenham thought that monosyllables offer a distinctive advantage for verse: they can be scanned indifferently, either long or short. Puttenham, it is true, contradicted himself when he also wrote that in pronouncing monosyllables, 'they do of necessity retaine a sharpe accent', a view shared by William Webbe and Roger Ascham. King James VI believed that monosyllables lack an intrinsic stress, but he found this a disadvantage and warned that monosyllabic lines should be avoided. William Camden took them to be 'vnfitting for verses and measures'.[67] Campion, the 'seraphic doctor of English prosody',[68] thought that English monosyllables are unfit to make dactylic verse, however versatile they may be in other metres.

An influential view emerged that monosyllabic lines in poems are rough, metrically ambiguous, and suited only for special purposes. In the Dedication to the *Æneis*, Dryden defended the monosyllabic opening line of his translation ('Arms, and the Man I sing, who forc'd by Fate') against the charge of harshness, while acknowledging the seriousness of the charge: 'it rarely happens, that a verse of monosyllables may sound harmoniously'. In a note to lines 9. 853–4, he wrote that, though the first line consists entirely of monosyllables, and both lines are very rough, this was a matter of choice, an instance where he chose to preserve harshness for special effect. Pope believed that 'Monosyllable-Lines, unless very artfully manag'd, are stiff, languishing, & hard.'[69] The warning from the *Essay on Criticism* became famous: 'And ten low words oft creep in one dull line.' Like Dryden, Pope defended certain monosyllabic lines (see the note to the *Odyssey* 11. 736) which serve the special purpose of conveying the sense of heaviness and difficulty. Thomas Gray regretted that English abounds in monosyllables, 'a defect which will for ever hinder it from adapting itself well to music, and must be consequently no small impediment to the sweetness and harmony of versification'.[70]

However, most of these prosodic generalizations are not true. Monosyllabic lines are frequent in English poetry, common in emphatic positions like the beginning and the end of poems, and constitute some of the finest lines of the language.[71] One in seven of Shakespeare's sonnets begins with a monosyllabic line, one in five ends with such a line, and one in twenty ends in a monosyllabic couplet. One in ten lines of Pope's *Epistle to Dr Arbuthnot* is monosyllabic. Some of the most powerful lines in *Paradise Regained* are monosyllabic ('I would be at the worst, worst is my Port', 3. 209; 'Tempt not the Lord thy God, he said and stood', 4. 558), and they are found in the more exalted language of *Paradise Lost*, too. Some of the most famous verses in the King James version of the Bible are monosyllabic ('And God said, Let there be light: and there was light. And God saw the light, that it was good'). Dickens not only has frequent recourse to iambic clauses and sentences, but also to iambic clauses in monosyllables: 'It was the best of times, it was the worst of times . . .' Swinburne, one of the most monosyllabic of all English poets, has monosyllabic lines in 'Hertha', 'Sapphics', and other non-iambic poems. Monosyllabic lines, monosyllables in verse, are simply too common, too various, to be helpfully discussed by reference to the intrinsic virtues or limitations of the monosyllable. The only generalization that seems to be right is Campion's: monosyllabic lines are in fact very rare in dactylic verse.

Although it would be a mistake to regard these disputes as an accurate description of prosody, they none the less document the history of the values and prejudices attached to monosyllables. Gascoigne praised monosyllables not only because of their metrical versatility, but also because 'the most aunciered words are of one syllable, so that the more monosyllables that you vse, the truer Englishman you shall seeme'. Puttenham equated monosyllables with 'the more part our naturall Saxon English'. In *Summer's Last Will and Testament*, Nashe had Orion praise dogs by pointing out that, among other virtues, 'They barke as good old Saxon as may be'. In fact, Nashe's attitude was more complex; in the preface to the second edition of *Christs Teares over Ierusalem*, he defended his compound words by writing, 'Our English tongue of all languages most swarmeth with the single money of monasillables, which are the onely scandall of it.' As with the debates on quantity, these arguments are involved in the attractions and dangers of English nationhood, as well as in the relations between ancient and modern; they reflect the same compound of desire, anxiety, and hostility provoked by Latin-speaking bodies in England generally. One other advantage was announced: both Richard Carew and William Camden thought that monosyllables were particularly effective for representing and enabling intellectual activity.[72]

At the end of the seventeenth century and through much of the eighteenth, monosyllables were set in a new context, and their advantages and disadvantages were perceived differently. Though suited to express laborious harshness, they were condemned in other contexts. Dryden complained that Holyday's translation of Juvenal was crowded with 'ill sounding Monosyllables, of which our Barbarous Language affords him a wild plenty'. He found that English monosyllables were 'clotted' or 'encumbered' with consonants, another obstacle to refined fluency. Pope found them stiff, languishing, and hard. Lowness was the main cause of literary anxiety in the period, and monosyllables were particularly liable to be low. Swift objected to the innovation that produced words like *Phizz*, *Hipps*, *Mobb*, *Pozz*, and *Rep*, 'when we are already over-loaded with Monosyllables, which are the Disgrace of our Language'.[73] They also lead to intellectual confusion; in *Gulliver's Travels*, the first project of the professors in Lagado is to shorten discourse by cutting polysyllables down to one (and by omitting verbs and participles since all things are but nouns). On the other hand, Dryden praised English because 'by reason of its monosyllables' it was far more 'compendious' than Italian, Spanish, or French. Smart located traditional Saxon virtues in them: 'For God has given us a language of monosyllables to prevent our clipping' (*Jubilate Agno*, B579). In his preface to the *Dictionary*, Johnson warned against the process by which English has departed from 'its original Teutonick character' toward French, 'from which it ought to be our endeavour to recall it, by making our ancient volumes the ground-work of style'. Latin did not pose a similar threat, and he imputed to it a historical priority equal to Saxon: 'Most of our syllables are *Roman*, and our words of one syllable are very often *Teutonick*.'

Johnson's equation was still widely accepted in the nineteenth century, though as hostility to Latin increased, so did hostility to English polysyllables. A new cluster of positive associations was attached to monosyllables: they constituted the language of feeling; guarded the virtues of the English nation; and were the means by which to instruct children, for whom now dozens of books written, or rewritten, in 'words of one syllable' were published.[74] In his essay on style (1852), Herbert Spencer sees in Saxon English the key cause of force in language, because the Saxon language which the child learns will always be more closely, more organically connected with particular ideas than Latin synonyms can be.[75] De Quincey (1845) sets out a magisterial description of the relations between latinate and Saxon English, and between monosyllables and polysyllables:[76]

Pathos, in situations which are homely, or at all connected with domestic affections, naturally moves by Saxon words. Lyrical emotion of every kind, which, (to merit the name of lyrical,) must be in the state of flux and reflux, or, generally, of agitation, also requires the Saxon element of our language. And why? Because the Saxon is the aboriginal element; the basis, and not the superstructure: consequently it comprehends all the ideas which are natural to the heart of man and to the elementary situations of life. And, although the Latin often furnishes us with duplicates of these ideas, yet the Saxon, or monosyllabic part, has the advantage of precedency in our use and knowledge; for it is the language of the nursery, whether for rich or poor, in which great philological academy no toleration is given to words in 'osity' or 'ation'. There is, therefore, a great advantage, as regards the consecration to our feelings, settled, by usage and custom, upon the Saxon strands, in the mixed yarn of our native tongue. And, universally, this may be remarked—that, wherever the passion of a poem is of that sort which uses, presumes, or postulates the ideas, without seeking to extend them, Saxon will be the 'cocoon', (to speak by the language applied to silk-worms,) which the poem spins for itself. But, on the other hand, where the motion of the feeling is by and through the ideas, where, (as in religious or meditative poetry—Young's, for instance, or Cowper's,) the pathos creeps and kindles underneath the very tissues of the thinking, there the Latin will predominate; and so much so that, whilst the flesh, the blood and the muscle, will be often almost exclusively Latin, the articulations only, or hinges of connection, will be Anglo-Saxon.

This division of labour, or division of the spoils, between Latin and Saxon remains popular today, but it took several centuries to evolve. De Quincey's description is unhappy when it tries to account for feeling mediated by thought. Latinate English is reserved for thought, or rather for thought that extends beyond the ideas of childhood, and Saxon English is assigned to feeling. Even with the exception made for religious and meditative poetry in which feeling is 'by and through' ideas, De Quincey fails to account for language in which feelings may be thought or thought felt. His argument is also unfortunate in having contributed to the cult of plain speaking by speaking of Saxon English as the essential component of English, and taking latinate English therefore to be dispensable. Still, it is no more inadequate than the theorizing in previous centuries about monosyllables, and is as useful in documenting habits of linguistic association.

Both Dryden and Pope describe particular monosyllabic lines in their translations excellently. To be unwilling to generalize about monosyllables does not imply that the two poets are wrong about their own lines, that a monosyllabic line never engages with the contemporary expectations about what it should and should not do. Like the etymology of a word, whose relevance in a particular context depends on the presence of other factors that actively allude to the etymology, a monosyllable or monosyllabic line in context may or may not advertise the fact of its Saxonness. The presence or absence of hiatus, quantity, aspirations, and the disposition of the secondary stresses may make a monosyllabic line rough or smooth; the presence of low monosyllables may make the line low, or monosyllables of sentiment make it sentimental; the presence of Biblical diction may make a monosyllabic line biblical, as in Swinburne's 'fighting and profane parody of the Old Testament', in which 'its lines are made of short English words like the short Roman swords'.[77] The Saxon element, as it is conceived at a particular moment, can be underlined, given a special, additional emphasis, by monosyllables.

Monosyllabic lines may also cut across the grain of expectations. Take a couplet from Ben Jonson's 'To William Camden':

What weight, and what authority in thy speech!
Man scarse can make that doubt, but thou canst teach.

The second line translates ten words of Pliny (*nihil est quod discere velis quod ille docere non possit*) into ten English monosyllables. To translate a concise Latin sentence into the same number of English words is very hard; to translate it into ten English monosyllables is an extraordinary accomplishment. The Latin coexists without effort or strain with the English. Authority, piety, and tradition have found a peaceful idiom, in which no quarrel arises between ancient and modern.

Or take this couplet from Aeneas's speech at the beginning of book 2 of the *Aeneid*, in Dryden's translation:

> A Peopl'd City made a Desart Place;
> All that I saw, and part of which I was:

Aeneas speaks English in the high style and with all the authority of a great commander, and he does this partly in monosyllables: 'quaeque ipse miserrima uidi et quorum pars magna fui' (All that I saw, and part of which I was). Dryden does not dislocate the English in order to suggest the presence and authority of Latin, because such a dislocation would acknowledge the contrast between English and Latin; rather they are presented as one.

Works entirely in monosyllables are much rarer than those with monosyllabic lines or sentences, if we discount children's books of the nineteenth century.[78] The most famous, perhaps best, monosyllabic poem is Chidiock Tichborne's elegy, which begins:[79]

> My prime of youth is but a frost of cares,
> My feast of joy is but a dish of paine:
> My crop of corne is but a field of tares,
> And al my good is but vaine hope of gaine.
> The day is past, and yet I saw no sunne;
> And now I liue, and now my life is done.

Each line is grammatically complete; each is divided into two parts, the second generally negating the expectation or promise of the first. The poem proceeds by relentlessly negating hopeful promise; perhaps some of the quality of inexorable doom derives from the unvarying sequence of ten monosyllables in each line. Still, one literary critic discusses the poem at length without mentioning that it is written entirely in monosyllables; in a way, this is a tribute to the poem's success, to the metrical variety within the set pattern.[80]

Even more remarkable than Tichborne's elegy is William Loe's *Songs of Sion* (1620), a book of eighty poems, mostly taken from scripture and 'metaphrased into words of one syllable of great Brittains language'.[81] When the book was rediscovered and printed for private circulation in 1870, the editor referred to the 'sweet, simple, pathetic strokes' of the poems and their 'quiet, child-like directness'. This may be the case with lines that serve as fillers, and with some of the repetitions, but it is more likely to be an accidental association of the Victorian age, in which so many monosyllabic primers for children were published. It is not true most of the time, and it is not true of these lines from Loe's metaphrase of Jeremiah 3: 1–3:

> I am the man O Lord
>   Haue felt thy wrath, thy rod:
> O send me helpe in this my woe
>   My Lord, my Christ, my God.
>
> Thy stormes and clouds of ire
>   Doe beate me day and night:
> Thou shewst me woe, and wast, and warre,
>   And hid'st me from the light.
>
> All the day long O Lord
>   Thine hand is turned gainst me:
> Noe helpe, noe hope, noe ioy, noe mirth
>   That I poore wretch can see.

In the dedicatory epistle to the first section, Loe explains that he presumed to metaphrase some passages of the Psalms

as an essay to know whether we might expresse our harts to God in our holy soliloquies, in monasillables in our owne mother tongue or no. It being a receaued opinion amongst many of those who seeme rather to be iuditious than caprichious, that heretofore our English tongue in the true idiome thereof, consisted altogether of monosillables, vntill it came to be blended and mingled with the commixture of exotique languages. And I my self haue seene all the Lord prayer vsed in the tyme of John Wickleefe to be expressed in words of one sillable.

His ambition was born out of the association of monosyllables, pure English, and national feeling; it also insists on a purified, monosyllabic Saxon language as the true language of the English church.

That is, the division between latinate and Saxon English had yet another function: it was applied to the religious divide in England. This is a topic which I will address in the next chapter from the other side of that divide, by looking at the highly latinate Catholic translation of the Bible and the attacks it provoked; in order to place it and other examples in the right context, we will need to consider an ambition that is directly opposite to that of language purism, the desire to dislocate English by following foreign models.

CHAPTER THREE

The Interference of Latin with English Literature

WHEN APPLIED TO language, the terms *foreign* and *native* refer both to a reality (for example, the foreign-language source behind a borrowing or an imitation) and to a perception of that reality (whether an expression is perceived to deviate from the norms of its language and conform to the norms of another). The path from etymological source to connotation is tortuous; to what degree a word is felt to be foreign varies with the tastes of each historical period, and with all that goes into forming taste, as well as with the judgements of particular readers. What is called native in one period may be called foreign in another. Johnson would have found incomprehensible the charge, increasingly frequent after his death, that he had betrayed English by writing in an English–Latin hybrid. Chaucer wrote with close attention to French and Italian literary models; he had no notion that he would come to be seen as a writer of pure English.

A foreign presence in a literary work may be perceived in manifold ways, or it may not be noticed at all. I propose to sketch four possible deployments of a foreign source within a literary work; then discuss a half-dozen examples of literature made to seem foreign; and finally consider at length a single latinism in order to illustrate from that perspective the main topic of the chapter: the ambition to dislocate the language of English literature by imitating foreign, and especially Latin, examples.

The first relation between foreign and native obtains when the foreign is present only as a source and does not interrupt the native language, does not cause it to deviate from its norms. Ben Jonson in 'Drinke to me, onely, with thine eyes' draws on Philostratus' *Epistles*; in fact all the lines can be traced to it. Here are the first four lines:

> Drinke to me, onely, with thine eyes,
> And I will pledge with mine;
> Or leave a kisse but in the cup,
> And Ile not looke for wine.

The Greek is only a source. Jonson calls the poem a song, a genre that does not alert a reader to the influence of ancient Greek; the subject and the conceits are not characteristic of the language; nor does the vocabulary, syntax, or prosody (Philostratus' *Epistles* were written in prose) suggest that the language is present. This adaptation, like Jonson's assimilation of Catullus in 'Kisse me, sweet', is supremely graceful. Nothing foreign remains to dislocate the texture or point away from the English words to another language. It is an ideally successful translation, according to one understanding of translation.

In the second relation the foreign is used as a means to deviate from the norms of ordinary language. By definition, the high style, grand style, the *genus sublime dicendi*, is not like the language in quotidian use; it functions by means of its unlikeness to common speech, and it succeeds or fails as it illuminates or obscures the ordinary. The use of foreign terms to create the high style has been discussed in most rhetorical handbooks since Aristotle (*Poetics* 22). *Paradise Lost* provides the most salient example in English, and the motivation for Milton's practice is succinctly described by Addison:

Another way of raising the Language, and giving it a Poetical Turn, is to make use of the Idioms of other Tongues. *Virgil* is full of the *Greek* Forms of Speech, which the Criticks call *Hellenisms*, as *Horace* in his Odes abounds with them much more than *Virgil*. I need not mention the several Dialects which *Homer* has made use of for this end. *Milton*, in conformity with the Practice of the Ancient Poets, and with *Aristotle*'s Rule has infused a great many *Latinisms*, as well as *Graecisms*, and sometimes *Hebraisms*, into the Language of his Poem . . . Under this Head may be reckoned the placing the Adjective after the Substantive, the transposition of Words, the turning the Adjective into a Substantive, with several other Foreign Modes of Speech, which this Poet has naturalized to give his Verse the greater Sound, and throw it out of Prose. (*Spectator* 285, 26 January 1712)

The style of *Paradise Lost* has also been resisted (notably by Johnson) for precisely the reason that Addison values it, for its deviating so markedly from ordinary language. English readers, in particular, have been suspicious of verse that has been thrown out of prose, made distant from the speaking voice. None the less, a prescriptive attitude insisting that poetry be like prose is parochial; after all, complaints that Milton was insensitive to or even ruthless about what constitutes ordinary English are not refuted or substantiated by liking or disliking the foreign expressions that distance his verse from prose. For Milton, as I will try to demonstrate below, foreignisms provided rich opportunities for logopoeia, 'the dance of the intelligence among words'.[1] The point to be made here is that the foreign may be used to alienate one's language from its common patterns, to make it strange, for which purpose Milton draws not only on Greek and Latin but also on Italian and Hebrew.

The third way that foreign and native might be related seems paradoxical: the foreign may have a crucial likeness to the native, or even be the means by which the native becomes itself, acquires its own nature. Ben Jonson, as we saw in the last chapter, wrote moral epigrams like 'To William Camden' that are not less Saxon, nor less monosyllabic, for their having been inspired by Latin. Pope described a certain English style as simultaneously Latin and English:[2]

> O come, that easy *Ciceronian* stile,
> So *Latin*, yet so *English* all the while

In the couplet, he was expressing contempt for the florid puerilities and flatteries of sermons and court speeches, but I would emphasize the word *easy*: the lack of ease which only a generation or so before had seemed to distinguish Latin from English, and latinate English from native English,[3] no longer does so, and ease is found to characterize both languages. German was believed to have a special affinity with ancient Greek, and from the eighteenth century on, Germans were told that imitating Greek was a good way to write purer German. In the nineteenth century, English writers were urged to write an English that more closely resembled German, or Anglo-Saxon, which was gaining for itself the status of 'Old English'. Conversely, too much nativeness might result in foreignness; this is a charge usually laid against Charles Doughty's *The Dawn in Britain*, and even Hopkins, who has been admired for his own stress on 'the naked thew and sinew of the English language' (for which he praised Dryden), has also been disparaged for turning his language into a 'muscle-bound monstrosity';[4] such evaluations, however, run the risk of taking native English as the *explanans* when it is an *explanandum*. The paradox whereby native becomes foreign or foreign becomes native partly reflects the traditional metaphysical instability of self and other, and it partly results from taking literally metaphors of language as an organism and so postulating sharp boundaries that keep languages distinct. The paradox has been explored most deeply, both in poetry and in theoretical essays, by Friedrich Hölderlin, to be discussed in Chapter 5. 'What is native must be learned as much as what is foreign', he writes; 'nothing is harder than the free use of the native'.[5]

The fourth way of relating foreign to native is to mark both style and subject as foreign. Milton's sonnet beginning 'Lawrence of vertuous Father vertuous son' takes over Horace's Latin syntax, from the first line of *Odes* 1. 16, a famous tag. He finds in Horace a means to return the sonnet to serious use after it had been debased during two centuries of Petrarchanisms (he is following the example of Italian writers like Bembo and Della Casa, who were similarly inspired by Horace). He draws here on the odes of invitation by Horace, as he draws on Horace's reputation for moral wisdom, as a judicious enjoyer of life's goods. However we interpret 'spare' in the penultimate line, either as 'forbear to' or as 'spare the time for', Horace limits the range of meanings, prohibits either meaning from being infected by licence on the one hand or asceticism on the other. Though the rest of the sonnet is thick with Horatian allusions, there is no more eruption of Latin into English after the first line, which has alerted us to the kind of sonnet that Milton is writing.

I distinguish this sort of dislocation from the second kind because in Milton's grand style the point is the dislocation itself, the deviation from contemporary usage, and the perspective that is gained as a result; in contrast, what is significant in the last sort is not only a deviation from the norms of usage but also an invocation of or allusion to something specifically foreign. When a culture sees itself standing in close relation to another time or another culture, the disruption of English along archaic or foreign patterns provides an opportunity to invoke the presence of the foreign culture. To make English sound like Greek or Latin may be a way of representing or commenting upon the Greece or Rome that formed part of a culture's self-understanding. The latinate syntax of the first line of Milton's sonnet is an allusion to Horace's Latin and also invokes Horace's Renaissance reputation for wisdom. Foreign aspects of the syntax of *Paradise Lost*, though they draw on the example of Greek,

Italian, and Latin models, do not typically constitute an allusion to them.

Four possibilities of relating foreign style to foreign substance have been sketched: in the first case, as in Jonson's 'Drinke to me, onely, with thine eyes', neither the language nor the subject invokes the foreign; in the second, Milton's grand style, the language is foreign, strange, but this is not a sign that points to a specific foreign presence; in the third, a foreign style is conceived as a key to the native being of one's language; in the fourth, both language and substance are foreign, as in the first line, but not the remainder, of Milton's sonnet.

Language interference, linguists explain, is exemplified by 'those instances of deviation from the norms of either language which occur in the speech of bilinguals as a result of their familiarity with more than one language'. [6] Though the term has been limited to errors and innovations made by non-native speakers of a language, literary analogues of the phenomenon also deserve attention, along with the diverse motivations for it—whether to establish a new norm, or for what it signifies in itself, or to invoke a foreign presence.[7] (Naturally, written literature may also try to record the language interference of particular speakers, as in the broken English of Friday and Queequeg.)

Let us start with interference in its most extreme literary forms. The two English works most famous for their deviation from the norms of English are Milton's *Paradise Lost* and Joyce's *Finnegans Wake*. From the start both works inspired violently antagonistic criticism as well as denunciations that they are not even written in English. Johnson's reservations about *Paradise Lost* are famous: 'he had formed his style by a perverse and pedantic principle. He was desirous to use English words with a foreign idiom'; he wrote in a '"Babylonish Dialect," in itself harsh and barbarous'. Johnson resists what he thinks is the call of Milton's language to obedience, admiration, and captivity. He objects to the strangeness and authority of Milton's verse, both of which are fundamental to it.[8] Foreign usages, moreover, help to create both those qualities: strangeness by the unfamiliar English, and authority by the example of the classical texts that lie in part behind the expression. However, foreignness is not only a means to enforce grandeur; it is also a rich poetic resource that Milton capitalizes on in many ways, providing him with some of his densest word-play, not simply grand in expression but also requiring the reader to pause and reflect.

Take a famous grecism from *Paradise Lost*. Eve plucks the fruit, eats (9. 791–2):

> Greedily she ingorg'd without restraint,
> And knew not eating Death:

Greek may use a participle after verbs of knowledge or perception, and the line, modelled after Greek, means 'and knew not that she ate Death'. But the unusual syntax is not limited to its Greek model; rather it concentrates several meanings in the line: Eve did not know (that is, she was ignorant for the last time) *while* she was eating death; she did not know *what* she did (she ate death); she did not know the *eating*, devouring power of death.

What is the point of the Greek presence? As a source, the Greek syntax suggested the possibility of the compact and dense verses. But the Greek has not entirely disappeared; the strangeness of the expression bears witness to a foreign element, which in this case is both Greek and Latin, Virgil having imitated the grecism and introduced it into his Latin (*Aeneid* 2. 377). Participating in the Renaissance aspiration to recreate ancient authority and deliberate magnificence, Milton imitates both languages at once. However, the authority or weight gained by such imitation does not stifle dissent, as Johnson believed; rather it focuses attention on syntax that rewards attention. The apparent paradox of the line invites reflection not submission. Nor is the strangeness of the expression a violent indifference to English. It emphasizes the momentous, mysterious nature of Eve's action: by eating the apple she is bringing death into the world.

Milton's genius is repeatedly engaged in adapting the classical languages to English and in adapting English to them. Sometimes he forces us to recognize the neutral etymological sense within English words that have fallen and acquired a sinister sense: 'with mazie error' (4. 239) or 'With Serpent errour wandring' (7. 302). He favours Latin constructions; indeed, 'paradise lost' is the Latin way of saying 'the loss of paradise'. His most powerful writing insists on the loss of paradise, to prevent paradise even from being imagined, except on condition of its imminent loss. Imitations of Greek and Latin syntax and vocabulary provided Milton with one means to accomplish this,[9] and they were instrumental in creating the high style itself, with its classical rhetoric, a style which none the less is scrutinized in the epic since it better suits the speech of Satan than of Christ. The accumulation of latinate words, the long periods, and the complex syntax have led some readers either to reject or to approve of the poem as 'un-English'.[10]

Finnegans Wake is more notorious. A few critics have found similarities between the two works; T. S. Eliot, for example, believes that both writers sacrifice the visual imagination for the auditory, and that both write their own language.[11] Yet in many respects Joyce's ambitions are the opposite of Milton's. Here is H. C. E. on trial in chapter 3 of the first book:

Thus the unfacts, did we possess them, are too imprecisely few to warrant our certitude, the evidencegivers by legpoll too untrustworthily irreperible where his adjugers are semmingly freak threes but his judicandees plainly minus twos. Nevertheless Madam's Toshowus waxes largely more lifeliked (entrance, one kudos; exits, free) and our notional gullery is now completely complacent, an exegious monument, aerily perennious.

In the paragraph Latin is present, Horace's Latin, from the first line of the last ode of his first published set of odes, a line which became a famous boast in the Renaissance, and also later, in Pushkin and as late as Pound: 'exegi monumentum aere perennius' (I have made a monument more lasting than bronze). It is a sentiment and an ambition which Milton could straightforwardly share. For Joyce, the Horatian tag which had been a proud boast of enduring artistic accomplishment has become airy and insubstantial. The monument that outlasts bronze is now exiguous, minute, and the bronze itself has become air; all that is solid has melted into air. And so has the rest of our gulling notions, whose contemporary spectral existence cannot compete with the hyperreality of the modern wax museum. From Horace, as from other Latin writers, Milton borrows syntax above all, as with 'Lawrence of vertuous Father vertuous son'. Joyce, on the other hand, borrows phonetics, the breaths of air that language is, 'exegi monumentum aere perennius', 'an exegious monument, aerily perennious'. Instead of Milton's English massively substantiated through Latin, Joyce's language plays over the broken phonemes of the world's speech, an unsubstantial language of trivial coincidence, the source of the ignorant articulate lies we tell each other in sharing grief and joy.[12]

The complaint 'That's not English!' has been directed at many targets besides Milton and Joyce, though they are the most famous.

Let us survey a half-dozen additional examples, in order to consider a wider range of motivations for making English foreign.

It will be necessary to navigate between a Scylla and a Charybdis. The Scylla comprises those readers and critics who demand that literature not diverge far from 'the real language of men', or that literary works be limited to words as they might conceivably, on some occasion, actually be spoken. This is a particularly strong bias in English literature, in which poetry (with the large exception of Milton) has kept close to prose, in which poetry, whenever it began to diverge from the spoken language, has been periodically renewed by being brought closer to the prose language of ordinary speech. Homer, in contrast, wrote in a synthetic language made up of dialects and archaisms in a combination which no one on earth ever spoke. The Charybdis consists of those who value divergence from ordinary usage for its own sake. In the recent anthology *Imagining Language* the editors write 'Deviations from the linguistic norm by literary works render them valuable'. Deviation, however, is nothing in itself; it may be valuable or pointlessly eccentric. A number of attempts to account for innovation in the arts founder because the question of value has been eliminated. Michel Serres, for example, drawing on metaphors from information theory, takes information to be encoded in difference and therefore takes deviations from norms as substantive; Ernst Gombrich gives a roughly analogous account of innovation in the arts as communication effected by the difference of a new signal from previous ones. Martin Heidegger believes when poets in a destitute time put language at risk, by taking it out of ordinary speech, they move beyond a particular horizon of being.[13] However, not all information is of equal value or of value at all, and not all deviations from ordinary speech have valuable implications. Attempts to avoid arguments about the value of an artwork by subsuming it within information theory or ontology are unhelpful because they end by defining difference as value, rather than arguing for its value. Let us turn to examples.

The first Catholic translation of the New Testament into English was published at Rheims in 1582 (the translation of the Old Testament followed in 1609–10 at Douay but was much less influential). It was mainly the work of Gregory Martin, who defended it vigorously in his preface and in subsequent polemics. The latinisms of the translation became notorious: 'Give vs to day our supersubstantial bread' (Matthew 6: 11); 'Haue care of him: and whatsoeuer thou shalt supererogate, I at my returne wil repay thee' (Luke 10: 35); 'he exinanited him self, taking the forme of a seruant, made into the similitude of men' (Philippians 2: 7). It adopted a latinate style as well as vocabulary: 'What is to me and thee woman?' (John 2: 4). In the twentieth century, the latinate reputation of the 'Rheims' New Testament has been qualified and contested. Where it has used vigorous Saxon diction, it has been applauded:[14] 'to blase abrode the word' (Mark 1: 45), 'and forthwith the wench rose vp, and walked' (Mark 5: 42), 'And doe ye al things without murmurings and staggerings' (Philippians 2: 14). Earlier in the sixteenth century, Protestant Bibles, too, had been obliged to introduce latinate vocabulary because English lacked the necessary ecclesiastical and theological terms,[15] and the comparative success of their latinate vocabulary, it has been argued, should not be invidiously compared to the Rheims failure because the Rheims never enjoyed the role of an official Bible.[16] Moreover, the considerable part played by the Rheims translation in the creation of the King James Bible has been revealed.[17]

None the less, the Rheims New Testament was intended to sound unlike normal English, and it was so received. It was repeatedly and furiously denounced for its dependence on terms designed to 'darken the sence' so that 'it may bee kept from being vnderstood'.[18] Gregory Martin defended his translation as vigorously as it was attacked, maintaining that it is better to write an ungainly, strange English than an elegant English that traduces scripture; better to preserve the difficulty of the original, forcing readers to wonder about the meaning of a passage, than to 'mollifie the speaches or phrases' or to use an English word with inappropriate and uncontrollable associations; better to preserve ambiguities in the translation than to remove them.[19]

The rationale for the practice is eminently defensible; but so is the rationale for the complementary practice of Tyndale and others. Translation involves unyielding cruces where one is required either to introduce a new technical term, and so not be understood, or to use an existing term in a new sense, and so be misunderstood. The Rheims translation should be evaluated by the integrity of the relation obtaining between its theory and practice. For example, true to his theory of translation, Martin writes 'supersubstantial bread', following Jerome's *panem supersubstantialem*, rather than the Greek. The Protestant case against the Vulgate focused on instances like this one where the discrepancy between the Latin and Greek texts was very great, and it is a mark of the integrity of the Rheims New Testament that it does not attempt to hide the difficulty; it includes a marginal note giving the Greek in this passage and in the analogous one in Luke (*panem quotidianum*, translated there as 'dayly bread'). On the other hand, Martin coins the verb 'supererogate' not to avoid the wrong connotation of an existing English word, but to introduce with questionable relevance a word with strong connotations of Catholic doctrine.

Martin expresses the hope that the strangeness of the translation will fade in time after repeated use. At other moments, however, he praises the remoteness of its style, and the reasons are clear: to make English follow the Latin of the Vulgate emphasizes the supremacy of the Vulgate; to choose English words modelled on traditional ecclesiastical terms acknowledges the validity of the tradition and remains within it; the difficulty of the latinate translation makes manifest the fact that lay readers need help and guidance; and obscurity is a necessary aspect of mystery. All these reasons incensed the reformers, who developed a powerfully influential rhetoric in order to repudiate the strange English of the Catholic bible, a rhetoric favouring terms of abuse like 'fustian', 'ink-horn', 'obscured', and 'barbarous', along with lists of unacceptable words.[20]

Because of the success of the anti-Rheims polemic, the association between latinate English and obfuscation was cemented; henceforth such English would often provoke the suspicion that it was masking illegitimate claims to authority. A decade later, the quarrel between Thomas Nashe, the dramatist and brilliant improviser, and Gabriel Harvey, the ambitious humanist, drew on the same abusive terms ('ink-horn', 'fustian') and likewise adduced lists of words that were not genuine English; it was influential in advancing another enduring prejudice against latinate English.[21] Nashe brilliantly skewered Harvey's idiom as the language of a pedant, a social climber who displayed his knowledge of Latin gratuitously in order to lay claim to a higher social status (a claim which his pedantry, his lack of social grace, continually frustrated). Aristophanes could not resist calling Euripides' mother a greengrocer; Nashe found it irresistible to point out that Harvey's father was a rope-maker. Nashe saw nothing shameful about rope-making—'Had I a Ropemaker to my father, & somebody cast it in my teeth, I would foorthwith haue write in praise of Ropemakers, & prou'd it by sound sillogistry to be one of the 7.

liberal sciences'[22]—but Harvey did feel shame, and his discomfiture was Nashe's delight. Perhaps Harvey came closest to following Nashe's advice when he responded to the many times Nashe had called him an ass by defending the 'most glorious Olde Asse'[23] at unamusing length. Harvey was far too laboured, too much like Milton's unwieldy elephant but without even the lithe proboscis, ever to make mirth happily. Nashe was quick to point out that Harvey was also unhappy in his lack of coins, 'the commodities of Santa Cruz':[24]

So blesse himself he could not, but beeing a little more roundly put to it, he was faine to confesse that he was a poore impecunious creature, & had not traffiqut a great while for anie of these commodities of *Santa Cruz*, but as soone as euer his rents came vp, which he expected euerie howre, (though I could neuer heare of anie he had, more than his ten shillings a yeare at *Trinitie Hall*, if he haue that,) he would most munificently congratulate, correspond, and simpathize with him in al interchangeable vicissitude of kindnes; & let not the current of time seeme to protractiue extended, or breed anie disvnion betwixth them, for he would accelerate & festinate his procrastinating ministers and commissaries in the countrey, by Letters as expedite as could bee. I giue him his true dialect and right varnish of elocution . . .

In Nashe's hands, Harvey's 'strange jargon',[25] motivated by his zeal to sound judicious, grave, and important, was shown to be an 'ambicious stratagem to aspire', and the 'affected accent of his speach' nothing more than a foppish attempt to distract attention from his true condition, penury.[26] In contrast, Harvey's attack on Nashe's language—'The ignorant Idiot . . . confuseth the artificiall wordes, which he neuer read'[27]—was pedantic and laboured, as we would expect since Harvey was clueless about the nature of the game that he was playing. Harvey may have seen himself engaged in a fierce humanist polemic, and he would have had respectable antecedents in this vein. He was not willing to see himself engaged in low comic abuse, and this assured Nashe the rhetorical victory. Nashe combined humanist polemic with late medieval flyting, exuberant latinate inkhornism with brash Saxon colloquialism. For the first time in English, a highly latinate style sounded extemporal,[28] coruscating, and nonchalant.

Inkhorn terms had been denounced heatedly since the middle of the sixteenth century; guides to rhetoric were explicitly concerned with the dangers they posed to writers.[29] In the literature of the sixteenth century, pedants were memorably shown in action, as when Pantagruel, exasperated by the Latinate French of a Limousin ('Nous transfretons la Sequane'), beats him until he talks naturally (*Pantagruel*, 2. 6); or when Holofernes applauds Armado's phrase 'the *posteriors* of this day' ('which the rude multitude call the afternoone'): 'The *posterior* of the day, most generous sir, is liable, congruent, and measurable for the after noone: the worde is well culd, chose, sweete, & apt I do assure you sir, I do assure' (*Love's Labour's Lost*, 5. 1).[30]

These two polemics in the latter half of the century helped to consolidate the mocking, suspicious rhetoric of unmasking that would be applied to latinate English styles suspected of obscurantist deceit or pompous vacuity. Certain ways of making English latinate were represented as a double betrayal, both of the language and of the country and its values. None the less, English latinate styles had a glorious career over the next two centuries, which saw Milton's monumental sublimity as well as Pope's playful brilliance, Clarendon's stately periods as well as Sterne's eccentric amusements. Only in the nineteenth century and after would languages other than Latin have this kind of influence on English writing.

Thomas Carlyle made his initial reputation on the strength of *Sartor Resartus*, but even enthusiastic readers and reviews had doubts about the style. The *North American Review* thought that it was written in 'a sort of Babylonish dialect . . . very strongly tinged throughout with the peculiar idiom of the German language'. In a private letter to Carlyle, later published in *The Life of John Sterling*, Sterling objected to the mannered, eccentric language of *Sartor Resartus*, including its superabundance of compound words, 'snow-and-rosebloom maiden' and many others, attractive in German but uncouth in English. In addition to the teutonisms, readers were confronted with writing that was aggressively different from Johnson's; instead of being carefully moulded within a period, sentences swept forward with headlong momentum. Replying to Sterling, Carlyle writes that there is now no time for 'mere dictionary Style', not with 'the whole structure of our Johnsonian English breaking up from its foundations'.[31] He found his style early, and having found it, in part by having imagined English in German as opposed to Latin terms, he used it in many contexts, whatever friends and critics might think of it. At the beginning of *The French Revolution*, Louis XV lies sick; is he the beneficiary of the prayers of his people?

Prayers? From a France smitten (by black-art) with plague after plague, and lying now in shame and pain, with a Harlot's foot on its neck, what prayer can come? Those lank scarecrows, that prowl hunger-stricken through all highways and byways of French Existence, will they pray? The dull millions that, in the workshop or furrowfield, grind fore-done at the wheel of Labour, like haltered gin-horses, if blind so much the quieter? Or they that in the Bicetre Hospital, 'eight to a bed', lie waiting their manu-mission? Dim are those heads of theirs, dull stagnant those hearts: to them the great Sovereign is known mainly as the great Regrater of Bread.

Alliteration, personification, inversion, archaisms, new compounds, loose sentences: all the characteristic features of Carlyle's style are present, and they all perform their frequent Carlylean function of conveying outrage, contempt, and violence. His writing derives its patent forcefulness from violating English patterns of speech in order to express violence. John Holloway has described the impression of violent energy in *The French Revolution*, whether depicted as misplaced and pitiful or terrible and splendid, as one of the major characteristics of his prose.[32] It might be compared to a series of editorial cartoons or satirical caricatures in which each scene is represented by a vigorous and striking vignette whose moral import is unquestionable and obvious. It is like a speech for the prosecution that does not need to engage with the case for the defence; or like a political speech not meant to persuade others but to strengthen the resolve of one's adherents.

However, in addition to its forensic function, Carlyle's rhetoric attempts to achieve a quite different effect: it seeks to be validated through the intense sincerity of the sage-prophet who is holding up his own moral outrage, angry contempt, self-abnegating admiration, or desperate pity to be admired and emulated. The double urgency of his prose, consisting of abrupt, intense vignettes and abrupt, intense emotions, became urgent by abandoning Latin models of periodic prose in favour of more Germanic ones. However, his source of urgency was timebound. When the Victorian cult of the sage faded away, so did the efficacy of much of Carlyle's writing, and his best writing, we might now judge, includes those passages where he is less hyperbolic, more measured, as in his depiction of Abbot Samson in *Past and Present* (as opposed to the heroes he praised in his lecture series), or his description of Coleridge in the *Life of Sterling* ('expressive of weakness under possibility of strength').

Another reason for including foreign linguistic features in a literary work motivates those translations in which the translator, instead of trying to assimilate the foreign original to the native resources of his language, attempts to preserve some marks of the foreign, or even, at the most ambitious, to change the nature of his own language to accommodate an alien pressure. This sort of translation runs different risks from the more common practice. If assimilative translation is in danger of misrepresenting the original as really the same sort of thing that we do, this other way of translating risks a different sort of misrepresentation, an exoticizing, even fetishizing, of the differences between another culture and our own. There is little point to preferring one practice over another on theoretical grounds. It is, obviously, harder to write well enough to change the norms of one's own language than it is to write competently within them, and most successful translations with greater ambitions than that of the crib have been assimilative. None the less, we have in English at least some great instances of this other way of translating, for example from Ezra Pound's *Confucian Odes*. Here is the last stanza of the first of the Greater Odes (235):[33]

> High destiny's not borne without its weight
> (equity lives not save by constant probe)
> Be not thy crash as Yin's from skies, foreseen.
> The working of Heaven hath neither sound nor smell,
> Be thy cut form of justice as Wen's was, shall rise
> ten thousand states, thine, and with candour in all.

Pound consulted previous translations in French, English, and Latin, but they lack the force of his version, in which he is able to make archaic diction and syntax appear as the natural vehicle to express enduring ancient truth, and in which the sense of an alien wisdom sounds plausible, even urgent, by means of an English remote from that of common speech. Pound's assumptions are Romantic, Wordsworthian, and Emersonian;[34] he is seeking a voice for these archaic poems that is to be heard as anonymous folk wisdom transmitting the voice of nature. None the less, the Confucian material inspired Pound to make something new, in which the Chinese has not disappeared into the English but continues to exert an imaginative pressure. Moreover, though one defence of fascism drew on organicist assumptions like Pound's, his best translations resist immediate assimilation to political purposes. Unlike, say, the Chinese emperors in *Thrones* who are sometimes little more than spokesmen for

Pound's fascist ideology, the emperors in this ode are more complex. Pound has expanded the original theme of the failure of regimes by laying stress on 'Yin's pride'. The militarism in the first part of the ode is followed by political failure in its conclusion; it has been noted that Pound, unlike other translators, emphasizes the emperor's democratic responsibilities.[35] Pound's rethinking of the ode led him to create within it a genuinely resistant foreign element; the strange and compressed syntax removes the ode from immediate and unreflective politics.

In the final example, the presence of foreign diction within an English poem does not point to another culture, but to another order of being. Hugh MacDiarmid's long poem 'On a Raised Beach' opens with this sentence:

> All is lithogenesis—or lochia,
> Carpolite fruit of the forbidden tree,
> Stones blacker than any in the Caaba,
> Cream-coloured caen-stone, chatoyant pieces,
> Celadon and corbeau, bistre and beige,
> Glaucous, hoar, enfouldered, cyathiform,
> Making mere faculae of the sun and moon
> I study you glout and gloss, but have
> No cadrans to adjust you with, and turn again
> From optik to haptik and like a blind man run
> My fingers over you, arris by arris, burr by burr,
> Slickensides, truité, rugas, foveoles,
> Bringing my aesthesis in vain to bear,
> An angle-titch to all your corrugations and coigns,
> Hatched foraminous cavo-rilievo of the world,
> Deictic, fiducial stones.

All the words in the sentence can be found in the *OED*, except for the two French words 'cadrans' and 'truité'. None the less, many of the other words that are present have scarcely been naturalized within English, being very close, or identical, to the Greek, Latin, French, and Italian words from which they are derived. MacDiarmid faces the alien and remote stony presences with a vocabulary that attempts to do justice to the heteroclite particularity of stone. The words, however, are from a human order not finally adequate to it. Initially, some of the vocabulary points to a religious dimension, like the black stone of the Ka'bah or the fruit of the forbidden tree; or at least potentially to some organic process, a lochia; finally, the words serve at least as witness to some immediate self-being, something deictic where meaning and being have not been sundered. It is natural that the speaker next asks who or what put the stone in place. The rest of the poem is concerned not with answering the question, but rejecting its premiss. Stone is stone: 'The hard fact. The inoppugnable reality.' It is truly alien from us—not a cipher of our hidden purposes. D. M. MacKinnon speaks of the 'atheist ontology' of the poem. In his meditation on the ancient rocks, MacDiarmid is 'delivered from a self-regarding anthropocentrism' and led to a 'serene atheism' through our irrelevance to geology which, however, is in no way irrelevant to us. MacDiarmid's hard, alien geological language is irrelevant to our ordinary purposes in speech, a realization that the inhuman is inhuman, not a secret deliverance.[36]

These examples offer diverse answers to the question of why authors sometimes choose to write in styles that deviate markedly from the norms of English. In *Paradise Lost*, Latin (especially) underwrites much of the verse, lending to the English a sense of Latin permanence and magnificence, and also, at times, of strangeness, all features of the high style; it is also a spur to Milton's logopoeic genius. The strange style of *Finnegans Wake* suggests hollowness, rejects permanence; it offers a cacophony of voices insubstantial as air. The English of the Rheims New Testament was programmatically made to be strange on the grounds that no available kind of English would be adequate to the task at hand; its opponents did not recognize such grounds, seeing only a pretext for obscurantism. Nashe and Harvey trade insults which maintain that bad latinate styles are a direct result of various moral failings. Carlyle exploits a potential mimesis: a style that is violently dislocated from the norms of polite prose and ordinary speech may effectively convey a sense of public violence and also a sense of personal urgency. MacDiarmid employs foreign quotations as well as the widest range of English vocabulary, in keeping with his call for 'A learned poetry wholly free | From the brutal love of ignorance'; among the many kinds of words in 'On a Raised Beach', he includes the technical language of geology, a vocabulary remote from what we know and can love, in order to insist on the remoteness of some orders of being. In Pound's archaisms, in his conditional syntax that sounds different from English conditional clauses, we may sense the pressure of foreign modes of perception.

To write an English that sounds like Latin may be a way to make present to the reader values embodied by Rome; likewise, to write German under the influence of Greek may be a way for a writer to communicate a vision of Greece. For this it is not inevitably necessary to adopt a style remote from the norms of one's language and in conformity with another; more commonly, particular instances of language interference are created for particular purposes within a work. Let us turn our attention to one of these instances, a single latinism that had a long career in English literature: the Latin *sunt qui*, meaning *there are those who* but in English sometimes translated more literally as *there are who*. Note that the more literal translation, in a sense, is less close to the Latin; by writing *there are who* the phrase is made into a sign of foreignness, unlike *sunt qui* in Latin; *there are who* is marked as strange English (though not very strange); it is made into a sign of Latin.

In Latin, *sunt qui* (with *est qui*) occurs in both poetry and prose and in a variety of genres; the syntax is neither elevated nor colloquial. It was often used in phrases like *there are those who say*, *there are some people who think*, etc., particularly useful in forensic, philosophical, and polemical writing: Cicero: *At etiam sunt, qui dicant, Quirites, a me eiectum in exilium esse Catilinam* ('Romans, there are some people who say that Catiline was banished by me', *Second oration against Catiline*); *Sunt enim qui discessum animi a corpore putent esse mortem; sunt qui nullum censeant fieri discessum . . .* ('There are some who think that death is the departure of the soul from the body; there are some who believe that no such departure takes place', *Tusculan Disputations*). The early church fathers found it no less useful in disputing points of theology, Augustine (in particular) favouring it, though he uses it post-classically with the indicative. In the Reformation, Jaroslav Pelikan argued,[37] Christian polemicists favoured it because of their own 'amnesia' about their past, their ignorance of their own sources and those of their opponents. The construction, however, has always had anonymity built into it, and certainly Erasmus (with whom *sunt qui* again takes the subjunctive) cannot be accused of amnesia about the past.

When the *Oxford English Dictionary* discusses the phrase in subsection 4(*f*) of the article on *there*, it is described as 'App. a Latinism, after *sunt qui dicunt*, and the like' (we may wonder, none the less, why *sunt qui dicunt* is given instead of *sunt qui dicant*). However, the subsections of section 4 have been arranged grammatically, not semantically, and as a result subsection 4(*f*) conflates a number of different kinds of usages, some having nothing to do with Latin.

The special function of *there* whereby it is 'used unemphatically to introduce a sentence or clause in which, for the sake of emphasis or preparing the hearer, the verb comes before the subject, as *there comes a time when*, etc., *there was heard a rumbling noise*' is discussed in section 4 of the article. The subsections are devoted to those times it is used with intransitive verbs, 4(*a*); transitive verbs, 4(*b*); with passive verbs, 4(*c*); in the phrases *there is* and *there are*, 4(*d*); followed by a relative clause in which the relative pronoun has been omitted, 4(*e*); and finally, in those cases where the antecedent, when it is a simple pronominal word ('usu. pl. e.g. *they, those, some*, rarely sing., e.g. *he, she, that*'), is omitted, 4(f). The *OED* gives about a column to section 4; the most recent edition of Quirk's grammar, in contrast, spends about ten pages on 'existential sentences' with *there*. So it is not surprising that some important distinctions are not made in the article. The author not only describes the syntax as 'App. a Latinism' but also asks the reader to 'Cf. *that* rel. pron. 3'. Both comments are valuable, but they rarely apply to the same citation.

Take the first quotation, from an alliterative romance translated (perhaps at secondhand) around 1400 from Guido delle Colonne's *Historia Destructionis Troiae* (1287). This enormously popular work was adapted into most of the European vernaculars, including Icelandic.[38] In the free English adaptation, the relevant couplet reads: 'There come out of castels & of cloise townes | ffrom the bowerdurs aboute, þat hom bale wroght' (ll. 12859–60). The *OED* is certainly correct that this involves a use of *there* followed by a pronoun without an antecedent; the syntax is equivalent to: *There come those that* . . . However, what does this have to do with the Latin *sunt qui dicunt*? The verb is *come*, not *are*, and besides, the English couplet, here as often in this loose translation, has no equivalent in the original Latin. We should conclude that the first quotation has nothing to do with the Latin phrase. Instead, it is an example of *that* rel. pron. 3(*b*): 'of persons: *that* = (the person) that, he (or him) that, one that; pl. (persons) that, they (them), or those who. Now only after *there are* and the like'. From *c*.1320 to before 1665—the time span of the citations given under *that* 3(*b*)—*that* meaning *those people that* was used in all sorts of contexts, one of which happens to be existential *there* sentences. The second quotation, also from the fifteenth century, runs 'There weren that dyd not so', and though the verb *be* makes the phrase closer to the Latin than the previous example, it is not particularly close. There is no sufficient or even good reason to call it a latinism; the English usage of *that* without antecedent together with the English expression *there are*, both long-standing, account for it easily. The next example is more ambiguous. Lord Berners's translation (before 1533) of the French translation (1531) of Antonio de Guevara's *Libro del Emperador Marco Aurelio* includes the sentence, 'There were that saied, that this ambassadour should be chastised'. The English translation went through more than a dozen editions. Its appeal was both in its 'hygh sentences' (i.e. *sententiae*) and 'high and sweete style'.[39] Given its high style, its roots in Renaissance humanism, its being advertised as the work of a Roman, and the fact that the verb used with the phrase is *say*, we have reasons in this instance to wonder if Latin is being invoked in the English.

The first unmistakable imitation in English of the *sunt qui* expression known to me occurs in George Turberville's translations of Mantuan's *Eclogues*, published in 1567:

> *There are that to their bloudy boordes our crushed bodies beare,*
> *And butcherlike (with greedy teeth) our rented corses teare.*
> *There are, I say, whom spitefull fiends vnto suche practise dryue:*

The Latin includes two *sunt qui*'s, so there can be no doubt that the English was made to serve as an equivalent to the Latin. This is also the first instance I have found where *who*[40] is used rather than *that*. Turberville uses the two pronouns interchangeably; perhaps he chose *whom* in the second instance because of the awkwardness of using *that* in an oblique case. Later, however, *there are who* came gradually to be preferred to *there are that* in those cases where Latin is to be emphasized or the style is to be elevated. Take, for example, Arthur Golding in his 1577 translation of Théodore de Bèze's *Abraham Sacrifiant* (in which the biblical story is influenced formally by Euripides' depiction of the sacrifice of Iphigenia): 'But yit I know there are whose foolish mind I I haue so turned quite against the kind, I That some . . . Had leuer serue a thowsand gods than one'. There is no equivalent to the 'sunt qui' in Bèze (and none in the French language?), and I doubt whether we should call it a latinism. Since *who* is declinable, it is more serviceable than *that* in the passage; perhaps, too, it was chosen to raise the style; perhaps it was a variant of the more common 'there are that'.

It is very difficult to make out whether an individual usage of the phrase in the sixteenth and early seventeenth century is a latinism or not. A. C. Partridge is more confident than he ought to be:[41] '*Omission of the demonstrative antedecent after 'there are' etc.* (Lat. *sunt qui dicunt*). This construction, with inverted order of the subject, seems to have been used to prepare the reader for a subject specially emphasized. It became common in the fifteenth century, but was obsolescent by the seventeenth.' Perhaps Partridge simply summarized the OED article, with its conflation of different kinds of *there are that*, its indifference to the difference between *who* and *that*, its failure to record the poetic afterlife of the phrase throughout the eighteenth century. In this period, the phrase (especially with *that*) was so common, in both poetry and prose, that it should not be understood as a latinism unless there is a good reason for doing so.

In the course of the seventeenth century, the timbre of the phrase altered; it became more latinate. The change was effected by two factors: the phrase, especially with *who* rather than *that*, became poetical, and it was repeatedly used in translations from Latin. Ben Jonson added a translation of Horace's *Satires* 2. 1 to his *Poetaster* in 1616. The satire begins:

> There are, to whom I seem excessive sour
> And past a satyre's law, t'extend my power ...

We are justified in responding to the phrase as a latinism for the excellent reason that it is a translation of the Horace's *sunt qui*. Like almost all Jonson's translations and in contrast to the adaptations and incorporations of his own verse, it is rather wooden, even stilted. The principled pedantry of his translations is the most likely motive for offering the literal English equivalent of the Latin construction. In order to introduce Horace with critical authority, Jonson keeps as close as possible to Latin. By making the English sound like Horace's Latin in this example, Jonson defers to and seeks to convey the authority of the Roman's own voice.

I know of two instances of this syntax in Jonson's prose. In the preface to *Volpone* (1605), he warns against malicious critics: 'there are, that professe to have a key for the decyphering of everything'. In *Timber* (1640), he praises those who master eloquence: 'Yet there are, who prove themselves Masters of her, and absolute Lords.' Note that the second instance is an adaptation of the elder Seneca; though *sunt qui* does not appear in the Latin, Jonson's *there are who* none the less appears in a Latin context. In the course of the seventeenth century, *there are who* increasingly appeared not just in Latin contexts but also in translations from Latin. From the eighteenth century, however, the syntax would become increasingly confined to poetry.[42] Likewise, *there are that*, which as Partridge noted was obsolescent in prose by the the seventeenth century, occurs as a latinism in a few poems of later periods.[43]

The close connection of this bit of syntax with translations from Latin helped to establish and maintain its use as a latinism and not merely a phrase with a Latin origin. After Jonson, Heywood (1625) and Sandys (1632) make use of it in translating Ovid, as Dryden does in translating Ovid (1693 and 1700), Juvenal (1693), and Virgil (1700), though nowhere that I have found in his own poetry.[44] In the eighteenth century, the syntax is often pressed into service not only in translations from Latin, but in particular in translations of Horace. In the preface to his *Dictionary*, Samuel Johnson warned against the great pest of translation: 'No book was ever turned from one language into another without imparting something of its native idiom; this is the most mischievous and comprehensive innovation.' The historical career of this construction illustrates this process whereby foreign syntax imparts something of its idiom to English. Johnson saw it only as pestiferous, but salutary instances can also be adduced.

Two early occurrences of the syntax (with *who*) in a poet's own work are found in Milton.[45] He capitalizes on the anonymity of the phrase. In defying Satan in *Paradise Lost*, 6, Abdiel says:

> but thou seest
> All are not of thy Train; there be who Faith
> Prefer, and Pietie to God, though then
> To thee not visible, when I alone
> Seemd in thy World erroneous to dissent
> From all: my Sect thou seest, now learn too late
> How few somtimes may know, when thousands err.

He combines humility and confidence. Humility before God, as often, is entirely compatible with absolute confidence before error. The faithful in their humility have no need to be proclaimed or even named; they will not be deceived and are content to be invisible to such as Satan. Their faith is a fact that does not require discussion or proof. The baldest statement of their faith will be the strongest ('there be who faith prefer'). In this respect, the passage is similar to Horace's *Epistles* i. 6, in which he uses the *sunt qui* to remind Numicius that there are those who can watch the sun, stars, and the movement of the seasons without fear. In Horace the phrase is evidence of the strength of those who have learnt philosophical detachment, and so have a strength that is content not to be named, that is unconcerned with praise or blame. The anonymity that is built into the syntax is a resource for Horace and for Milton, as well as for English poets after Milton.

In *Samson Agonistes*, the chorus affirms:

> Just are the ways of God,
> And justifiable to Men;
> Unless there be who think not God at all,
> If any be, they walk obscure;
> For of such Doctrine never was there School,
> But the heart of the Fool,
> And no man therein Doctor but himself.

'Unless there be who think not God at all' gives a double dose of Latin syntax, with *there be who* and *think not God*.[46] In this case, the anonymity of the construction helps to convey incredulity, a potential of which subsequent English poets will avail themselves. Moreover, the compressed syntax borders on obscurity in order to make palpable a sense of the contradiction inherent in atheism; even the description of the atheist is obscure. The line is doubled in another sense, since the two latinisms are also grecisms. *Sunt qui*, in Greek, is εἰσὶν οἵ (less commonly ἔστιν οἵ). In his recreation of Greek tragedy, and in an imitation of a Greek chorus, Milton appropriately invokes Greek, as well as Latin.

Fifty years later, Pope exploits the Latin phrase fully and repeatedly. He draws on it four times in his imitations of Horace, and several times in his other poetry. Dryden, we recall, used it only in his translations, and this is evidence, not conclusive but suggestive, that he did not entirely accept it as English. Pope, though he was not the first to employ it in a translation of Horace, emphatically stamped it as Horatian[47] because of the success of his Horatian imitations.

Pope plays with Horace's Latin, at times offering interlingual puns. His contemporary readers knew the Latin original (printed *en face* with his imitations), and they could hear him out-Latining the original. The Latin of Horace's *Satires* and *Epistles* is far from elevated; instead, it is a language for conversation, friendly intimacy, gentle mockery, and self-mockery. Pope elevates the diction. He opens his imitation of *Satires* 2. 1 thus:

> There are (I scarce can think it, but am told)
> There are to whom my Satire seems too bold . . .

Here, by interrupting and prolonging the construction with a parenthetical aside, he focuses the attention on its conclusion, and *sunt quibus* is all the more forced into view. The aside changes Horace's straightforward statement ('there are some people to whom I seem too bold') into one of mock incredulity. It is witty, even sportive, but also ready for battle.

A passage from Horace's *Epistles* 1. 6 provides Pope with an opportunity to soar:

> 'Not to Admire, is all the Art I know,
> To make men happy, and to keep them so.'
> [Plain Truth, dear MURRAY, needs no flow'rs of speech,
> So take it in the very words of *Creech*.]
>   This Vault of Air, this congregated Ball,
> Self-centred Sun, and Stars that rise and fall,
> There are, my Friend! whose philosophic eyes
> Look thro', and trust the Ruler with his Skies,
> To him commit the hour, the day, the year,
> And view this dreadful All without a fear.

Although Pope mocks his predecessor in translation, Creech in fact is closer to Horace's style than Pope is. Creech translates:

> Not to admire, as most are wont to do,
> It is the only method that I know,
> To make Men happy, and to keep 'em so.

This imitates the plain style of Milton's *Paradise Regained*, a passage in praise of the prophets' 'majestic unaffected style' (4. 362–3):

> In them is plainest taught, and easiest learnt,
> What makes a Nation happy, and keeps it so.

Pope has none of this. Creech's plain speaking is represented as merely dull. After Creech's plain words and the parenthetical jab at him, Pope plays up the Latin original. Instead of a straightforward 'Some view this glittering Sun, and glorious Stars, | And all the various Seasons free from fears' (Creech), Pope changes Horace's regular

Latin syntax *sunt qui* governing the lines into an elaborate Latinism, interrupted by an address, ('There are, my Friend! whose philosophical eyes') and places it in the centre, an order which also imitates the Latin placement of the words. The effect of grandeur and gorgeousness diminishes and mocks Creech, and sets forth a different stylistic and cultural ideal. The latinate English bears witness to a Rome where the emphasis is placed on urbanity and correctness. Pope's great statement about English literature is his imitation of Horace's *Epistle* 2. 1, where he relates correctness to the precarious and perpetually threatened achievement of civilization, balanced as it is between ossified dullness and anarchic energy. Correctness translates into a style influenced by and responding to Horace, whose creation of a pure diction and fluent metre became a standard for English, and whose urbanity and wit in the *Odes* was a model for Pope's poetry, 'Serenely pure, and yet divinely strong | Rich with the Treasures of each foreign Tongue' (from his imitation of *Epistles* 2. 2).

When Pope uses the phrase in his own poetry, Horace is often close in spirit. In the 'Epistle to Dr Arbuthnot', he alludes to Horace in a number of ways:

> There are, who to my Person pay their court,
> I cough like *Horace*, and tho' lean, am short . . .

Pope presumes the reader's acceptance of three facts about Horace: that he was fat; and short; and coughed. That he was fat and short he himself admits (*Epistles* 1. 20. 24, *Epistles* 1. 4. 15); the cough is puzzling. In a note to the Twickenham edition, John Butt writes that Horace refers to his cough in *Satires* 1. 9. 32. Untrue; in that passage, Horace recalls a prophecy made when he was a boy that he would not be done in by poison, the sword, pleurisy, cough, or the gout, but destroyed by a prattler. Pope seems to have conjured an asthmatic Horace in order to be able to share another trait with him. The ostensible reason for introducing Horace at this moment is to emphasize his and Pope's physical ridiculousness. Then the first line of the couplet expresses incredulity: my person would be the least likely candidate for patron, yet there are who pay court to it, even though I am asthmatic and dwarfish. A deeper reason for introducing Horace is to invoke the constant Horatian concern for moral independence. Butt's instinct in citing *Satires* 1. 9 is sound, since it is particularly in that satire (as also in *Satires* 1. 6) that Horace explicitly describes and resents the inconveniences he is subject to by those who attempt to pay court to him. In two lines, Pope identifies himself with Horace physically, morally, and linguistically.

In the nineteenth century, this syntax appeared less often in translation (though it is not uncommon in William Gifford's translation of Juvenal and Persius); on the other hand, it became a standard, even hackneyed, part of poetic diction and on a few occasions a spur to remarkable achievement. It was common in the writing of some very minor poets, in Bernard Barton's metrical effusions, the poetastery of Robert Montgomery, and the poems of Aubrey de Vere.

Wordsworth's 'Ode to Duty' is a return to the plain style:

> There are who ask not if thine eye
> Be on them; who, in love and truth,
> Where no misgiving is, rely
> Upon the genial sense of youth:
> Glad Hearts! without reproach or blot;
> Who do thy work, and know it not:
> Oh! If through confidence misplaced
> They fail, thy saving arms, dread Power! around them cast.

Like Milton, Wordsworth adapts the intrinsic anonymity of the syntax to his own purposes. The unselfconscious reliance on youth's genial sense is a simple gift of nature. An explicit naming would be self-conscious; it would complicate the gift. Moreover, by not placing this reliance in an individual, Wordsworth presents it as an unconscious force of nature.

The phrase also fits in with other purposes at work in the poem. 'Ode to Duty' is one of two odes in the *Poems* of 1807; the immortality ode (then simply called 'Ode') is the other. The volume is framed by the Horatian ode near the beginning and the Pindaric ode at the end. The Horatian lineage of the 'Ode to Duty' is further emphasized by its stanza form, derived from Gray's 'Ode to Adversity', which has in turn Horace's *Odes* 1. 35 as a source. Wordsworth made the stoic element explicit when he added an epigraph from Seneca in 1836. The poem's moral sources, however, are German as well as Horatian. Duty preserves the stars and keeps the ancient heavens fresh and strong, in a possible echo[48] of the famous sentence in the conclusion of *The Critique of Pure Reason*: 'Two things fill the mind with ever-increasing awe and wonder, the more often and the more intensely the mind of thought is drawn to them: the starry heavens above me and the moral law within me'. The status of moral duty after the loss of a primal and intuitive connection with nature and the fall into self-consciousness is a central theme in German philosophy and Romantic poetry. The point is that Wordsworth's Latin phrasing of the Romantic moral position harmonizes his sources. Wordsworth has found the right way to express simultaneously two different moral traditions and present them as inseparable.

Especially in his later poetry, Wordsworth correlates this construction with the happy, wise unselfconsciousness of the simple:

> There are whose calmer mind it would content
> To be an unculled floweret of the glen
>
> ('The River Duddon', 7. 11–12)

> There are who to a birthday strain
> Confine not harp and voice,
> But evermore throughout thy reign
> Are grateful and rejoice!
>
> ('To May', 5–8)

> There are to whom the garden, grove, and field,
> Perpetual lessons of forbearance yield
>
> ('Humanity', 105–6)

It is as though Wordsworth would make the grammatical absence of the antecedent subject equivalent to the absence of subjectivity. The effect is gained at some cost, since these poems lack the corrective that is present in the 'Ode to Duty', the idea that intuitive confidence may be misplaced or fail, that instinct and moral action may not be one. Moreover, Wordsworth's veneration of the spiritual virtues of anonymous people is very different from Milton's celebration of Abdiel's spiritual elite. It is not free from the bullying inherent in appealing to a conveniently mute moral majority whose behaviour is offered as exemplary by a self-appointed spokesman.

Landor likes the phrase, unsurprisingly, but he does not appear to make much of it ('There are who would retaliate, Gallus'). Although it is my thesis that this bit of Latin syntax is most creatively deployed in English poetry that invokes Rome for moral or political reasons (as with Pope's continual reference to Horace, or Wordsworth's stoic sources in the 'Ode to Duty'), I do not suggest for a moment that every *there are who* in a Latin context will be impressive. Nor do I maintain that it necessarily evokes Rome, since in at least one lyric it moves out of any Roman context: 'Love is enough: ho ye who seek saving, I Go no further; come hither; there have been who have found it' (the last of the 'Love is enough' lyrics in William Morris, *Love is Enough*).

George Crabbe is the third major English poet (after Pope and Wordsworth) for whom the *sunt qui* is a favourite usage. I count eleven instances in *The Borough* (1810) alone. I do not see that Rome, in particular, is invoked. Rather it is the claustrophobic,[49] embittered, sometimes envious, sometimes empathetic, somewhat paranoid tone that we associate with the use of 'they' without antecedent. ('They get all the breaks'. 'They're doomed'. 'They'll stop at nothing'. 'How do they get away with it?' 'They don't stand a chance'.)

> ... There are who hold manorial Courts,
> Or whom the trust of powerful Friends supports
>
> (6. 85–6)

> There are beside, whom powerful Friends advance,
> Whom Fashion favours, Persons, Patrons, Chance:
>
> (7. 57–8)

> There are who labour through the Year, and yet
> No more have gain'd them—not to be in Debt
>
> (8. 41–2)

> There are who names in Shame or Fear assume
>
> (12. 193)

> ... and can there be who take
> Infernal pains, the sleeping Vice to wake?
>
> (24. 170–1)

Though there is no explicit appeal to Roman matters, the sense of oppression routinely associated with both Rome and Latin in the nineteenth century is part of the effectiveness of *there are who* in Crabbe's hands. A similar sense of Roman tyranny may have motivated Keats's lines at the beginning of book iii of *Endymion*: 'There are who lord it o'er their fellow-men'. It is repeated often in Crabbe, and the psychology of the poem provides some justification for the obsessive frequency of the phrase.

Kipling's parodies of Horace show him attentive to the mechanics of Horace's style. The 'translation' of *Odes* 5. 3 begins:

> There are whose study is of smells,
> And to attentive schools rehearse
> How something mixed with something else
> Makes something worse.

The opening words 'there are whose' announces as effectively as the subtitled reference to Horace's non-existent book 5 that the poem is Horatian. It is light, but for two reasons we ought to hesitate to call it frivolous. First, it follows the story 'Regulus', where schoolboys painfully construe the Regulus ode (3. 5). The schoolmaster believes that, despite their feeble grasp of grammar, some essential qualities penetrate into their character: 'balance, proportion, perspective'. The Regulus ode has a particular significance since the Roman hero was often associated with British figures of self-sacrifice, like General Gordon at Khartoum. Moreover, in the final stanza where we see the poet 'sunk in thought profound | Of what the unaltering gods require', the parody strikes a note of high seriousness which many nineteenth-century readers no longer found in Horace. Kipling unites the public Horace of the Roman odes and private Horace of intimate and friendly address. The ideal of reverence and public duty exemplified by Regulus was made attractive by this intimacy, as well as by the sentimental nostalgia motivating the schoolboy play of 'A Translation'. Language play is universal;[50] interlingual puns, along with mock latinate diction and even mock grecisms,[51] have been enjoyed since the Renaissance. Still, a girl can't go on laughing all the time. The Anglo-Latin *sunt qui* play in both Pope and Kipling was meant not just to be enjoyed but to be enjoyed within a political context.

> I allude to William Empson:
>
> No man is sure he does not need to climb.
> It is not human to feel safely placed.
> 'A girl can't go on laughing all the time'.
>
> Wrecked by their games and jeering at their prime
> There are who can, but who can praise their taste?
> No man is sure he does not need to climb.
>
> ('Reflection from Anita Loos')

Expanding the syntax, and paraphrasing, I might offer this reading: 'Anita Loos has said "A girl can't go on laughing all the time"; still, there are girls who can go on laughing all the time, but they are wrecked by their games and when they are at their prime they jeer at it, and who could praise their taste?' Many such versions are permitted by the grammar. What is essential is that Loos's remark and Empson's syntactically dense justification of it are given equal priority. Her words are illustrated by the following *sunt qui* sentence, which in its turn gains a direct appeal through the colloquial immediacy of the sentence it justifies. None the less, readers may feel that Empson's intended balance of apparent simplicity and apparent complexity is a rhetorical sleight of hand. 'A girl can't go on laughing all the time' lends itself to being understood in a variety of ways, as a stoical remark, an appeal to common sense, an avoidance of bad form, moodiness not in need of justification, etc. In the next two lines, however, the final clause 'but who can praise their taste?' impoverishes Loos's sentence by making taste so emphatically involved in it. It suggests that fun should be abandoned when it is in bad taste, a simplistic reduction of her words.

J. V. Cunningham turns to the *sunt qui* in his lament which develops a theme in Horace (and elsewhere) of the ridiculousness of the aged lover, *senesco sed amo*. His 'The Aged Lover Discourses in the Flat Style' begins:

> There are, perhaps, whom passion gives a grace,
> Who fuse and part as dancers on the stage,
> But that is not for me, not at my age,
> Not with my bony shoulders and fat face.
> Yet in my clumsiness I found a place
> And use for passion: with it I ignore
> My gaucheries and yours, and feel no more
> The awkwardness of the absurd embrace.

The *sunt qui* has something of the force of a generalized allusion to Horace, that is, an invocation of Horace, as it had for Pope and for Kipling, two other devoted readers of Horace. By means of the latinism, the sonnet uses Horace in the complex and ironic way that Horace himself used literary and mythological references, simultaneously distancing and intensifying an experience. 'There are, perhaps, whom' aims to cauterize any suggestion of self-pity arising from 'not at my age' (so, too, does 'fat face', a pre-emptive strike against a euphemistic or vague description of ageing). Changes in register from latinate to Saxon may allow for the truthful and more passionate expression of sentimentality, nostalgia, self-pity, recognizing their claims and rejecting their pretensions; at worst, however, they permit a speaker to indulge in them while at the same time, via latinate ironies, feeling superior to those who indulge in them. With 'perhaps' added to the nameless ones who fuse and part like dancers, Cunningham distances himself from a contemplation of sexual beauty, by doubting that it really exists, but he also shows that he is attracted to it terribly. In this respect, it is close to a quatrain from Hardy's 'A Sign-Seeker':

> —There are who, rapt to heights of trancelike trust,
> These tokens claim to feel and see,
> Read radiant hints of times to be—
> Of heart to heart returning.

Hardy's 'claim' is meant to restrain himself from giving the assent he longs to give to a religious trust permitting heart to return to heart. In both cases, distance, envy, and mistrust are conveyed through the latinate syntax that has been used for so many purposes since Milton.

The latinism owes the breadth of its semantic reach to the number of roles Rome has played in English representations. It has been used to facilitate witty, urbane exchanges; to impress a sense of duty; underline imperial responsibility; create an atmosphere of oppression. The kind of Rome invoked depended on the long history of the reception of antiquity in England. While latinate English was a correlate to the presence of Rome in the English imagination, language interference was a rich poetic resource.

CHAPTER FOUR

Some Greek Influences on English Poetry

SINCE THE RENAISSANCE, Latin has exerted a continual pressure on Western literature; Greek, in contrast, has been only intermittently present, and even when it has been influential, the nature of its influence is hard to pin down. There is no English grecism equivalent in scope and importance to the latinism *there are who*. The Miltonic grecism in which *know* is followed by a participle, as at *Paradise Lost*, 9.792 ('knew not eating Death') and at *Samson Agonistes*, l. 1549 ('My Countreymen, whom here I knew remaining'), scarcely exists in any other poet, and it does not carry particular weight in *Samson Agonistes*. Until the nineteenth century, Milton's drama was the sole eminent example of an English recreation of the language and form of Greek tragedy, and it is perhaps the greatest response ever made in English to Greek. The ancient language provided Milton with a ground on which to rework radically the language of English drama, so that he could create a new tragic drama, unadorned, magnificent, and bring into being an alternative to Shakespearean high tragedy. None the less, because of its singularity, its indebtedness to several languages (the choruses, for example, draw not only on Greek choral odes but also on the Italian canzone and the Psalms), and the fact that, unlike *Paradise Lost*, it does not direct attention to foreign presences within its language, the play is elusive in its relation to Greek.[1]

Therefore, our topic is best pursued not by looking at a particular grecism or a Greek-influenced work, but by examining aspects of the language of English poetry that have been inspired by the ancient language. In Greek, the abundance and variety of compound epithets ('*rosy-fingered* dawn'), poetic negative or privative adjectives ('the *unfruitful* sea'), and metres have frequently been noted and have sometimes spurred writers to emulate them within their own literary languages. At times, imitating Greek has been a means by which poets have explored the alien value, desired or threatening, of Greece.

The Compound Epithet

During the Renaissance, Greek was praised for its ready formation of compound words; emboldened by this precedent French and English poets, especially, formed new compounds and in particular many new compound epithets.[2] One kind of compound epithet drew especially on the Greek example: the *epitheton ornans*, the decorative, sometimes very beautiful, epithet, often compound, that does not typically advance the narrative or create dramatic tension, though it can be used tenderly and poignantly.[3] In particular, the compound epithets in Homer inspired numerous imitators.

In English this compound epithet was sometimes both an imitation of the Greek language and part of a statement about pagan mythology. Milton's early poetry is rich in compounds and especially compound epithets, and many of the most striking of these are decorative in the Greek way. In *A Maske Presented at Ludlow Castle* (*Comus*), they are actively involved in determining the relation between pagan and Christian: they exemplify the seductive danger of the former but may also be used properly in the service of the latter. In his later poetry, Milton lost his confidence that they could be used in this way and with a few exceptions abandoned the decorative compound epithet. When Romantic writers rediscovered Greece, they also rediscovered the compound epithet. Both Shelley and Keats used these epithets to relate their language to their visions of pagan antiquity. In the next generation, Hopkins (like Milton) was both attracted by and distrustful of the beauty they promised.

The facility of Greek for forming compounds was emphasized in Western Europe at least from the early sixteenth century. Reviewing his career, Erasmus recalled in 1523 that he had abandoned an early attempt to translate a piece by Lucian because 'there was no hope of reproducing in Latin the happy formation of compound words so noticeable in Greek vocabulary, while had I expressed each Greek word in several Latin ones, the point of the whole poem would be lost'; he went on to note how often poems like the Homeric hymns 'consist of such compound epithets of the gods put together in a traditional way'.[4] In France in mid-century, the poets of the Pléiade were being urged to imitate this Greek richness of compounds in their vernacular. In the *Deffence* (1549), Du Bellay advised poets to be bold: 'inventer, adopter & composer à l'immitation des Grecz quelquez motz Francoys', just as Cicero (and Virgil) had done in Latin. It is not clear from the context whether 'composer' means to create in general or to create compound words specifically; at any rate, only a few years later Du Bellay was defending his use of compound adjectives like *pié-sonnant*, *porte-lois*, and *porte-ciel* to translate Virgil's compound epithets.[5] Du Bellay's advice was reiterated by Ronsard in the *Abbregé de l'Art poëtique* of 1565, in which he advised, 'Tu composeras hardiment des mots à l'imitation des Grecs & Latins'.[6] In 1579 Henri Estienne was claiming that among the many reasons French was superior to Italian was the fact that French formed compounds almost as easily as Greek.[7]

Ronsard's compound adjectives were more numerous and more original than Du Bellay's. Consider a sonnet from the first book of the *Amours* (1552), the one beginning:

> Fier Aquilon, horreur de la Scythie,
>   La chasse-nuë & l'esbranle-rocher,
>   L'irrite-mer . . .

The second edition appeared in the next year with a commentary by Muret, who admired the compound epithets of this poem which had been 'heureusement composez à la maniere Grecque, pour signifier les effets du vent Borée'. Muret was undoubtedly overeager to find Greek behind Ronsard's words; he adduced, for example, an irrelevant line from Aratus in connection with 'chasse-nuë'.[8] None the less, the association of compound epithets with Greek was not farfetched; it was a common observation of the period, and it applied with particular force to Ronsard, whose devotion to Homer and Pindar predisposed him towards such usage. Even so, he sometimes had second thoughts about his epithets and, by the time of the *Abbregé* at least, he rejected the free Greek use of them, insisting that they should be an integral part of the context.[9]

Other French writers were profligate in the use of compound epithets. The most notorious excesses were those of Du Bartas. In book 6 ('Babilone', ll. 349–52) of *Le Seconde semaine* (1584), he paused while extolling the virtues of Hebrew to praise Greek:

> . . . avec ses Synonymes,
> Epithetes hardis, metaphores sublimes,
> Ses couplements des mots, ses divers tems, ses cas,
> Et mille autres beautez dont on fait tant de cas.

Du Bartas, however, did not limit himself to admiring Greek for its *couplements des mots*; he made compound epithets a regular and extravagant feature of his epic:

> Le feu donne-clarté, porte-chaud, iette-flame,
> Source de mouuement, chasse-ordure, donne-ame . . .
>
> (First Week, Second Day, 857–8)

> Ie te salue, ô Terre, ô Terre porte-grains,
> Porte-or, porte-santé, porte-habits, porte-humains,
> Porte fruicts, porte-tours . . .
>
> (First Week, Third Day, 851–3)[10]

Toward the end of the sixteenth century and under French influence, English writers and translators in their turn began to reflect on the capacity of their language to form compounds. As in France, it was the epithet that was most frequently compounded, and Greek was an indispensable model and point of comparison. Puttenham, in the *Arte of English Poesie* (1589), believed the Greeks were a happy people because their language 'allowed them to inuent any new name they listed, and to peece many words together to make of them one entire, much more significative than the single word'. In the *Defence of Poesie* (1595), Sidney praised English because it almost approaches Greek in its capacity for compounding words. English, he wrote, is 'perticularly happy in compositions of two or three wordes togither, neare the Greeke, farre beyonde the Latine, which is one of the greatest bewties can be in a language'. In the *Excellencie of the English tongue* (written about 1595, published 1631), Richard Carew described the peculiar grace that English has in the composition of words, 'a like significancy, and more shorte then the Greekes'. The praise of Greek in an early translation of Du Bartas's 'Babilon' by the Anglo-Saxon scholar William Lisle would have been familiar:[11]

> . . . hir Synonymons,
> Hir lofty Metaphors, hir bould Epithetons,
> Hir compounding of words, hir tenses and hir cases,
> And of so great request a thousand other graces:

In his Cambridge comedy *Lingua*, written some time after 1602 and
subsequently printed on half a dozen occasions, Thomas Tomkis
(also spelt Tomkins, but not the musician) described the language:
'The learned Greek rich in fit epithets, I blest in the lovely marriage of
pure words.'

The practice of compounding epithets in English kept pace with
this theorizing about them. Sidney, following the example of the
French, has often been credited with introducing them into English,
initially it seems by Joseph Hall, who in a satire of 1598 complained
about the extravagant overuse of them; they had degenerated from
'the grace of that new elegance':

> Which sweet *Philisides* fetch't of late from *France*,
> That well beseem'd his high-stil'd *Arcady*,
> Tho others marre it with much liberty;
> In Epithets to ioyne two words in one,
> Forsooth for Adiectiues cannot stand alone;
> As a great Poet could of *Bacchus* say,
> That he was *Semele-femori-gena*.

('Semele-thigh-brood' compressed the story of Bacchus' birth into
three words; the 'great Poet' who coined the epithet was Scaliger.)
Hall was perhaps symbolically right to credit Sidney with the innovation. *Astrophil and Stella* as well as some of the 'plaine-singing'
poems from *Arcadia* are thick with compounds and particularly
diverse in compound epithets, the latter including examples of the
favourite French variety, verb plus noun, like *pass-praise hue, kisse-
cheeke teares*, and *scorn-gold haire*. However, it would be mistaken
to give exclusive credit for this innovation to Sidney or even to the
influential French precedent. Compounds are easily formed in Old
and Middle English, and though the many Elizabethan classicizing
compound epithets were new, Sidney's compound epithets were
anticipated to a degree by Nicholas Grimald's,[12] while those of
Spenser and of Shakespeare's early poems were not obviously
indebted to Sidney's example.

In the two decades around 1600, Sidney, Spenser, and Shakespeare created an enduring poetic diction. All three were a prime
source of compound epithets, as was the powerful influence of the
translations by Chapman (who compounded boldly and felt free to
insert his own compounds) and the many English translations of Du
Bartas.[13] These poets and translators created compounds that would

be picked up by later writers, they established the dominant patterns for the formation of compound epithets, and they demonstrated the purposes to which these epithets can be put.

What are these purposes? Aristotle wrote that compound words and plentiful epithets suit passionate speech, and one purpose of compound epithets has been to raise the rhetorical level of writing, to animate it, to indicate a greater degree of emotional involvement in it.[14] Impassioned rhetoric, characterized by energeia, we find in Sidney's *sun-burnd brain*, *sobd-out-words*, *soule-invading voice*; Spenser's *hart-burning Hate*, *hartfretting payne*, *heart-gnawing griefe*; and Shakespeare's *lust-dieted man*, *dog-harted daughters*, *toad-spotted traytor*.[15] Others of their compound epithets exemplify a complementary rhetorical principle, enargeia, implying vividness, phanopoeia, or decorative beauty.[16] Sidney's *flamie-glistring lights* and *rose-enameld skies* are examples; along with Spenser's *sea-shouldring Whales*, which so excited Keats when he read it that he acted out the part of a whale lifting the sea as it rose; and the *earth-delving Conies* and *deaw-bedabbled wretch* of Shakespeare.[17]

Compound epithets tend to belong to one or the other sort, but this is not an absolute distinction since a poet may form a compound epithet that is both impassioned and descriptive. Perhaps Keats and Yeats provide the strongest examples, especially on those occasions when their descriptions bear the weight of a suggested or embedded mythology. Should Keats's epithets fail to give delight, the emotional and intellectual structure of his odes would fail. 'That dolphin-torn, that gong-tormented sea', the dense, final line of Yeats's 'Byzantium', appeals to the eye and ear with great enargeia while it evokes through alliteration and energeia the torment of being torn: in his scheme, between Self and Soul, fire and water, nature and art, body and spirit. Although that torment is itself being 'broken' by the marbles of the dancing floor, and although the rest of the poem is devoted to the resolution of human division, the single last line is weighty enough to change the centre of gravity of the poem, putting its accent on the world's mire and taking it away from Byzantium. The significance of the enargeia–energeia distinction, in relation to our topic, is that the descriptive, 'enargetic', poetical compound epithet was understood to be Greek. Because of that understanding, these epithets could become a means to relate Greek mythology and beauty. In some of his poetry, Milton used them beautifully in order to warn against their beauty, their seductiveness.

Compound epithets may perform a variety of functions besides animating rhetoric or stimulating the visual imagination. They may be classicizing, as Spenser's *rosy-fingred* (*Fairie Queene* I. 2. 7. 1) and similar epithets. By translating a classical epithet in an allusion to Greek mythology near the beginning of his poem, Spenser clearly indicated his ambition to create a work not inferior in status to the great epics of classical antiquity.[18] Perhaps the poets of the Pléiade were more strictly classicizing in their compound epithets than their English counterparts.[19] Other compound epithets may be allegorizing (the *pure-ey'd Faith* and *white-handed Hope* of *Comus*); like mythological epithets, allegorical ones depend on a shared imaginative understanding of the world. More generally, they may give a physical description of an abstraction, as Shakespeare did when he made jealousy *greene-eyed* (*Merchant of Venice*, 3. 2). Or they may be an attempt to elevate the style by making it less like prose, an aspiration that sometimes overlapped with the classicizing ambition. In the preface to his translation of the *Iliad*, Alexander Pope imputed this purpose, among others, to Homer:[20]

To throw his Language more out of Prose, *Homer* seems to have affected the *Compound-Epithets*. This was a sort of Composition peculiarly proper to Poetry, not only as it heighten'd the *Diction*, but as it assisted and fill'd the *Numbers* with greater Sound and Pomp, and likewise conduced in some measure to thicken the *Images*. On this last Consideration, I cannot but attribute these also to the Fruitfulness of his Invention, since (as he has manag'd them) they are a sort of supernumerary Pictures of the Persons or Things to which they are join'd.

The compound epithets in Homer have always raised questions for those emulating him; controversies over their true function have always been heated. In response to Perrault who dismissed them as often tedious and unnecessary, Boileau described the compound epithets of the heroes and gods as a kind of surname;[21] Pope, later in his preface, imagined them to be a kind of solemn and reverential part of their name, which to omit would have been offensive. Their function in oral composition was not clearly understood before the work of Milman Parry in the twentieth century, though it was also necessary, decades after Parry's early death, for Adam Parry to demonstrate the incapacity of a strictly oral-formulaic approach to account for Homer's poetry.[22] Despite this historical variety of interpretations, the compound epithets in Homer always gave European poets an influential precedent to include epithets not strictly or organically demanded by the narrative, especially if they stimulated the visual imagination.

In his early poetry Milton was attracted to words as visual stimuli, and he saw in them a possibility to force a confrontation between pagan and Christian. Throughout his poetry, Milton loved to bring about such confrontations, and particularly in the form of collisions. In book 1 of *Paradise Lost*, he recalled the classical myth of Hephaestus flung out of Olympus by Zeus:

> ... from Morn
> To Noon he fell, from Noon to dewy Eve,
> A Summers day; and with the setting Sun
> Dropt from the Zenith like a falling Star,
> On *Lemnos* th' *Ægæan* Ile: thus they relate,
> Erring.

Milton tells the ancient fable beautifully; none the less, the fable is untrue or at most a garbled version of the Christian truth, and Milton immediately dismisses it. In 'On the Morning of Christs Nativity', Christ put the false pagan gods to flight. He could therefore depict a scene from Greek mythology in all its beauty (using the Greek decorative compound epithet) because it could no longer seduce, its falseness having been revealed.

> With flowre-inwov'n tresses torn
> The Nimphs in twilight shade of tangled thickets mourn.

In *Comus*, the central collision is the seduction attempted by Comus and the spiritual and moral resistance of the Lady, who is none the less physically paralysed by him. From the 'divine volumes of *Plato*' Milton had learnt 'of chastity and love, I meane that which is truly so, whose charming cup is only vertue which she bears in her hand to those who are worthy. The rest are cheated with a thick intoxicating potion which a certaine Sorceresse the abuser of loves name carries about.'[23] The allegory of the masque is Platonic in its depiction of the merely animal existence of those who live the life of the senses; however, Milton does not simply repeat Platonic ideas. Where Plato sought in intellect a means to bypass all experience that is mediated by the senses, Milton distinguishes between two kinds of sensory experience: that which reveals the presence of God and that which directs man away from God and makes him bestial.

Johnson thought it was one of the most 'truly poetical' of works, and he went on to explain what he meant by 'poetical': 'allusions, images, and decorative epithets embellish almost every period with lavish decoration'.[24] The decorative compound epithets in the work are both numerous and striking; they are very frequent, and they are frequently original (the poem contains the greatest number of Milton's coinages[25]). One way Milton uses them is to contrast the characters. For example, compounds in ill- and well-, analogues to the many Greek compounds in $\delta\upsilon\sigma$- and $\epsilon\dot{\upsilon}$-, are almost never spoken by Comus. The moral evaluations implicit in 'ill manag'd Merriment' (171), 'ill greeting touch' (405), 'wel-govern'd and wise appetit' (704) are outside his scope. He uses this kind of compound adjective only once, and when he does he draws only on the amoral, instrumental sense of 'well': he plans to insinuate himself into the confidence of the 'easie hearted man' (163) by means of 'wel plac't words of glozing courtesie' (161). What is most significant about these compounds is the way Milton keeps evaluations like 'ill managed' and 'wel-govern'd' from sounding like crabbed moralizing. The poem defends chastity as one aspect of the wise self-governance which prevents the exploitation of many for the sake of the pleasure of the few. Chastity is primal self-control, and the chaste man will eschew all forms of excess, luxury, and superfluity:

> If every just man that now pines with want
> Had but a moderate, and beseeming share
> Of that which lewdy-pamper'd Luxurie
> Now heaps upon some few with vast excesse,
> Natures full blessings would be well dispenc't.
> In unsuperfluous even proportion . . .
>
> (767–72)

Milton, that is, connects the 'easie hearted man' not with joy (Comus' seductive lie) but with ' hard besetting need' (856) and so exposes the false pretence by which luxury is made to be so tempting.

Some decorative epithets in *Comus* are sensuous in Milton's positive sense, free from the imputation of depraved indulgence, innocent of the danger that leads man away from God. The Spirit and the Lady describe nature's innocent beauty with striking epithets: 'violet-imbroider'd vale' (233), 'Knot-grass dew-besprent' (541), 'amber-dropping haire' (862), 'coral-paven bed' (886). Yet when these epithets are applied to pagan divinities, they intensify the potential conflict between Christian and pagan. When he wrote the masque, Milton believed it was possible to distinguish those truthful aspects of pagan mythology (which could be read as allegories of Christian truths) from other, sinister aspects. The virgin goddess Artemis, the 'silver-shafted Queene' (441) could be easily assimilated to the Christian defence of chastity. Likewise the Spirit need not hesitate to acknowledge the 'blu-hair'd deities' who rule England in Neptune's behalf (29) or to invoke '*Thetis* tinsel-slipper'd feet' (876) and other divinities. However, when Comus refers to the 'flowrie-kirtl'd *Naiades*' (253), one of the most famous of Milton's epithets, the depiction occurs in the sinister context of Circe. The very attractiveness of this description shows Milton's success in making evil tempting. Comus' praise of the Lady's beauty is itself beautiful, but the compound epithets he invents in praise of her body—'vermeil-tinctur'd lip' (751) and 'Love-darting eyes' (752)—are designed to seduce her. The language of 'vermeil-tinctur'd lip' is later implicitly rejected by Sabrina, when she refers, not less beautifully though with less ostentation, to the Lady's 'rubied lip' (914). Compound epithets require, and invite, vigilance to distinguish just praise from flattery intended to seduce, to dissever, that is, the sensuous from the sensual.

Milton included very few decorative compound epithets in his longer poems. Two occur in *Paradise Lost*, 5.38–43:

> Why sleepst thou Eve? now is the pleasant time,
> The cool, the silent, save where silence yields
> To the night-warbling Bird, that now awake
> Tunes sweetest his love-labor'd song; now reignes
> Full Orb'd the Moon, and with more pleasing light
> Shadowie sets off the face of things . . .

Of these lines Archie Burnett writes: 'The beguiling suavity of this Satanic serenade to Eve in her dream is rendered suspiciously unctuous by the profusion of compound adjectives alien to the poem's prevailing style.'[26] In his greatest works, Milton has qualified and even abandoned the Renaissance hope for the comity of ancient and modern and has reverted to a traditional Christian understanding of pagan eloquence: like the captive woman of Deuteronomy 21, who may be married once her head and eyebrows have been shaved, so ancient grandeur and beauty, clipped and pared, can be put to Christian purposes.[27] Milton makes the decorative compound epithet participate in the highest ambitions of his poetry.

The change from the 'superfluity' of double epithets in *Comus* (as Coleridge put it, who believed that Milton's subsequent abandonment of them was exemplary[28]) to almost an absence of them in the longer works paralleled a change in literary fashion in the course of the seventeenth century. In Cowley's *Poems* of 1656, compound epithets were prominent, and in *The English Parnassus* of 1657 (reprinted in 1677 and 1678), Joshua Poole gave many and varied examples. On the other hand, John Ogilby's translations of Homer (1660 and 1665), to say nothing of Hobbes's version of the *Odyssey* (1676), curtailed them severely. This became the dominant attitude, influenced by a change in French fashion: compound epithets in French had been an object of caricature at least since Desmarets de Saint-Sorlin ridiculed them in *Les Visionnaires* (1638), and the critics René Rapin and Dominique Bouhours among others continued to judge them uncouth. In 1677, Dryden censured the unlucky attempts by Sidney and the translator of Du Bartas to create in English the 'frequent and elegant' compound epithets of Greek. Pope, we saw, had a similar attitude to Dryden's, admiring the Greek capacity for forming compound epithets but believing they seldom worked in English; in practice, though, Pope was somewhat more hospitable to them than Dryden. Johnson was magisterial in theory and consistent in practice. 'We have long ago seen *white-rob'd* innocence, and *flower-bespangled* meads',[29] he said in dismissal of a minor poet, and sedulously avoided such lapses in his own poetry.

Even though compound epithets were often rejected as antiquarian or self-indulgent within the major tradition of poetry in the eighteenth century, with its emphasis on perspicuous writing, they were welcomed by lesser poets. Thomson was especially concerned to create suggestive and decorative compound epithets, as were Collins and Gray, who followed (with more discretion) the example set by the *Seasons*.[30] Thomson's descriptions and descriptive epithets ('close-embowering woods', 'dusky-mantled lawn') were the most attractive part of his poem; some of his epithets proved to be enduring (Gray adopted 'many-twinkling' and 'sea-encircled' in a single poem; Wordsworth took over 'sole-sitting'). However, the epithets have only a distant and indirect relation to Greek. The same is true also of the Pindaric odes of Collins and Gray, for example, the 'Ode to Liberty' and 'The Progress of Poesy'. In these odes there are many compound epithets, some visually striking ('light-embroidered sky', 'fiery-tressed Dane' in Collins; 'many-twinkling feet' in Gray), and in that respect they succeed in being reminiscent of Pindar; in addition, the poets offered much Greek in their notes to the odes. None the less, the language of their poems is not particularly Greek, and most of the epithets are taken or modified from English sources, not invented or translated. Even Cowper, who loved Homer's compound epithets, cut many of them from the second edition of his translation of the *Iliad*.

Wordsworth, with his compound epithets, followed the pattern which Coleridge found exemplary: they are common in the early work ('Evening Walk', 'Descriptive Sketches'), but in *Lyrical Ballads* and his subsequent work, when he had freed himself from the influence of eighteenth-century lyric mannerisms, he largely eliminated them. Coleridge himself, though he claimed that he pruned the double epithets from his first book of poems 'with no sparing hand', kept many of them in the book's second edition. One of his most influential compound epithets occurs in his prose; Greek gave him 'myriad-minded', from the Byzantine word μυριόνους, an epithet which he bestowed on Shakespeare in *Biographia Literaria* and which Tennyson and Swinburne later used in poetry. Such epithets took on a new importance in the generation after Wordsworth and Coleridge, in the work of Shelley and especially Keats, the first poet since Milton to establish a relation with Greek mythology through a language influenced by Greek, primarily in the use of compound epithets.

Shelley wrote in distinct styles. In the next chapter, it will be argued that two styles of English poetry developed in the nineteenth century under the influence of Greek. The first was a new and stricter neo-classicism largely derived from Winckelmann and his idealization of the 'noble simplicity and tranquil grandeur' of the Greeks; in literature, this corresponded to a style which emphasized swiftness and clarity, simplicity, crystalline transparency. When Shelley wrote in this vein, he emphasized verbs over epithets and took care to limit the number of compound epithets. In his version of the Homeric hymn to Hermes, he included only thirty compound adjectives; the original had 161 (Chapman has seventy-seven). Of the 227 compound epithets in the Greek of those Homeric hymns which Shelley translated, he rendered only forty by English compounds, adding nineteen more of his own (Chapman's corresponding figures are fifty and fifty-nine).[31] In this respect, he followed the example of the

Orphic hymns translated by Thomas Taylor, who had despaired of translating the epithets:[32]

Thus most of the compound epithets of which the following Hymns chiefly consist, though very beautiful in the Greek language, yet, when translated into ours, lose all their propriety and force. In their native language, as in a prolific soil, they diffuse their sweets with full-blown elegance, but shrink like the sensitive plant at the touch of the verbal critic, or the close translator.

The major tonal effects for which Shelley as translator is striving— the urbane story-telling of the 'Hymn to Mercury', reverence and simple gratitude in 'To the Earth, Mother of All'—are not conveyed by compound epithets in these translations, some of the finest translations from Greek in the nineteenth century. The hymn to the earth has twice as many verbs as adjectives, and the adjectives are often plain (*mild, ripe, fair, happy, fresh, lovely*, etc.) because they are meant to be taken without stopping to reflect, in order to suggest an easy, familiar, and happy rootedness in the world.

The choruses about ancient Greece in *Hellas* are perhaps Shelley's most famous lyrics in this style. Light, sunrise, the crystalline sea, splendour are celebrated and made manifest in ancient Greece. The emphasis is on the harmony of the whole, not on descriptive detail. There are no compound epithets in those choruses, few in the other choruses, and only eighteen in the drama.

The second style influenced by Greek was developed as a Romantic reaction against the neo-classicism and French fashions of the eighteenth century. Greek and Elizabethan tragedy were believed, despite their differences, to form a single coherent alternative to neo-classical and especially French drama, which was by now regarded as enfeebled, rule-bound, and derivative. Shelley also wrote in this style; *Prometheus Unbound* is the most prominent English Romantic example in which Greek and Elizabethan models have been combined. Although *Hellas* and *Prometheus Unbound* are each given the subtitle 'lyrical drama', their style is dissimilar since they conform to different understandings of Greek lyric style. *Hellas* avoids compound epithets, while *Prometheus Unbound* is filled with them.[33]

In both dramas, as in both styles generally, however, Shelley fails to form effective compound epithets. Take the following examples: from *Prometheus Unbound*, 'crystal-wingèd snow' (1. 385), 'tempest-wingèd chariots' (2. 4. 93), 'rainbow-wingèd steeds' (2. 4.

130), 'insects rainbow-winged' (3. 3. 92), and 'tempest-wingèd ship (4. 409); from *Hellas*, 'tempest-winged cities' (300), 'seraph-winged Victory' (448), 'eagle winged victory' (715), with which we might compare the 'splendour-wingèd worlds' and 'seraph-wingèd Victory' of the so-called 'Prologue to Hellas' (54, 102), first published in 1862. Though compound epithets in '-winged' occur in Greek (as they do in English),[34] and though other epithets in the plays may have been taken directly from Greek sources,[35] the connection to Greek remains superficial. Shelley varies the '-winged' epithets to little purpose; he merely recycles them. Moreover, the epithets lack vividness in their own right; with the exception of 'insects rainbow-winged', none of them encourages exact visualization. It is as if Shelley's imagination regarded visual details as interchangeable. In his best work, this is not the case: the hard and hateful details of oppression inspire vivid depictions in 'The Mask of Anarchy' and 'The Triumph of Life'; his close friendship with the Gisbornes led to the marvellous 'still life' of Henry Revely's workroom described in the 'Letter to Maria Gisborne'.[36] But those descriptions avoid compound epithets. Shelley's compound epithets tend either to be forgettable, like the ones in '-winged', or so anxious to demonstrate their Greek foreignness (like the 'eagle-baffling mountain' and 'moon-freezing crystals' at the beginning of *Prometheus Unbound*) that they are insufficiently perceived within English. That is, they provoke a feeling of strangeness—essential to vivid descriptions—but the strangeness lies in our response to the particular words, not to the scene.

Keats's greatest epithets, in contrast, elicit the response, 'How strange, how delightful, how true'. Madeleine's 'azure-lidded sleep' evokes the delicate blue veining of the relaxed, closed eyelid; in seeing it in memory or imagination, we participate in the erotic intimacy which Keats describes. The 'far-foamed sands' has a strange power in context, mingling visual, auditory, and tactile imagery.[37] Oceanus caught murmurs from the world's shore with his tongue. We not only see the vast expanse of shore, but hear the muffled sound of the world through it, and imagine the foam as a tongue flickering over it, lapping it. Psyche's 'soft-conched ear' presents an initial oxymoron, just as the senses do. Keats want us to experience the synaesthesia, resolved only after we distinguish between the soft texture and the conched shape of the ear. This last epithet has been condemned as jarring and awkward, but such an objection misses not only the synaesthesia but also a central feature of Keats's poetry: his delightful epithets are sometimes awkward in order to keep readers aware of the potential awkwardness of delight—as in watching a sleeping lover, or moving your tongue across a surface, or finding an ear beautiful—so that we may unperplex delight from its sticky neighbours, prurience, embarrassment, voyeurism, infantilism, and others. The epithets go wrong when they are linguistically strange but visually conventional; the 'cirque-couchant' snake is no more than a coiled snake (Keats has no interest in the heraldic implications of his coinage).[38]

The sensory brilliance of Keats's epithets was widely appreciated, after his death. In reading them, Tennyson was confirmed in his own love of suggestive and minutely described landscapes.[39] In a discussion about the exquisite fineness of pine trees in *Modern Painters*, Ruskin praised him for putting 'nearly all that may be said of the pine into one verse . . . though they are only figurative pines of which he is speaking'.[40] Ruskin had in mind these lines from the 'Ode to Psyche':

> Far, far around shall those dark-cluster'd trees
> Fledge the wild-ridged mountains steep by steep.

For Ruskin, this natural description is consummate, even though description is only Keats's purpose in a secondary sense; the primary purpose of the compound epithets is to evoke the wild and dark of the mind.

Keats never learnt Greek.[41] Greekless, he none the less depicted himself as an Odyssean hero in 'On First Looking into Chapman's Homer'; the phrases 'Much have I travell'd' and 'many . . . kingdoms seen' recall the opening of the *Odyssey*.[42] In the sonnet, Keats proclaims the value not only of Homer and Chapman's translation but of his own intuitive affinity ('almost consanguinity'[43]) with Greece, which enabled him to bypass Pope and discover Homer directly. In his compound epithets Keats is likewise both Greek and Greekless. A few of these may have been inspired by Chapman; some have parallels in Greek; he also uses them in Greek ways, for vivid descriptions and for epithets of divinities.[44] None the less, their deepest connection to Greece is not philological but mythological. Ruskin told his readers that they would gain 'a more truthful idea of the nature of Greek religion and legend from the poems of Keats . . . than from frigid scholarship, however extensive'.[45] Ruskin did not consider the potential contribution of non-frigid scholarship; still, he responded to something essential: the reimagining of a Greek religious sense.

Keats's compound epithets are particularly adroit in depicting the world in such a way that myth is suggested by it or embedded in it.[46]

Keats and Milton have complementary relations to Greece. Milton repudiated it because it had produced beauty but not truth. Milton's poetic honesty lay in recreating so compellingly the beauty that is to be rejected, thereby making evident just how much sensual abstention Christian truth demands. He drew on the decorative Greek compound epithets for this purpose, primarily in *Comus* and the 'Nativity Ode', but even occasionally in the later poetry where they are very scarce; think of the seductive description of Athens, the eye of Greece, 'where the *Attic* Bird | Trills her thick-warbl'd notes the summer long' (*Paradise Regained*, 4. 245–6). Keats in turn repudiated Milton's repudiation and sought to restore a pagan religious sense, to insist on the truth of beauty. His poetic honesty was analogous to Milton's; it lay in his acknowledgement of the possibilities of untruthfulness in the equation of truth, beauty, and happiness. Sometimes this takes the form it did in the verse epistle to Reynolds, with its vision of 'eternal fierce destruction' at the core of nature, of nature without beauty or beneficence. Even in poems where Keats is committed to what he saw as the Greek 'Religion of the Beautiful, the Religion of Joy,'[47] he does not suppress his doubts and self-divisions. Of Lamia it was succinctly said that 'Keats himself did not know whether she was a thing of beauty or a thing of bale.'[48] Contradictory impulses also run through *Endymion* and the two versions of *Hyperion*.

In the 'Ode to Psyche', the recovery and worship of the neglected Psyche are fraught with darkness, some of which is conveyed by the compound epithets that so impressed Ruskin. The ode is an agon in which Keats engages with Milton. Literary critics have pointed specifically to the indebtedness of Keats's language to the stanzas in Milton's 'Nativity Ode' in which Greek divinities lament their own imminent demise.[49] Keats draws on Milton's language in order to repudiate Milton's moralism. Whereas the demise of the pagan gods is Milton's subject, Keats intends to institute a new worship of Psyche. In Milton's poem the 'pale-eyed priest' no longer receives inspiration, while Keats is to become the 'pale-mouthed priest' whom Psyche needs. Compound epithets in Keats do more, however, than allude to and rewrite Milton. They are mythological, not only in the sense of conveying the known attributes of mythic figures, but also in that they make landscape articulate. The ode opens with a picture of erotic happiness (and not merely pleasure): Psyche and Cupid in each other's arms, blissful, untroubled. They lay 'calm-breathing' in 'soft-handed slumber' amid 'cool-rooted flowers, fragrant-eyed'. Later in the poem the landscape is darker: Keats resolves to build a temple for Psyche in some untrodden region of his mind, where his thoughts will be 'dark-cluster'd trees' that 'fledge the wild-ridged mountains'. Then the picture lightens: 'moss-lain Dryads' will be lulled to sleep there; Keats will dress a rosy sanctuary; the gardener Fancy will breed ever new flowers; all will be soft delight. Another shift: all will be soft delight—or rather, all will be whatever soft delight shadowy thoughts can win. The ode is incoherent; the relations between senses and thought, between love, body, and spirit, between myth and reality, are inconsistent, and their relative value is unstable. But it is an honest failure. Keats starts not with a mythological fiat but with an experience, a vision of erotic happiness so awesome that it seems to be of eternal value. Rather than assert a mythological or Platonic equivalent to that experience, Keats explores it, acknowledging the unhappiness the lover may suffer from so intensely valuing the experience; he shows how much it may cost.

In the next generation, Tennyson and Browning became the Victorian masters of compound epithets. However, though they both read Greek passionately, the ancient language rarely inspired their best coinages directly. Rarely, not never: with the 'many-fountained Ida' of 'Œnone', Tennyson translates a specific Homeric epithet and introduces a formal distance into Œnone's cry of pain, giving to it some of the plangency of formal keening ('O mother Ida, many-fountained Ida, | Dear mother Ida, harken ere I die'). Still, for the most part his epithets neither draw on Greek nor obtrude Greek on the reader. Consider the descriptive compound epithets of 'The Lotos-Eaters', which convey not myth but mood (like Theocritus, Tennsyon makes the most sophisticated and appealing use of the pathetic fallacy): 'slow-dropping veils of thinnest lawn'; 'in the stream the long-leaved flowers weep'; 'the folded leaf is . . . Sun-steeped at noon, and in the moon | Nightly dew-fed'; 'The full-juiced apple, waxing over-mellow'; 'the thick-twinèd vine'; 'To watch the emerald-coloured water falling'.[50] In contrast, Browning often intends that his compound epithets not be fully integrated into the texture of his verse; they are meant to stand out. In some descriptive passages, they are notable for their strangeness and excess, like the jennet that is 'black-barred, cream-coated and pink eye-balled' in 'The Flight of the Duchess'. Translation from Greek offers plenty of scope for such experimentation, but Browning's version of the *Agamemnon*—done 'in as Greek a fashion as English will bear'— does not match his ambition. Its literalism leads mostly to an obscure, uniformly elevated translationese. For example, the 'two-throned, two-sceptred' Atreidai, the 'wind-abating sacrifice', and Agamemnon's 'vice-devising miserable mood' invoke details that could just as well be told without the compounds.[51] In general, we may conclude that Browning does not know what to do with the foreignness he so desires.

Gerard Hopkins hated Greek mythology but admired its beauty. Words fail him 'to express the loathing and horror' with which he thinks of Greek mythology and religion; on the other hand, he agrees 'with the rest of the world in admiring its beauty'.[52] For Hopkins, beauty is dangerous: 'I think then no one can admire beauty of the body more than I do, and it is of course a comfort to find beauty in a friend or a friend in beauty. But this kind of beauty is dangerous'.[53] 'This kind of beauty' refers not only to sexual attractiveness but to all natural beauty, and not because nature produces beautiful evil (nature, he writes, is incapable of doing so), but because the human will, infected by sin, will abuse beauty, nature's good. For both Keats and Hopkins, beauty is supercharged with meaning, but where Keats connects it to truth and happiness, Hopkins sees in it either God's grace or Satan's lure. For both poets, it is revealed with particular intensity in erotic experience, but this experience has radically different meanings for them. Hopkins sets himself expressly against Keats: 'His poems, I know, are very sensuous and indeed they are sensual. This sensuality is their fault'. [54]

Some of Hopkins's compound epithets are acute and heightened descriptions of natural beauty. They are Keatsian, and more, in the intensity of their response to landscape, to the richly compacted sensory stimulation of nature, which Hopkins recreates in richly compacted epithets.[55] Let us consider three passages from *The Wreck of the Deutschland*, in which a 'lush-kept plush-capped sloe', 'down-dugged ground-hugged grey', and 'crimson-cresseted east' respectively appear. In them Hopkins is also reacting against Keats, and he makes the epithets undergo a scrutiny foreign to Keats's purposes.

The sloe, mouthed to flesh-burst, draws on Keats's lines from the *Ode on Melancholy* where melancholy is seen only by him 'whose

strenuous tongue I Can burst Joy's grape against his palate fine'. But
the sloe itself cancels any Keatsian expectation of delectability since
its bitterness contrasts so sharply with the grape's sweetness. Hopkins's choice of a sloe confuses the reader's expectations of sour and
sweet:

> Oh,
> We lash with the best or worst
> Word last! How a lush-kept plush-capped sloe
> Will, mouthed to flesh-burst,
> Gush!—flush the man, the being with it, sour or sweet,
> Brim, in a flásh, fúll!

In this stanza, the last words and final mental state of the dying have
all their popular Victorian significance—compare the death-bed
scenes in Dickens, even the death of Lucy in *Dracula*[56]—as well as
constituting the climax of life in both Evangelical and Catholic
traditions. Our being is fulfilled in our last words in a way we can
understand by imagining, even exaggerating, how the sloe flushes us;
as they are best ('Bring me a priest!') or worst, so our being will be
filled sweet or sour. The last words of the drowned nun were her best:
'O Chríst, Chríst, come quíckly'. Hopkins sets out the relation that
truly obtains between worst and best and sweet and sour. The sloe,
in his description, looks sweet, but it is sour; the sacrifice appears to
be the worst but is the best. The sour worst in appearance is the sweet
best in Christ's reality.

In the next passage, Hopkins carefully directs the movement from
delight in a natural scene to delight in what is beyond the senses.
Stanza 26:

> For how to the heart's cheering
> The down-dugged ground-hugged grey
> Hovers off, the jay-blue heavens appearing
> Of pied and peeled May!
> Blue-beating and hoary-glow height; or night, still higher,
> With bélled fíre and the móth-soft Mílky Wáy.
> What bý your méasure is the héaven of desíre,
> The tréasure never éyesight gót, nor was éver guessed whát for the héaring?

The advent of spring cheers the heart, but the stanza does not leave
us to enjoy spring or the night-time; our thoughts and our delight
move finally to what is beyond the senses. Moreover, by virtue of
their position within the poem's argument, these lines further keep

natural beauty from being celebrated for its own sake apart from God. The previous stanza ends with the question whether the nun cried out to Christ out of her eager desire to attain heaven; Hopkins depicts the treasure of heaven in this stanza; but then in the next he rejects this explanation. 'The jáding and jár of the cárt, Time's tásking' are the circumstances in which one would ask for death, 'Not danger, electrical-horror'. Hopkins is maintaining that it is the dull, daily grind that turns one's mind to entertain thoughts of death, and even to desire death, and not 'danger' or 'electrical-horror'. It is a lapse in his moral imagination. He is unable to imagine that a person drowning for hours may finally wish for death. Out of his own need to repudiate a wish for death in response to the daily jading and jar of life, he makes her emotionally exempt from the immense exhaustion of dying.

The 'crímson-cresseted east' comes in the last stanza of the poem. The beautiful dawn is also the Easter of resurrection; the crimson is sky-tint and Christ's sacrifice of blood. Hopkins makes landscape articulate in his own way: nature becomes a witness to God's purpose.

Like Milton and Keats, Hopkins finds in decorative compound epithets a means to dramatize the moral status of mortal beauty. He is just as bold in forming other compounds. Greek gave him some precedent for his word-formation and abrupt phrasing. Aeschylus, in particular, provided him with an exemplar of verse boldly compounded, under stress, and in earnest—a theme for the next chapter.

Compound epithets continue to be engaged with mythology in two modernist poets. The first of Pound's *Cantos* rewrites Odysseus' descent into hell; it introduces us to Circe, 'the trim-coifed goddess' and to the peopled cities of the Kimmerian lands 'Covered with close-webbed mist'. The epithets help to set the scene and are suggestive of Greek, but they have only a minor function in this canto and are dropped in his major restatements of Greek myth, cantos 17 and 47 for example (with one exception: 'green-gray dust'). Yeats's forceful epithets—'the mackerel-crowded seas' ('Sailing to Byzantium') and 'the haystack- and roof-levelling wind' ('A Prayer for my Daughter') to 'That dolphin-torn, that gong-tormented sea'—animate his mythologizing but are conceptually fairly obvious (crowds of mackerel implying the fertility of youth, the displacing of the compound 'haystack-levelling' into separate words corresponding to the havoc caused by the wind). 'That dolphin-torn, that gong-tormented sea' is unique in Yeats's œuvre for its combination of rhetorical forcefulness and conceptual density. The Renaissance and the nineteenth century, the periods when English literature was most intensely involved with Greek, were the ones when the compound epithets were most charged with activity.

Negative Adjectives

Negative or privative adjectives, that is, words in 'un-' and '-less' and so on, are easily created in Greek, and some of them form part of Greek's distinctive poetic vocabulary.[57] The standard epithet for sea in Homer is ἀτρύγετος; its meaning is uncertain but since ancient times it has been understood as 'barren' or 'unfruitful'.[58] Shelley probably had it in mind when he wrote in *Prometheus Unbound* (3. 2. 49): 'It is the unpastured sea hungering for calm'.[59] In the same play, he turns to negative adjectives to produce oxymorons in a form common in Greek tragedy:[60] 'unseasonable seasons' (2. 4. 52), 'faithless faith' (3. 3. 130). His coinage *garlandless* (3. 4. 186) translates the ἀστέφανος of Greek tragedy, and other negatives in the play also have Greek equivalents.

It has several times been suggested that groups of privative adjectives in English follow Greek patterns. Milton's editors, commenting on the five occasions in his verse when he links consecutively three or more negative adjectives,[61] point to the possible influence of Greek tragedy.[62] Some editors add examples from Greek prose and English instances from Spenser, Shakespeare, and Fairfax's translation of Tasso.[63] To these influences should be added Homer's example at *Iliad* 9. 63. It is my impression that negative triplets (to say nothing of larger groups) are relatively uncommon in English literature between Milton and the nineteenth century.[64] In the thirteen-book *Prelude*, Wordsworth finds four occasions for them (only two of them survive in the fourteen-book version, to which he adds one new triplet).[65] He echoes Milton in his creation of a new sublime, an equivalent to high epic diction; in this sense, he may have been influenced by Greek at second hand. With other negative series of the period, I can find no Greek influence whatever; for instance, neither Byron's description of a waste world 'Seasonless, herbless, treeless, manless, lifeless' ('Darkness', l. 71) nor Thackeray's picture of Miss Crawley as 'graceless, thankless, religionless' (*Vanity Fair*, ch. 14) has any relation to Greek. On the other hand, when Shelley writes in *Prometheus Unbound*, 3. 4. 193–8:

> The loathsome mask has fallen, the man remains
> Sceptreless, free, uncircumscribed, but man
> Equal, unclassed, tribeless, and nationless,
> Exempt from awe, worship, degree, the king
> Over himself; just, gentle, wise: but man
> Passionless?

the play itself, in its indebtedness to Greek tragedy, encourages us to perceive a connection to Greek. Moreover, 'unclassed, tribeless, and nationless' parallels the man in Homer who is ἀφρήτωρ, ἀθέμιστος, ἀνέστιος (clanless, lawless, hearthless). Though Shelley has expanded the Homeric triad into a much longer sequence of negatives, we may still hear the Homeric allusion: Shelley has turned Homer's curse into utopian redemption. In a chorus from Arnold's *Merope* (ll. 629–30), the heart of man is 'unplumb'd, | Unscaled, untrodden'; in Swinburne's 'Sapphics' (ll. 73–4), the ghosts of outcast women return 'unassuaged, unheard of, | Unbeloved, unseen', and 'implacable' Aphrodite makes her appearance 'with hair unbound and feet unsandalled' (ll. 9–10). In these instances, no allusion to Greek is present, but the Greek atmosphere of both works is partly created by this echo of a characteristic Greek formation.

In his study of Milton's lexis, Thomas Corns notes Milton's predilection for negative affixation; he assembles instances of negatives in groups of two to four elements, in both the poetry and the prose; and he draws attention to the neologisms in 'un-'. He asks the key question: 'Milton's enthusiasm for such compounds fascinates—why should he, more than most, define what is by what is not?'; he does not, however, attempt an answer, and his emphasis on definition excessively restricts the activity of Milton's negatives.[66]

Some of Milton's editors have claimed that the negative adjectives add emphasis. A group of such adjectives might be more emphatic than a single one, but then again, the aggregate might diffuse the emphasis. A rare or novel privative may emphatically call attention to itself, but it may only be superficially eccentric; or it may not call attention to itself in the first place. None of Browning's twelve privative neologisms in '-less' (*abashless, disguiseless, drugless . . .*) receives special emphasis or attracts particular attention. Hopkins, in contrast, favours active negatives describing a process rather than passive ones indicating a state: *unchilding, unfathering, unleaving,* not *childless, fatherless, leafless.* He introduces unusual negatives where a less marked form would fail to convey the full extent of negation. To be lost to Christ is actively to be somewhere else, *in Unchrist;* the destruction of poplars is also a destruction of an inscape and a haecceitas, and so strokes of havoc *unselve* the scene the poplars created; *disremembering,* in the 'metamorphic power of Hopkins' context', changes its meaning, which is no longer simply 'failing to remember' but rather 'dismembering the memory'.[67]

Some things in life are understood as the negation of something else, virginity, for example, or unselfconsciousness, say, or oppression. These are the concerns of the three poets in English who pre-eminently draw on negated words: Milton, Wordsworth, and Shelley. In Milton's imagination, the negation (as Comus describes it) or the abstention required by virginity has a positive, almost absolute, value. Sin, too, has an almost absolute value in his mind. Though sin is the negation of righteousness, righteousness itself is revealed only in its resistance to that negation. His many negatives in *Comus* serve to bring out the many kinds of negations involved in the drama: virginity ('thou unblemish't forme of Chastitie', 'unpolluted temple of the mind '), its apparent vulnerability ('all unguarded Ladie', 'haplesse virgin', 'unarmed weaknesse of one virgin | Alone, and helplesse'), vice's attempted negation of virtue ('unprincipl'd', 'bold Incontinence', 'unchast looks', 'shameless brows', 'Intemperance') and virtue's active resistance to vice ('uninchanted eye', 'unconquer'd virgin ', 'dauntlesse hardihood'). The argument of the masque establishes the virgin as innocent, that is, not nocent, not causing injury.

Milton's good emerges out of unceasing warfare with evil. It is not defined but it is proved by what it is not. The 'irrefutable grammar of Abdiel's defiance'[68] contains Milton's longest sequence of negatives:

> So spake the Seraph *Abdiel* faithful found,
> Among the faithless, faithful only hee;
> Among innumerable false, unmov'd,
> Unshak'n, unseduc'd, unterrifi'd
> His Loyaltie he kept, his Love, his Zeale;

> (*Paradise Lost*, 5. 896–900)

In many poets, things imagined negatively may be expressed by negated words. Pope is not especially fond of such negations, but he provides something like an infinitely sublimed strip-tease at the end of canto i of *The Rape of the Lock*: the toilet is 'unveil'd', the nymph's head is 'uncover'd', she 'unlocks' her box of gems. Keats in the three negatives of 'Ode on a Grecian Urn' characterizes the eternity of art's truth and beauty by contrasting and negating our experience of them in life: 'Thou still unravish'd bride of quietness'; 'Heard melodies are sweet, but those unheard | Are sweeter'; 'happy melodist, unwearied'. In life, melodies are heard, melodists become weary, and urns are ravaged by time. The choice of *unravish'd* for the more obvious *unravaged* brings a rich ambivalence into the understanding of experience, so that it comprises consummation as well as destruction. It is in Wordsworth and Shelley, however, that negation is a principal means for expressing their concerns.

The Prelude, like (and unlike) Milton's epic, describes the Fall. Wordsworth describes the fallen state in negative terms: to fall is to be deprived of something essential: nature. The poem opens with the poet able to shake off, as if by miraculous gift, 'That burthen of my own unnatural self' (1.21; I quote from the 1850 edition). Science, misprized, becomes unnatural (3. 421–3). Or it tempts us to lose our corporate human soul, as in the confused attempt to 'unsoul' with 'syllogistic words' the mysteries of being which make one brotherhood of us (12. 81–7). The unfallen state is likewise described negatively, but with a different semantic emphasis: to be unfallen is to be unspoilt, uncorrupted by something, for example, self-consciousness. 'I held unconscious intercourse with beauty | Old as creation' (1. 562–3); 'unconscious love and reverence | Of human nature' (8. 278–9). Science also threatens, and Wordsworth praises Coleridge to whom, 'unblinded' by the formal arts of science, the unity of all has been revealed (2. 220–1).

Wordsworth's genius lies not in this simple polarity, but his charting of the dense, difficult relations between nature, consciousness, and our moral being. At one moment in the poem, he turns to three negatives to express the complex relation between unfallen (though inordinate) then and fallen (though tutored) now: 'things viewed | By Poets in old time . . . | May in these tutored days no more be seen | With undisordered sight' (3. 153–7). The stress on negatives is sometimes like his stress on the words *bare* or *naked*, meaning at once both destitute and essential. Wordsworth intends to record 'meek Worth | Left to Herself, unheard of and unknown'. Part of the value of meek worth lies in its anonymity. In his noble (if idealized) tribute to Mary Robinson, deceived by John Hatfield in a fake wedding, Wordsworth observes her discretion, the justice of her opinions, her delicate reserve, patience, and humility of mind 'Unspoiled by commendation' (7. 310–15).[69] Earlier in the poem, the veteran tells Wordsworth his history, 'unmoved, | And with a quiet uncomplaining voice, | A stately air of mild indifference' (4. 417–19). He fails to be 'solemn and sublime' because he has been deprived even of feeling his own experience, though his trust in God is unshaken. Mary, 'a meek spirit suffering inwardly', and the veteran with 'ghastly mildness' have had their humanity hideously negated and yet are most essentially human.

Shelley draws most effectively on negated words for several purposes. Sometimes they emphasize patient, constant resistance to evil: *undeclining, unvanquished, unrepentant, unextinguished, unrepressed, unexhausted* (*Prometheus Unbound*, 1. 281, 1. 315, 1. 427, 3. 1. 5, 3. 1. 17, 3. 3. 36). In particular, when Shelley in *The Mask of Anarchy* calls for a massive public demonstration, he insists that it remain peaceful despite risk of massacre. Hatred must not be returned in kind because the mind that hates is in bondage to its hate; it is love that breaks the bonds. The weapons of 'unvanquished war' are non-violent. Shelley tells the people to let Panic pass 'disregarded' through them, to remain 'undismayed' by it (ll. 323, 326). Non-violence is to be an active good, not a passive absence of evil.

At other times they perform the central act of Shelley's Platonic metaphysics: lifting the veil of sensory reality. John Buxton analyses *Prometheus Unbound*:[70]

Shelley sees the poet's experience as moving always from the 'yellow bees in the ivy-bloom' to the intellectual, ideal world of Platonic forms 'more real than living man' [1. 745, 748]. This idealism leads to the tenuous quality of many of Shelley's epithets, but also, beyond this, to an idiosyncratic liking for negative epithets. By this means he strips away the sensuous character of experience, which he regards as a hindrance to the perception of truth, just as Blake did; for to him

> The deep truth is imageless [2. 4. 116].

A negative epithet denies the presence of the attribute which the positive describes, and is far more effective than mere omission ... By these negatives Shelley breaks down

> the veil and the bar
> Of things which seem and are [2. 3. 59–60],

the veil—it is one of his favorite images—suspended by the sense between *videri* and *esse*, appearance and reality … For Shelley, the veil was the interposition of the material world between finite mind and Platonic idea; it was also the obscuring effect of concrete imagery, with its appeal to our senses, which his negative epithets were intended to remove. They withdraw the veil of sense-perception.

Demogorgon, who is potential being and therefore beyond the perception of the senses, is likewise described negatively, along with the attributeless attributes of his world: *ungazed upon and shapeless* (2. 4. 5) *unbeheld* (3. 1. 23, 3. 1. 45), *unknown* (2. 1. 190), *unbodied* (3. 1. 44). In the 'lampless deep' (4. 245) and 'lampless caves of unimagined being' (4. 378), Shelley is retelling Plato's myth of the cave. The lamp is the source of the light by which the senses perceive, and Demogorgon's realm is not illuminated by the light of mere seeming. The Being of beings is necessarily lampless, without illumination.

Timothy Webb points to other purposes motivating Shelley's negatives. Life-denying Jupiter negates the good of the world, which is therefore best described negatively, as it is in Prometheus' opening speech. Prometheus' resistance takes the form not only of defiance but also unbroken endurance, a negation of Jupiter's negation; so 'his eyes remain *tearless*, his head is *undeclining*, he is *the Invincible*'.[71] None the less, the negatives in *Prometheus Unbound* sometimes reflect Shelley's poetic immaturity. With epithets like *foodless*, *wingless*, and *windless*, he shows himself investing and invested in eighteenth-century poetic vocabulary, which he is able to turn to his own account some of the time, for example by connecting *foodless* specifically with famine, *wingless* with the failure to transcend, and *windless* with a condition beyond mutability. However, he uses *foodless* on four occasions, *windless* on five occasions, and *wingless* on three, attenuating their impact and relying more on their status as poeticized diction than on their sense. These occasional lapses of diction are accompanied by a more fundamental failure. Shelley's vision is utopian, not satiric, and yet it is defined more by the negation of current injustices than by any affirmation. Throughout the play, the redeemed future is described in negative terms: 'Heaven's kingless throne' (2. 4. 149), the sea henceforth 'unstain'd with blood' (3. 2. 20), and the title itself, *Prometheus Unbound*. The climactic speech at the end of Act 3, quoted above, gives five negatives in two lines (*sceptreless, uncircumscribed, unclassed, tribeless*, and *nation-*

less). Prometheus prophesies that lovely apparitions will visit, the immortal progeny of 'Painting, Sculpture and rapt Poesy | And arts, though unimagined, yet to be'. The fourth act is intended to realize the prophecy, to give a joyful picture of the redeemed future; however, in it Shelley offers us 'unimagined being' (4. 378), 'unimaginable shapes' (4. 244), 'unimagined gems' (4. 281). On these terms, which are the terms he himself established, Shelley's imagination has failed.

Metres

At the end of 'A Grammar of the English Tongue' introducing his dictionary, Johnson described the metrical options available to poets: iambic verse of four, six, eight, or twelve syllables; and trochaic verse of three, five, or seven. He noted in smaller type that other lengths had been used in the past, including the Alexandrine ('now only used to diversify heroick lines'), and that the anapestic measure, very quick and lively, was much used in songs. Already by the middle decades of the eighteenth century, writers on prosody found this regularization of metre to be impoverishing; in response, they insisted on the necessary liberties of occasionally substituting a trisyllabic foot and of shifting the stress.[72] The anapest would begin to be freed from its associations with light verse; Shenstone used anapests for landscapes and Cowper for somber religious themes. These trends persisted into the nineteenth century. Wordsworth's and Coleridge's ballads, under the influence of the accentual metre of popular ballads, often found room for trisyllabic feet. With 'The Destruction of Sennacherib', Byron gave a new prominence to anapestic verse, which Swinburne, especially, developed with a new assurance and intensity in a number of poems.[73]

Greek poetry, with one of the most complex prosodies of all Western languages, influenced the metres of English poets at the time when they were reading Greek most intensively. To praise Greek for its musical qualities had been commonplace since at least the eighteenth century.[74] Sometimes its metres were directly adopted. English sapphics had hitherto followed the pattern of the Latin metre, with a long fourth foot and a relatively rigid caesura. In English, such a rhythm often sounded unnatural; one of the most impressive English poems in sapphics derives its power from the unnatural tension between the metre and the word rhythms. In Cowper's 'Lines Written During a Period of Insanity', God's judgement inexorably overrides the poet's ejaculations of despair as the metre overrides the words; he is made to conform to an order from which a damned man is forever excluded. The rhythm of Swinburne's 'Sapphics', in contrast, recreates a fluid Greek movement. The diction is occasionally clichéd and merely picturesque, but in his hands English moves in a new, Greek way: ποικιλόθρον' ἀθανάτ' Ἀφρόδιτα, 'Saw the white implacable Aphrodite', 'Saw the hair unbound and the feet unsandalled'.[75] Alcaic verse, rare in English, common in Horace, was common in Greek but very little survives; none the less, Tennyson intended the alcaics of 'Milton' to reproduce a Greek movement, 'much freer and lighter' than Horace's, which Tennyson had already represented in 'The Daisy' and 'To the Rev. F. D. Maurice'. His boldest attempt at naturalizing a classical metre was the experimental adaptation of galliambics, 'Boädicea', more convincing than Meredith's attempt in 'Phaéthôn'.

No metre received greater attention in the nineteenth century than dactylic hexameter. Though Homer's verse was the dominant example, the metre in other languages were also influential: Latin of course, but also German. Klopstock's epic *Der Messias* (1749–73), Voss's Homeric translations (*Odyssey*, 1781 and *Iliad*, 1793), and Goethe's *Hermann und Dorothea* (1798) brought it into vogue. Coleridge translated a couplet by Schiller in order both to describe and to exemplify it. An English translation of Klopstock helped inspire Southey's attempt to naturalize the metre in 'A Vision of Judgement' (1821); the German achievement led him to believe that he could succeed with it in English where Sidney, Richard Stanihurst, and Abraham Fraunce had failed. The immense popular success of Longfellow's *Evangeline* (1847) forced the metre on Victorian attention generally. In literary circles, the 'hexameter controversy' dominated the middle decades of the century.[76] Southey had anticipated most of the major points of contention: as spondees are rare in English, perhaps trochees should be allowed to substitute for them; always to begin with a stressed foot in long poems strikes the English ear as unnatural, so perhaps lines should on occasion begin with an unstressed foot. In contrast to German, Greek, and Latin, English does not abound in polysyllabic words, so the feet rely too heavily on monosyllables. In practice, different solutions were found to these difficulties. Charles Kingsley in 'Andromeda' (1858), 'taking Homer as the ideal', strove for metrical rigour and resisted trochees, initial unstressed syllables, and other licences.[77] In *Amours de Voyage* (1858) Clough took the opposite course, allowing for frequent substitutions, iambic, trochaic, and anapestic. His loosening of the foot enhanced the conversational rhythm of the poem; it also emphasized the remoteness of Homer even while insisting on the abiding presence of antiquity, mediated through Rome ('Budding, unfolding, and falling, decaying and flowering ever').

Southey did not raise the question of the proper role of quantity in English hexameters, a topic much disputed in the period. Victorian theorists of prosody proclaimed from time to time the impossibility of quantitative verse in English, or even the non-existence of quantity in English. On the other hand, Kingsley believed himself to be writing quantitative verse in 'Andromeda'. Tennyson's 'Experiments in Quantity' show the most careful attention to it. I favour a middle ground in this dispute (which shows no sign of ending). Cowper's observation on translating Homer is succinct and accurate: 'without close attention to syllabic quantity in the construction of our verse, we can give it neither melody nor dignity'. Three forms of close attention suggest themselves: first, syllables obviously long ought normally to receive a stress; second, quantity may sometimes be used effectively to distinguish primary from secondary stresses; third, whole lines may be made emphatic through the use of obviously long syllables, as in Milton: 'wild uproar | Stood rul'd, stood vast infinitude confin'd'.

Closely related to the hexameter is the elegiac couplet, consisting of one line of dactylic hexameter and one line of two 'halves' of dactylic hexameter separated by a caesura. It is perhaps best known in English through Coleridge's version of Schiller:

> In the hexameter rises the fountain's silvery column;
> In the pentameter aye falling in melody back.

> x ⌣ ⌣ | x ⌣ ⌣ | x ⌣ ⌣ | x x | x ⌣ ⌣ | x x
> x ⌣ ⌣ | x ⌣ ⌣ | x ‖ x ⌣ ⌣ | x ⌣ ⌣ | x

It is the metre of Ovid's elegies, though these had almost always been translated into English heroic couplets. Rare in English, despite a few experiments in the Renaissance, it was used in a few nineteenth-century poems, such as Browning's 'Ixion' (pronounced 'Ixíon'): a poem that suffers especially from the monotonous regularity of the caesura in the second line. His 'Abt Vogler' opens with an elegiac couplet (minus the final syllable of the first line), but then the poem breaks from the strict form, lines begin with unstressed syllables, iambic and other feet are substituted; the form is recovered in the second stanza, but promptly dissolves again, not to reappear. The movement is as slippery as Abt Vogler's extemporizing and spiritualizing. In *Amours de Voyages*, at the beginning and end of each of the five parts (with the exception of the final section), Clough writes a brief, reflective section in elegiac couplets. These take fewer metrical liberties than do his hexameters, though they treat quantity freely; they are used more solemnly, and their tone is more elevated:

> *Is it illusion? or does there a spirit from perfecter ages*
>   *Here, even yet, amid loss, change, and corruption, abide?*
> *Does there a spirit we know not, though seek, though we find,*
>   *comprehend not,*
>   *Here to entice and confuse, tempt and evade us, abide?*

Clough perplexes the syntax here in order to observe the demands of the metre, but also to vary the caesura and suggest the spiritual confusions of the modern world.

Swinburne's 'Hesperia' is a version of the elegiac couplet, subject to one modification: the anacrusis. The term belongs especially to an obsolete account of classical prosody and refers to a putative unstressed syllable before the first foot which does not count in the scansion of the poem.[78] It is now a matter of controversy whether the term is even applicable to poetry in English since the Renaissance. An iambic line that begins with two unstressed syllables might be described either as anacrustic or as beginning with an anapestic substitution for the initial iamb. The metre of Blake's 'Tyger' is trochaic; how do we account for the last line of the first stanza: 'Could frame thy fearful symmetry?' We may either call 'could' an anacrustic syllable, or find that Blake switched to iambics in the last line. Nothing forces us to posit the anacrusis; in the nineteenth century, however, everyone who received a classical education scanned Greek poetry with attention to the anacrusis. It was not then a recondite term. In *New Grub Street*, Gissing makes it a key part of the discussion on Greek metres between Reardon and Biffen through which they find relief from their misery ('the two men talked Greek metres as if they lived in a world where the only hunger known could be satisfied by grand or sweet cadences', ch. 10). Whether the English hexameter should be anacrustic exercised theorists and critics. It is not surprising, then, to find that English poets of this period would sometimes employ the anacrusis in their own verse; it is particularly common in Shelley and in Browning.[79] In 'Hesperia', Swinburne deploys the anacrusis in an unconventional way. Not only is it found at the beginning of many lines, both the hexameter and the 'pentameter', but it frequently also occurs after the caesura in the latter. In my edition of Swinburne's *Poems and Ballads* (Penguin, 2000), I failed to scan the poem correctly because I did not recognize the anacrusis after the caesura. Gilbert Murray offered the correct scansion (the anacruses are italicized in these lines 29–36):[80]

Fair as a rose is on earth, as a rose under water in prison
    That stretches and swings to the slow passionate pulse of the sea,
Closed up from the air and the sun, but alive, as a ghost re-arisen,
    Pale as the love that revives *as a* ghost re-arisen in me.
From the bountiful infinite West, from the happy memorial places
    Full of the stately repose *and the* lordly delight of the dead,
Where the Fortunate Islands are lit with the light of ineffable faces,
    And the sound of a sea without wind *is a*bout them, and sunset is red.

The effect of the anacrusis is to convert dactyls into anapests and trochees into iambs. Since Swinburne rejects dactyls and spondees of the hexameter as unnatural and abhorrent (he allows that Kingsley's 'Andromeda' is the 'one good poem extant in that pernicious metre'), the anacrusis allows him to write in a more natural rhythm. Even so, 'Hesperia' is monotonous and rambling; 'too long, too vague', he described it in 1887. Some of the greatest German poems, on the other hand, were written in elegiac couplets: Hölderlin's 'Brot und Wein', Goethe's 'Euphrosyne' and *Römische Elegien*, Schiller's 'Spaziergang', and others. I do not know why it counts for so little in English poetry.[81]

The influence of Greek prosody on English poets was mediated by the understandings and misunderstandings that obtained at the time. The anacrusis offers one example of how that understanding influenced English verse. A second example is the metrical foot that used to be known as the paeon (and is now usually seen as a resolved cretic). The paeon referred to a foot of four syllables with one long syllable; if the long was on the first syllable, it was known as the first paeon; if on the second, the second paeon; etc. (I take it that the fourth paeon might sound something like the opening of Beethoven's Fifth Symphony). Should we wish to read Hopkins's sprung rhythm in terms of syllabic feet rather than accentually, we would find the first paeon in 'The Wreck of the Deutschland'; Hopkins announced in his preface on rhythm that the first paeon was the upper limit for the length of a foot within his sprung rhythm. Studies of English prosody have located occasional paeonic substitution across a range of nineteenth-century verse, though it is often the case that the usual contractions would turn them into anapests or dactyls. Poe's 'Ulalume' has several first paeons, if we do not contract the pronunciation: 'The leaves they were *withering and* sere' and 'Our *memories were treacherous and* sere'.[82] Not just paeonic feet but also paeonic verse is ambiguous and open to interpretation, since the paeons tend to be heard as units of two trochaic or two iambic feet. On the other hand, some trochaics sound like paeons; the catalectic tetrameter of Browning's 'A Toccata of Galuppi's', in which a heavy stress falls solely on every other stressed syllable, may be heard as third paeonic: 'O Galúppi, Baldassáro, this is véry sad to fínd!' The most famous poem in which paeons play a direct role is Meredith's 'Love in the Valley'. Its rhythm is complex and resists formulation. Still, the first paeon can be heard as a regular, distinct element, especially in the first version of the poem:

Under yonder beech-tree *standing on the* green-sward,
   Couch'd with her arms be*hind her little* head,   [or two trochees]
Her knees folded up, and her *tresses on her* bosom,
   Lies my young love *sleeping in the* shade.
Had I the heart to *slide one arm* beneath her!   [or two trochees]
   Press her dreaming lips as her waist I folded slow,
Waking on the instant she *could not but em*brace me—
   Ah! would she hold me, and *never let me* go?

A third obsolete concept present in nineteenth-century theories of Greek prosody proved influential: logaoedic verse. The Greek word meant 'prose-verse', and it was first applied by ancient metrists who no longer understood the metrical principles involved. Persistent efforts were made to define and describe logaoedic verse in the nineteenth century; the concept has now disappeared.[83] The *OED* defines it as the epithet of 'various metres in which dactyls are combined with trochees' and gives 1844 as the date of the first citation. The second quotation refers to 'anapaestic logaoedics', which is only apparently in contradiction to the dictionary's definition since they can often be converted to logaoedic dactylics (via the anacrusis). The

OED article is at best misleading; none of the quotations illustrates the meaning of the term. Those interested in the matter would be better served by consulting, for example, Hermann's *Elementa Doctrinae Metricae* (1817). The abridged English translation of 1830 not only explains fully the logaoedic metre as it was then understood (in the chapters entitled 'Of Logaœdic Dactylics' and 'Of Logaœdic Anapæstics') but also antedates the *OED*'s first citation.

We do not need to linger in the graveyard of obsolete theories of prosody, and in any case I lack the technical knowledge to serve as a guide. The inspiration which Shelley, Browning, and Swinburne derived from their understanding of Greek prosody is a more promising and more productive topic. Logaoedic verse combined dactyls and trochees. Shelley introduced a new movement into English verse by combining anapests and iambs. In 'The Cloud' and 'The Sensitive-Plant', neither iambs nor anapests form the basis of the verse-line, into which occasional substitutions are permitted; rather, they both occur with approximately equal frequency and in any position in the line. 'The Sensitive-Plant' is written almost entirely in quatrains of tetrameter lines made up of iambs and anapests. The combination produces a rhythm that ranges from light verse (traditionally associated with anapests) to folk ballad and to tragedy ('the metres induce a dream, not a pre-Raphaelite swoon'[84]):

> Then the rain came down, and the broken stalks
> Were bent and tangled across the walks;
> And the leafless network of parasite bowers
> Massed into ruin; and all sweet flowers.

In the irregular stanza of 'The Hymn of Pan', Shelley triumphantly demonstrates the metrical variety of iambic-anapestic verse. In Browning's 'Abt Vogler', the metre becomes difficult to scan after the opening lines modelled on the elegiac couplet; still, it remains possible to perceive six feet in the subsequent lines combining iambs and trochees on the one hand with anapests and dactyls on the other, though with the anacrusis and the continual shifts of foot, the precise scansion is open to doubt. Hopkins offers a translation of sprung rhythm into logaoedic terms, but it is more natural to read it accentually (as with rhythmic prose, nursery rhymes, weather saws); the translation is laboured and gratuitous. Swinburne, in 'Hymn to Proserpine' and 'Dolores' and in some of the choruses in *Atalanta in Calydon*, wrote the most famous and most successful English poems in logaoedic verse. His 'new words, in classic guise'[85] create new metrical possibilities inspired by Greek lyric:

> And they laughed, changing hands in the measure,
>   And they mixed and made peace after strife;
> Pain melted in tears, and was pleasure;
>   Death tingled with blood, and was life.

> ('Dolores', 177–80)

> When the hounds of spring are on winter's traces,
>   The mother of months in meadow or plain
> Fills the shadows and windy places
>   With lisp of leaves and ripple of rain...

> (*Atalanta in Calydon*, 65–8)

Some complex Greek metres have been echoed in these combinations of anapests and iambs. Swinburne's 'Fleeter of foot than the fleet-foot kid' (*Atalanta*, p. 106) has a metrical analogue to a line in Aeschylus' *Seven Against Thebes*, and in Shelley's 'Hymn of Pan' several lines possess recognizable metrical units from Greek poetry.[86] Because the subject and literary form of both works are derived from Greece, readers may, understandably, hear in them metrical echoes of Greek poetry. But English poems in logaoedic verse do not usually imitate specific Greek metres; they are examples of metrical invention by poets who trained their ear on Greek poetry. Ear-training, in Latin and often in Greek, was an exercise which all classically inducted Englishmen received. W. H. Auden once remarked that the minor poets of the nineteenth century frequently had a prosodic mastery superior to poets of the twentieth century, while their command of diction was often inferior. He attributed both facts to the long school and university hours so many nineteenth-century poets spent writing classical verse (they would be beaten for a false quantity, not for failing to find the *mot juste*).[87] It was as a spur to prosodic subtlety and invention that Greek exercised its most salutary influence on English poetry.

CHAPTER FIVE

Apollo, Dionysus, and Nineteenth-Century English and German Poetry

IN *The Birth of Tragedy* (1872), Friedrich Nietzsche made a contrast that has since become famous. The greatness of Greek tragedy—he means the tragedies of Aeschylus and Sophocles—is rooted not only in the Apollonian impulse towards light, clarity, and distinct and articulated form but equally in the Dionysian drive to ecstasy, drunkenness, and all forms of enthusiasm (etymologically, the fact of being ἔνθεος, possessed by a god). Nietzsche would continue to think throughout his career about art and its relation to life, and he would change his mind repeatedly about the relative values of the two impulses and their relation to each other. Yet a basic distinction between them is central to his aesthetics, as it had been for Schopenhauer (in the form of the *principium individuationis* and the Will) and as it would be for Heidegger (in the form of being as revelation and of Being which both reveals and conceals).[1]

By placing the poles of his aesthetics under the twin aspect of Apollo and Dionysus, Nietzsche inherited and transformed a legacy of German literate culture which had been obsessed for more than a century with Greece and specifically with two competing versions of ancient Greece. The first was most influentially expressed in the writings of Johann Joachim Winckelmann. In a polemical essay of 1755, 'Gedanken über die Nachahmung der Griechischen Werke in der Malerei und Bildhauerkunst' ('Reflections on the Imitation of Greek Works in Painting and Sculpture'), he insisted on the superiority of Greece to Rome, maintaining that an ideal of aesthetic lucidity and clarity was uniquely embodied in Greek art, which ought therefore to be exclusively followed by contemporary artists. To express this ideal he coined the phrase 'eine edle Einfalt und eine stille

Grösse' ('a noble simplicity and a quiet greatness'). That phrase in particular became an effective neo-classical slogan. He compared the experience of beauty conveyed by Greek art with such experiences as contemplating a calm sea and tasting pure water,[2] and this was the ideal adopted by many artists throughout Europe in the second half of the eighteenth century. Lessing and Herder would subsequently adopt Winckelmann's Greek priority and to some extent his interpretation of the Greek ideal; Lessing even agreed with Winckelmann that the frenzied piece of hellenistic sculpture known as the Laocoon was expressive of serenity and restraint.

This ideal Greece, with its emphasis on clarity and harmony, was central not only to aesthetic considerations, but also to moral, political, and philosophical debate. An eighteenth-century experiment in moral philosophy, now largely forgotten, attempted to vindicate moral beauty, to valorize beautiful souls. It drew largely on Shaftesbury but also on an ideal which kept its Greek name, *kalokagathia*, 'beauty-and-goodness', taken to be the harmonious blending of goodness and beauty. Wieland's *Geschichte des Agathon* told the story of a beautiful soul, and elsewhere Wieland, Lessing, and Herder debated the concept of *kalokagathia*.[3] Greek harmony, especially harmony with nature, was a constant theme of Schiller's theoretical writing ('Über naive und sentimentalische Dichtung', the sixth letter of the *Über die ästhetische Erziehung des Menschen*), and the longing for a harmony now lost to the world found one of its most powerful expressions in his elegy 'Die Götter Griechenlands'. Wilhelm von Humboldt and Friedrich Schlegel took Greece to be an exemplary model not only for the harmonious development of the individual but also for German culture as a whole; this Greece became a nationalist paradigm for a desiderated Germany. Goethe ranged over most of these concerns, entertaining at different periods of his career diverse attitudes towards Greece, but Winckelmann, however complex and oblique Goethe's relation to him, had largely set the terms in which Greece was to be understood, and the *Iphigenie auf Tauris*, written in Goethe's most classicizing phase, was (and is) the most prominent literary work inspired by the idea of Greece that derived from Winckelmann.[4]

A counterimage was pitched against Winckelmann's ideal and the classicism of the Enlightenment by Johann Georg Hamann.[5] In the *Sokratische Merkwürdigkeiten* (1759), he presented a Socrates who was at the furthest remove from the Enlightenment hero of rationalism. The tract had new implications for aesthetics (Socrates' *daemon* was equated with the newly important sense of genius), but also for morality and politics, since his polemic was an attempt to expose what he considered to be the fraudulent Enlightenment claims of objectivity and universality. A more direct precursor of Nietzsche's Dionysian Greece was envisioned by Friedrich Hölderlin, though he called it 'Apollonian', and opposed it to the 'Junonian' qualities of sobriety and restraint. The self-control, harmony, measure, and coolness of the Greeks was a self-defensive reaction against their natural propensity towards passionate, self-destroying inebriation. The task of the constitutionally sober West was the reverse of the Greek one: they had to recover Apollonian passion. After Hölderlin, it was probably in Heinrich von Kleist's tragedy *Penthesilea* (1808) that this violent, tragically self-destructive Greece was most explicitly depicted; it has even been suggested that Kleist deliberately sought to revoke Goethe's *Iphigenie*, like Leverkühn in Thomas Mann's *Doktor Faustus* who intended to revoke Beethoven's Ninth Symphony.[6]

The two German versions of Greece, however, are not always exclusively conceptual; they are sometimes also linguistic; in some works, that is, Greece is invoked (or revoked) through German influenced by Greek. Since the seventeenth century, the inner affinity between Greek and German had often been asserted, and from the eighteenth century on the Greek language was regularly held up for imitation.[7] It is useful to distinguish the two kinds of Greek influence in German literature that were established by the end of the eighteenth century. The first places a premium on clarity, calmness, and simplicity; the style to imitate is the smooth Homeric–Sophoclean one; the vision of Greece invoked by the style derives from Winckelmann; and Goethe's *Iphigenie* is the most striking literary example. The second kind is paratactical, abrupt; it elides transitions and prefers a logic of images to a controlling syntax; the models here are Aeschylus and Pindar. This Greece is imagined above all in the hymns of Hölderlin.[8]

The two stylistic ideals can be related to traditional rhetorical categories. Cicero writes in the *Orator*:[9]

The orators of the grandiloquent style, if I may use an old word, showed splendid power of thought and majesty of diction; they were forceful, versatile, copious and grave, trained and equipped to arouse and sway the emotions; some attained their effects by a rough, severe, harsh style, without regular construction or rounded periods; others used a smooth, ordered sentence-structure with a periodic cadence.

Applied retrospectively to Greek literature, this contrast can be seen in the styles of Aeschylus and Sophocles. Already in Aristophanes' *Frogs* we have the view of Aeschylus as 'unbridled, out of control, and unchecked' (838), a poet whose expressions are 'bolted together' (ῥήματα γομφοπαγῆ, 825), in contrast to Sophocles, the implicit standard. Quintilian passes the influential judgement on Aeschylus: 'he is lofty, dignified, grandiloquent often to a fault, but frequently uncouth and inharmonious'.[10] Pindar's style is often described in similar terms; he is abrupt, grandiloquent, and lacks logical constructions. Horace draws on this view in the *Odes* 4. 2, where Pindar is likened to a swollen river rushing forth without restraint. The contrast is usually made with Sophocles, and sometimes with Homer, both frequently presented as transparent and harmonious.[11]

This distinction between smooth and rough styles can be used for many purposes, and has been so employed at different times. In troubadour lyric the division between poetry in the complex style and in the simple, popular style (*trobar clus* and *trobar leu*) can distinguish smooth poems of delight in nature and amorous melancholy from rough poems of violent passion or hermetic thought.[12] Christian poets have used this stylistic opposition to differentiate, for example, living in humble submission to God's will from living in the anxious or tormented awareness of sin. John Donne writes in both styles, in the smooth way of 'La Corona' and in the harsh way of the Holy Sonnets. Nor is the contrast between rough and smooth styles limited to verbal artworks; recent scholarship traces the emergence of the rough style in Titian and Rembrandt, in particular, not to an idiosyncratic personal development but to contemporary ideas about the 'smooth and rough manners'.

Part of the difficulty for English readers in coming to grips with the contrast between smooth and rough literary styles is the dominating example of Shakespeare: he actively inhibits readers from imagining how a grand style, the *genus sublime dicendi*, may also be a plain style. Macbeth (1. 7) fears that Duncan's virtues

> Will pleade like Angels, Trumpet-tongu'd against
> The deepe damnation of his taking off:
> And Pitty, like a naked New-borne-Babe,
> Striding the blast, or Heauens Cherubin, hors'd

> Vpon the sightlesse Curriors of the Ayre,
> Shall blow the horrid deed in euery eye,
> That teares shall drowne the winde. I haue no Spurre
> To pricke the sides of my intent, but onely
> Vaulting Ambition, which ore-leapes it selfe,
> And falles on th' other.

Shakespeare's language is so characteristically dense with semantic overtones and undertones, so packed with metaphors pressed for all they are worth, that an aesthetic sense formed by reading him may not be able to respond to the plainness, for example, of Sophocles' language.[13] Of course there are overpowering moments of plain language in Shakespeare ('I cannot but remember such things were | That were most precious to me'), but they are intermittent. Perhaps it is only Milton's *Samson Agonistes* that gives an English reader a sense of plain language working at a high pitch of intensity (ll. 590–8):

> All otherwise to me my thoughts portend,
> That these dark orbs no more shall treat with light,
> Nor th' other light of life continue long,
> But yield to double darkness nigh at hand:
> So much I feel my genial spirits droop,
> My hopes all flat, nature within me seems
> In all her functions weary of her self;
> My race of glory run, and race of shame,
> And I shall shortly be with them that rest.

Milton read Greek with passionate attention, and in this respect his style serves as an appropriate prelude to the styles of two intense German readers of Greek, Hölderlin and Goethe. Goethe's *Iphigenie* does not lose touch with Sophocles; Hölderlin's hymns follow Pindar's example. Let us begin by comparing two short lyrics—among the most famous short lyrics in German—in order to illustrate the contrast.

Goethe's 'Wandrers Nachtlied' ('Wayfarer's Night Song', 1780):

> Über allen Gipfeln
> Ist Ruh,
> In allen Wipfeln
> Spürest du
> Kaum einen Hauch;
> Die Vögelein schweigen im Walde.
> Warte nur, balde
> Ruhest du auch.

Over all the peaks it is silent, in all the tree-tops you scarcely notice a breath. The little birds are quiet in the woods. Just wait, soon you too will be silent.

Stillness is the poem's subject and means of expression. The syntactical action is minimal: the poem begins and ends with quiet; a breath of wind is scarcely to be noticed in the tree-tops; and the little birds are silent. The style is one of direct and simple utterance, unhurried progression, and freedom from strain. At the end of the poem death does not rip apart the fabric of stillness, does not irrupt into the quiet scene but is another manifestation of stillness. Nothing jarring or unharmonious is admitted, yet death is not excluded: the aesthetic is that of Winckelmann's Greece. Goethe read widely in Greek lyric, and he would have known Alcman's fragment on nature asleep (εὕδουσι δ᾽ ὀρέων κορυφαί, 'the mountain tops are asleep', εὕδουσι δ᾽ οἰωνῶν φῦλα τανυπτερύγων, 'the tribes of the long-winged birds are asleep') which is echoed here.[14]

Hölderlin's 'Hälfte des Lebens' (1802–3):

> Mit gelben Birnen hänget
> Und voll mit wilden Rosen
> Das Land in den See,
> Ihr holden Schwäne,
> Und trunken von Küssen
> Tunkt ihr das Haupt
> Ins heilignüchterne Wasser.
>
> Weh mir, wo nehm' ich, wenn
> Es Winter ist, die Blumen, und wo
> Den Sonnenschein,
> Und Schatten der Erde?
> Die Mauern stehn
> Sprachlos und kalt, im Winde
> Klirren die Fahnen.

With yellow pears hangs, and filled with wild roses, the land into the lake, you gracious swans, and drunk with kisses you dunk your heads into the holysober water.

Alas, where am I to find, when it is winter, flowers, and where the sunshine, and shadows of the earth? The walls stand speechless and cold, in the wind the weathervanes clatter.

The compound adjective 'heilignüchtern', 'holysober', relates the poem to Hölderlin's meditations on Greece. 'Holy', as in the holy pathos of Apollo, is glossed by a twentieth-century translator and poet as 'the ecstatic otherness of divine elemental being';[15] it is compacted with the Junonian sobriety of the Hesperian poet in the dense epithet. The logic of the poem, in a sense, is as simple as that of Goethe's: winter follows summer, just as in Goethe's lyric night follows day. The syntax of the two poems, however, is vastly different. Instead of using syntax to order his utterance harmoniously and with great transparency, Hölderlin interrupts and contorts the syntax. By twisting the word order, unexpectedly addressing the swans, and by doing away with grammatical transitions, Hölderlin mimes the struggle against the simple, fatal logic of his poem. 'Holy' and 'sober', epithets of the two versions of Greece, are joined in the poem's syntax and meaning.

It is sobriety that governs Goethe's *Iphigenie* (the prose version dates from 1779, the verse drama from 1786–7). He calls it a 'Schauspiel' rather than a tragedy, and he follows the French convention of act and scene divisions. None the less, the play adopts many Greek conventions: stichomythia, occasional sententiousness, lyrics approximating the use of choral odes, a recognition scene, and other devices. His vocabulary sometimes translates Greek words and phrases.[16] The frequent compound epithets contribute to the Greek feeling of the play; it was Voss's translation of Homer that inspired the introduction of so many of them.[17] Other Greek expressions are reproduced: the many instances of *Haupt* (κάρα) to refer to a person, or the occasional examples of *liebes Herz* (φίλον ἦτορ, φίλη κραδίη) to refer to oneself. At a critical moment, when Iphigenia (rather than lie to Thoas, king of the Taurians) risks the safety of herself, her brother and his friend, and their companions, she tells him: 'Allein Euch leg' ich's auf die Kniee!', a direct imitation of the Homeric phrase θεῶν ἐν γούνασι κεῖται. Goethe dressed his actors in Greek costume for his production of the play.[18] The general treatment of the story derives from Euripides, the account of the curse of the House of Atreus from Aeschylus' *Agamemnon*, and the dramatic situation of Iphigenia from Sophocles' *Antigone*.[19]

These are repeated signals that Goethe is imitating a Greek tragedy. However, in order to understand his purpose, we must see how he relates an imitation of Greek to an invocation of Greece. A single ideal of style, Winckelmann's, governs both language and ideology in the play. Calmness and quiet are essential qualities in both Winckelmann and in *Iphigenie auf Tauris*. The words 'still', 'gelassen', and 'ruhig' occur throughout the play. The syntax is mostly straightforward, the word order unconvoluted, and the diction free from neologisms. Schiller speaks of the great 'Ruhe' of the play,[20] and G. H. Lewes in his *Life of Goethe* refers to the 'simplicity of its action', the 'calmness in the dialogue', and the 'limpid clearness of its language'.[21]

Goethe's style in the work emphasizes clarity and simplicity. It is the language of 'Rat, Mäßigung und Weisheit und Geduld' (l. 332). The style is a correlative to the theme. Gods speak to us through our hearts, when our hearts are clear:

> THOAS: Es spricht kein Gott; es spricht dein eignes Herz.
> IPHIGENIE: Sie reden nur durch unser Herz zu uns.
>
> (493–4)

THOAS: No god is speaking; it is your own heart speaking.
IPHIGENIE: They speak to us only through our hearts

> THOAS: Du glaubst, es höre
> Der rohe Skythe, der Barbar, die Stimme
> Der Wahrheit und der Menschlichkeit, die Atreus,
> Der Grieche, nicht vernahm?
>
> IPHIGENIE: Es hört sie jeder,
> Geboren unter jedem Himmel, dem
> Des Lebens Quelle durch den Busen rein
> Und ungehindert fließt.
>
> (1936–42)

THOAS: Do you think that the brute Scythian, the barbarian, will hear the voice of truth and humanity while Atreus, the Greek, did not?
IPHIGENIE: Everyone born under this sky hears it through whose breast the well of life flows free and unhindered.

Iphigenia in the second exchange offers the critical qualification. Everyone can hear the voice of truth and humanity; everyone, that is, through whose breast the fountain of life flows pure and unhindered. Only the 'pure and unhindered' heart hears the gods truly. Passion deafens us to the voice of the gods and makes us confound our desires with theirs. Cruel gods, Iphigenia says, are only the illusory projection of cruel men (ll. 523–5); the gods are not cruel, they love mortals and aid them (ll. 554–5).[22] The passion of Thoas and the madness of Orestes keep them from hearing the truth that their hearts would tell them: the gods are good, a moral order exists, and is humane. An ordered and harmonious existence, clarity, purity, gentleness, and tranquillity are offered as universal values of civilized humanity, from whose ranks the barbarian Thoas and the madman Orestes are excluded until, under the influence of Iphigenia's 'schöne Seele' ('beautiful soul', l. 1493), they behave properly.

There is little in my summary to distinguish the style and substance of the play from the pseudo-classicism of a 'plaster-of-Paris statuary to which Goethe's taste was by no means immune'.[23] The power of his drama derives not only from its lyrical expression of a certain hellenic ideal of civilization, but from the fact that he subjects that ideal to sustained criticism. For example, at the end of Act 4, Iphigenia sings the *Parzenlied* (the song of the Parcae, the goddesses of Fate); in it the gods are depicted as powers who rule as it pleases them, mostly unconcerned with human affairs, and whose unending festival is not interrupted by mortal demands for justice. Just before she sings, she prays that the Olympians will save their image in her soul ('Und rettet euer Bild in meiner Seele', l. 1717), yet the song itself demonstrates that they are unconcerned with their image in her soul. We misread the play if we think that Goethe is simply endorsing Iphigenia's beliefs.

Consider barbarian and madman, classic test-cases for the claims of civilization. In the play, the civilized values of Iphigenia educate and humanize the barbarian king, who abandons the old laws of vengeance and blood sacrifice. Her method is her 'gentle persuasion' (l. 125). The conflict, however, is not only between civilization and barbarism; it is also between civilization and exploitation that masks itself as civilization. It is the mark of the civilized man to be calm, but Pylades too is described as calm, repeatedly, and on different occasions he calms both Iphigenia and Orestes. Yet this calmness is the shallow calm of self-confident cunning and exploitation. Despite his calm heart Pylades like Thoas confuses his heart's demands with the will of the gods.[24] Like Thoas, Pylades appeals to necessity to justify his course of action.[25] But unlike the barbarian ruler, for whom his word is his bond and who uses language sparingly and in earnest, Orestes' friend is willing to use any means, say anything, to get what he wants.[26] Moreover, Thoas sacrifices more of himself than the Greeks do, and at the end his actions show him to be more humane than the representatives of civilization. Goethe goes to great lengths to distinguish between the coercive deceit of Pylades and the gentle persuasion of Iphigenia (who none the less depends on Pylades and praises him, though she will not in the end lie for him, despite being tempted[27]); he confronts the emanation of civilization with its specter.

At the heart of Orestes' nightmare (Act 3, scene 2) is a vision of universal reconciliation. In the afterworld, Thyestes and Atreus walk as friends, and the children play around them; Agamemnon and Clytemnestra hold hands; and Orestes imagines his mother welcoming him. Orestes is alone in this scene, so no one hears him, yet his words bear critically on the moral choices of the drama. Iphigenia is successful; Thoas yields to gentle persuasion. What if he had not yielded? What is the status of civilized values when confronted with obdurately inhumane values? The play gives no direct answer to this question, but nor does it simply avoid it. Orestes' vision of the murdered reconciled with the murderer, the cannibalized with the cannibal, shows unblinkingly how atrocity must be absorbed and forgiven before allegedly humane values can be truly humane. The Greeks dismiss the vision as madness, and it may be madness; but if it is, their pretensions to universal humanity are deluded or fraudulent.

Criticism of *Iphigenie* depends crucially on the relation of the dominant movement of the play to its moments of self-critique. For Erich Heller, there is no relation: 'The reality of evil asserts itself poetically on only three occasions, which are scattered about the play like three erratic blocks in the gentle groves of human kindness.'[28] For Theodor Adorno, the play has a fraudulent resolution that disguises the fact that the king is being exploited; however, laying stress on the monologue of Orestes' madness, Adorno argues that its utopian vision of total reconciliation transcends the doctrine of humanity and exposes its limitations.[29] Probably a critical consensus will not emerge about the relation of the action to the play's self-scrutiny. As in book vi of *Wilhelm Meisters Lehrjahre*, which gives the most fully realized literary description of a 'beautiful soul' but also searchingly and implicitly criticizes it by confronting it with the different moral choices of the uncle,[30] readers are confronted with diverse positions unresolved in the 'moral beauty' of a single character.

The Greek influence on Goethe's style has been thoroughly absorbed in his German. Since lucidity and calmness are the criteria, the Greek has not been allowed to dislocate the German to register the shock of the foreign. Hölderlin's later poetry takes the opposite approach. A key document is the letter of 1801 to Casimire Ulrich Bohlendorff:[31]

Nothing is harder for us to learn than the free use of what is native to us. And I think that clarity of representation is to us originally as natural as the fire from heaven was to the Greeks. Precisely for this reason, they can be surpassed in comely passion, which you sustain, rather than in that Homeric presence of mind and gift for representing things.

It sounds paradoxical. But I say it again and offer it for your reflection and use: a peculiarly native quality becomes less salient as the cultivation of the mind proceeds. Therefore the Greeks are in less degree masters of holy pathos, because it was innate in them, whereas they excel, from Homer onward, because this extraordinary man had the profundity and greatness of soul to acquire for his Apollonian realm the occidental Junonian restraint, and thus truly to make the alien his own.

With us the opposite is the case.

The task of the modern poet (for whom sobriety is innate) is to aspire to holy pathos, to Apollonian fire, rather than to Homeric clarity. This is also the task of the translator; Hölderlin's translation of Sophocles is meant to recover the divine fire underneath the Junonian restraint,[32] to encounter 'primitive renewing fury'.[33]

Before his attempt to recreate this holy pathos behind the Homeric presence of mind and Sophoclean 'excess of form' (a form and style so perfect that it conceals the divine fire), Hölderlin turned to Pindar. He translated more than 2,000 lines in the spring and summer of 1800.[34] The translations are famously unreadable, despite passages of perfect lucidity (such as the end of *Pythian* 8). At times mechanically, he was attempting to assert the affinity between Greek and German, and sacrificed everything to that end—German diction, word order, and syntax had to submit to the Greek original.[35] It was an experiment from which he learnt not only the similarities but also the limits of the affinity between the languages;[36] they also prepared the ground for the great translations of Sophocles after 1801. These latter translations made explicit the 'Oriental' passion beneath the 'Hesperian' sober surface by their dislocation of ordinary German into a wild language full of strange new words, exorbitant hyperbaton, and (during the last revisions of 1803–4) etymological and interpretive leaps. The strangeness of the language was both a recovery and recreation of the passion hidden to later readers by the perfection of Sophoclean form and an insistence on its essentially foreign character. His Sophocles did not assimilate the original into German but preserved its foreign character.[37] He wrote to Bohlendorff that poets succeed in what is foreign to them, not native. First though, the foreign must be recognized as foreign, as something other. Hölderlin's greatest poetry came from this recognition, that this something—the divine fire—was missing, that it could not be assimilated easily and perhaps could not be recovered at all.

This distancing of the foreign can be seen in small details as well as in the overall scheme of his poems.[38] Whereas Goethe's compound epithets are rarely coined—he takes them from the familiar German Greece of Voss and Wieland in order to situate the action in a familiar landscape—Hölderlin's compound epithets are frequently new and daring;[39] they insist on the strangeness of Greece. When he applies the Greek epithets to German places, he indicates both the distance between them and the hope of closing the distance, in an intimation of the possible rebirth of Greece in Germany.[40]

These experiments in translation trained Hölderlin in making logical leaps and sudden shifts; the literal rendering of Greek forced him to write this way. They heighten the level of diction by their remove from prosaic expression; more importantly, 'the discreet suppression of the logical and syntactical links between one image or idea and another' create logical gaps that are 'the stylistic counterpart of the mysteries to which the hymns allude'.[41] The disruptions of ordinary German syntax and word order are both the dislocations of passionate utterance and the expression of the foreignness. Take the lyric beginning 'Reif sind, in Feuer getaucht . . .'

> Reif sind, in Feuer getaucht, gekochet
> Die Frücht und auf der Erde geprüfet und ein Gesetz ist
> Dass alles hineingeht, Schlangen gleich,
> Prophetisch, träumend auf
> Den Hügeln des Himmels. Und vieles
> Wie auf den Schultern eine
> Last von Scheitern ist
> Zu behalten. Aber bös sind
> Die Pfade. Nämlich unrecht,
> Wie Rosse, gehn die gefangenen
> Element' und alten
> Gesetze der Erd. Und immer
> Ins Ungebundene gehet eine Sehnsucht. Vieles aber ist
> Zu behalten. Und Not die Treue.
> Vorwärts aber und rückwärts wollen wir
> Nicht sehn. Uns wiegen lassen, wie
> Auf schwankem Kahne der See.

Ripe are, dipped in fire, cooked the fruits and tested on the earth, and it is a law that everything goes in, like snakes, prophetically, dreaming on the hills of heaven. And much, like a burden of logs on the shoulders, is to be retained. But evil are the paths. For like steeds they go wrong, the elements and the old laws of the earth. And always into that which is not bound goes a yearning. But much is to be retained. And the need is faithfulness. But backwards and forwards we will not look. Let us be cradled, as on the rocking boat of the sea.

Fire and earth, the two poles between which mortal lives are lived, are sharply counterpointed in the lyric and at the end apparently resolved in an image of a small boat and the sea. Fire, which for Hölderlin is how divinity makes itself known, brings fruit to ripeness, but the men who seek it are in danger of going astray, going beyond bounds. It is essential to resist such temptation, to maintain loyalty to the earth, to the conditions on which life is given to humans, including the law that everything returns into the earth. Easier said than done, however, because the earthly elements and the laws themselves seem to go astray, and our own desire goes too far. No matter: there is still much on earth to keep faith with, so long as we look neither backwards (into a golden age of Greece) nor forwards (into a possible rebirth). In the last image, such fidelity to earthly life as the proper medium through which divinity is encountered is represented by the image of the *Kahne* (a rowboat or skiff) rocked by the ocean. The image is charged with an ambiguous emotional force. Ostensibly, it indicates a peaceful resolution to the conflicting impulses of the poem, but it also suggests drift and even foundering, not least because the lyric itself has rocked back and forth so violently between two poles, alternating 'And . . .', 'But . . .', 'And . . .', 'But . . .', 'And . . .', 'But . . .'

The language of the passage moves under great strain. The dislocations of word order and the paratactical forcing together of diverse elements is both the correlative of the mystery and uncertainty of the struggle between earth and heaven's fire and the means to simulate a voice trying to make sense out of the experience. Lessing praised Greek for its ability to follow the natural order of thought,[42] and here the intense dislocation of the language (as in the translations from Greek) represents the speaker's natural expression of unnatural strain; he attempts to describe as best he can the experience as it happens. Note too that the employment of 'nämlich', 'aber', and 'und' in the passage, in imitation of Greek particles,[43] is a means to move from private logic to public explanation; they give the sense of struggling to be as clear as possible in the midst of the mystery. They are another example of the way he seeks to create a sense of community for his vision.[44]

Some editors and critics have seen this lyric as constituting the first stanza of the third version of the late hymn 'Mnemosyne', though others have disagreed; the question is not likely to be settled on editorial grounds alone.[45] Whether it is an independent lyric or a first stanza, however, the passage resembles the other stanzas of 'Mnemosyne' in its emotional logic. If it does constitute the first stanza, the second then follows with 'Wie aber liebes?' ('But how dear one?'), how is it possible not to look towards past and future but to keep faith with the earth only? The answer comes immediately after: 'Sonnenschein | Am Boden sehen wir und trockenen Staub | Und heimatlich die Schatten der Wälder' ('Sunshine | on the ground we see and dry dust | and the shadows of the woods'). The answer itself then comes to seem inadequate, as some aspects of earthly life—the snow shining brightly on the green meadow of the Alps—point to what is noble-minded, to the place where a wanderer (a name for the poet in Hölderlin's language) speaks of what is not present, as a grave speaks of what is not present, a wanderer who is 'Fern ahnend mit | Dem andern' ('Distantly foreboding with | The other one'). Hölderlin then turns sharply again, adding the blunt question 'aber was ist dies?' ('but what is this?') which brings the stanza to an end. In that question contrary impulses are again balanced, the scepticism of 'what is this that we should be so mindful of it?' as well as the perplexed admiration of 'what thing is this?' (Mark 1: 27, 'was ist dies?').

The last stanza invokes Greece, but differently from Hölderlin's usual depiction of Greece as earth transfigured by heaven's fire. The first sentence begins, 'Am Feigenbaum ist mein | Achilles mir gestorben' ('At the figtree my Achilles died to me'). The deaths of two other Greek heroes follow: Ajax, who went mad with anger after not being awarded the arms of Achilles and then committed suicide, and Patroclus, who wore Achilles' armour into battle and died there. Ajax died of the roar at his temples, 'An Schläfen Sausen ist . . . gestorben', in a frenzy, having gone beyond all bounds; Patroclus died obedient to the needs of the Greeks, opposing even Achilles' own unbounded rage. 'Und es starben | Noch andere viel', and there died many others too. In the contrast between Ajax and Patroclus, what had been experienced as two antithetical poles of being, heavenly fire and earthly sobriety, are now described as equivalent, likewise fatal. This scrutiny of Apollonian fire, of his own poetic impulse, is heightened at the end of the poem, where Mnemosyne, memory herself, has died. In 'Brot und Wein', Hölderlin had answered the question 'What are poets for?' by insisting that poets are bearers of a sacred mission: they keep faith with lost divinity by mourning it, and so preserve it in the only way possible, by experiencing as intensely as possible its absence. But at the end of 'Mnemosyne' even mourning is out of place. The gods become angry if a man does not pull himself together and spare his soul. It is true that some do not pull themselves together, do not reconcile themselves, as it is true that this excess may be unavoidable, but this does not form the tragic burden of a spiritual elite; it is not even a cause for mourning, nor does it justify the remembrance implicit in mourning.

> Himmlische nämlich sind
> Unwillig, wenn einer nicht die Seele schonend sich
> Zusammengenommen, aber er muss doch; dem
> Gleich fehlet die Trauer.

In the lyric (or lyrics), Hölderlin returns to the Greece which he intuited and to which he bore witness in a German acting under the pressure of Greek. Like Goethe in *Iphigenie*, though with a commitment to 'Dionysian' rather than 'Apollonian' Greece, he offers a poem that is its own most searching critique.

There was no one like Hamann or Hölderlin in England, and nothing like the reaction against Winckelmann's Greece, until the second half of the nineteenth century. Pater in the 1870s, drawing on contemporary anthropology and possibly on Nietzsche at some remove, may have been the first in England to write explicitly about the darker side of Greek religion.[46] Matthew Arnold's 'sweetness and light'[47] always dominated the English response to Greece, characteristic not only of Victorian hellenism but of the Grecian taste at the beginning of the century when Winckelmann's version of Greek antiquity was diffused in England by artists like Flaxman and Fuseli, by historians like John Gillies, by translations of August Schlegel's lectures on drama, and also in translations of Goethe and others. It easily mingled with a British neo-classicism evolving in response to the findings of archaeologists (published, for example, in *The*

Antiquities of Athens and *Ionian Antiquities*), to a new evaluation of Homer (Robert Wood), to Greek vase painting (Sir William Hamilton's celebrated collection), and to the Greek revival in architecture. It was the 'Apollonian' Greece that dominated the English imagination in the nineteenth century.[48]

Even so, this is not the whole story of British hellenism. In Germany, it is not just that writers theorized about two Greeces; it is also the case that two literary styles influenced by Greek were developed; moreover, in Goethe and Hölderlin, style under the influence of Greek was made to relate to and reflect on the vision of Greece. In England, even though an alternative to Apollonian Greece was not formulated conceptually, both styles, a smooth high style under the influence of Homer and Sophocles and a rough high style modelled especially on Aeschylus, were influential in poetry. The dominant 'Apollonian' style in painting, sculpture, poetry, and English culture has been closely studied; I propose to focus on the alternative style, one that emphasizes parataxis, agglutination, and abruption rather than lucidity, translucence, and clarity. Three authors in particular will claim our attention: Shelley, Swinburne, and Hopkins, all of whom read Aeschylus in Greek with great excitement and intensity. In Shelley's *Prometheus Unbound*, an Aeschylean style that heaped together multiple images helped to create a sense of the fractured multiplicity of being; in *Atalanta in Calydon*, Swinburne discovered that the disintegrated self, divided against itself in a world of division, could be dramatized through a paratactical style influenced by Aeschylus; and Hopkins, who thought Aeschylus unique among pagans for his earnestness, learnt in part from him how to create a style expressive of a self under pressure that is entirely in earnest.

Since Aeschylus was the Greek writer to whom these poets were most attracted, let us consider an example of his poetry. In the choruses of the *Agamemnon*, he is famous for making a logic of images dominate syntactical logic. In the second stasimon, after describing the carnage Helen caused, the chorus tells a story: a man reared a lion cub in his house; the cub was fawning at first but later slaughtered the inhabitants of the house. The story is told with imagery that mixes gentleness and violence, but the associations cannot be pressed into logical exactitude. Helen cannot be conveyed in that way. The parallel between the lion and Helen is only approximate; in other ways, it resembles Clytemnestra. It makes an unbidden feast 'with sheep-killing destruction'; then the sheep disappear and men are killed. An image appears and then is dropped or merged into another. Aeschylus 'does not trust the logic of syntax to convey the logic of his meaning', Martin West writes.[49] The Chorus, 'as so often in Aeschylus, lets free a shifting cloud-pattern of suggestions and ampler truth' (John Jones).[50] This story is relatively straightforward, by Aeschylean standards; sometimes the choruses adopt the deliberately elusive language of prophecy, in which connections are made or suggested between events that remain obstinately unconnected by syntax, or even logic.[51] Such confusion, however, is part of the immediate dramatic purpose. In such passages 'what matters most of all is the nature of the aggregate music, the total mood of the sequence, with its violent juxtapositions of gentleness and viciousness, of grace and horror'.[52]

It may seem odd to claim the rough, Aeschylean style as an influence on Shelley. The two choruses about ancient Greece in *Hellas* (1822), for example, are far removed from any dark or disturbed hellenism; instead, Greece is connected to light, sunrise from the sea, glorious states shining like mountains in the morn (ll. 682–6). Athens is a place of brightness and the 'chrystalline' (l. 698) clarity of pure thought; it is an unchanging reminder of the potential for human achievement. The style of these choruses likewise aspires to the clarity of the Greek ideal. There are no compound epithets in either chorus, and in fact few epithets at all. There is little descriptive detail; the focus is general, on the harmony of the whole. The vocabulary is familiar and free from coinages. Clarity and harmony characterize both the style and the ideal.

This is a style which, John Buxton argued, Shelley developed from his reading of Sophocles in particular, though Homer might equally be invoked. An 'imaginative bareness' characterizes the style; epithets and neologisms are avoided in favour of direct statements dominated by verbs, rifts are not typically loaded with ore, and the atmosphere is clear, translucent, and bright. Shelley himself would press that style into the service of a kind of Platonism, one in which 'supreme beauty itself' can be depicted, as it is in Shelley's translation of Plato's *Symposium* (211e), as 'simple, pure, uncontaminated with the intermixture of human flesh and colours, and all other idle and unreal shapes attendant on mortality'. Shelley's favourite way to express the supreme beauty itself is to contrast white light with light divided into its spectral colours.

> The One remains, the many change and pass;
> Heaven's light forever shines, Earth's shadows fly;
> Life, like a dome of many-coloured glass,
> Stains the white radiance of Eternity . . .

(Adonais, ll. 460–3)

The metaphors of whiteness and of transparent brightness recur throughout *Prometheus Unbound* (1820). The Chorus of Spirits breathes the atmosphere of human thought, whether in its dim, dank, and grey manifestation, or

> Be it bright as all between
> Cloudless skies and windless streams
> Silent, liquid and serene—

(1. 680–2)

Demogorgon's realm, 'where the air is no prism' (2. 3. 74), is the place where 'there is One pervading, One alone' (2. 3. 79). When Jupiter is deposed and Prometheus and Asia are reunited (3. 4. 100–5), the earth's atmosphere is altered, 'thus no longer distorting sunlight into varied colors and a glare that hides realities'.[53] Once man no longer distorts 'this true fair world of things', he will perceive a 'Sea reflecting Love', 'smooth, serene and even', darting 'radiance and light' (4. 384–7). And in the regenerated cosmos, an infant sits within the moon:

> Within it sits a winged Infant, *white*
> Its countenance, like the *whiteness* of bright snow,
> Its plumes are as feathers of sunny frost,
> Its limbs gleam *white*, through the wind-flowing folds
> Of its *white* robe, woof of aetherial pearl.
> Its hair is *white*,—the brightness of *white* light
> Scattered in strings . . .

(4. 219–24; italics added)

For Shelley serene clarity and single whiteness are to constitute—by the fiat of repetition—both style and faith.

Yet early reviewers and critics responded to contrary qualities in the play: the 'hectic flutter' in the speech,[54] the violent opposition of words and sentiments,[55] the 'jumble of words and heterogeneous ideas',[56] and the 'unwieldy abundance of incoherent words and images'.[57] Instead of whiteness, the play's kaleidoscope of colours was remarked on, and disparaged, by some early readers. One critic, counting seven colours and nearly as many shades of colour in eleven lines of Asia's description of spring (2. 1. 17–27) accused Shelley of looking through a prism rather than spectacles.[58] Two styles are at work in the play, the limpid and transparent style of Sophocles as well as the rough and hectic style of Aeschylus and the Elizabethan dramatists.

Prometheus Unbound is a hybrid and draws on several styles. The form of the play (its division into acts and scenes) and much of the diction is Elizabethan and Jacobean. At times, as with the downfall of Jupiter in the first scene of Act 3, the language and dramatic situation might pass as a pastiche of Jacobean revenge drama, with a few Platonic touches. Shelley also includes songs in the drama, like many English playwrights; his chorus of Furies and Spirits (unlike the choruses of *Hellas*) bears no resemblance to Greek drama. Other features of the play, however, do derive from Greek practice, from both Greek styles: the smooth, limpid, and transparent style as well as the hectic, jumbled, and abundant style that gained support from the Romantic conflation of Aeschylus and Shakespeare.[59] The title of the play declares its relation to Aeschylus.[60] The dense compound epithets and negative adjectives, as we saw in Chapter 4, seek to recreate the texture of Greek, and specifically Aeschylean, tragedy; they are also Elizabethan. Likewise, the hectic flutter, the jumble, and the unwieldy abundance of the play are at once Aeschylean and Elizabethan.

That jumbled style (recall that Aristophanes called Aeschylus' style 'bolted-together') is intended to embody the manifold qualities of the world as we experience it and to be in counterpoint with the style of Platonic unity. The two styles are for Shelley those of the One and the Many, and their relation to each other is the central problem of the play.

To create the style of manifold sense impressions, Shelley relies on compound epithets (which bolt together diverse sense impressions, simultaneously perceived or imagined); he is equally reliant on another grammatical entity: the relative clause. Take *Prometheus Unbound*, 2. 1. 27–9 (I have used italic for the relative clauses and italic underlined for relative clauses within relative clauses):

> I feel, I see
> Those eyes *which burn through smiles <u>that fade in tears</u>*
> Like stars *half quenched in mists of silver dew.*

The purpose is to produce rapidly the sequence of actions and images Shelley needs (eyes, smiles, tears, stars, mists of silver dew) to convey a sense of fragile and evanescent beauty. The syntax of the main clause is simple and direct (subject, verb, object), doing little more than emote (I feel, I see); the emphasis is on the shifting display.

Sometimes the syntax is overwhelmed by this shifting display of images presented in relative clauses. When a faun describes the hydrogen cycle, the verse is made largely from such clauses:

> The bubbles *which the enchantment of the sun*
> *Sucks from the pale water-flowers* <u>*that pave*</u>
> <u>*The oozy bottom of clear lakes and pools*</u>
> Are the pavilions *where such dwell and float*
> *Under the green and golden atmosphere*
> <u>*Which noontide kindles through the woven leaves.*</u>
> And when these burst, and the thin fiery air,
> *The which they breathed within those lucent domes,*
> Ascends to flow like meteors through the night,
> They ride on it . . .
>
> (2. 2. 71–80)

Shelley's infolding in this way gives great freedom to the clauses, allowing them to move easily in unpredictable directions. The overall syntax is still simple: bubbles are pavilions where the spirits dwell and float; when the bubbles burst and the air escapes from them, the spirits ride on them. Yet the proliferation of relative clauses continually interrupts the syntax and prevents it from exercising a governing force.[61] Attention is therefore taken away from the syntactical statement and directed to the sequence of images: bubbles, sun, pale water-flowers, oozy bottom, etc. The passage is likely to have eluded readers unfamiliar with the science of his day. The style, in the continual shifts of attention conveyed by the relative clauses, deliberately makes the connections even more elusive, to present the hydrogen cycle as a mystery (which can none the less be apprehended). The elusiveness of the syntax places a new weight on the images, which are Shelley's means to embody an apprehension of the many, that is the many parts of the whole. The focus on the multiplicity of things is further emphasized by epithets, particularly those referring to colour: 'pale', 'green and golden', 'thin fiery', and 'lucent'. Individuated qualities are given; the whiteness and brightness of the whole are for the time forgotten.

Early reviewers of *Prometheus Unbound* sometimes accused Shelley of writing nonsense. W. S. Walker in *The Quarterly Review* (October 1821) wrote that readers of Shelley's poetry are 'dazzled by the multitude of words which sound as if they denoted something grand or splendid . . . but when the procession has gone by, and the tumult of it is over, not a trace of it remains upon the memory'.[62] In more recent times, F. R. Leavis influentially restated early criticism of Shelley's vagueness and incoherence, arguing that Shelley's best poetry, like 'Ode to the West Wind', works only by very general connections. He writes:[63] 'This poetry induces—depends for its success on inducing—a kind of attention that doesn't bring the critical intelligence into view: the imagery feels right, the associations work appropriately, if (as it takes conscious resistance not to do) one accepts the immediate feeling and doesn't slow down to think.' His criticism has been answered on two separate grounds. First, the charges of vagueness and incoherence have been rebutted. Patricia Hodgart defends the stanza of the 'Ode to the West Wind' that Leavis criticizes, and she makes the case that the imagery is precise with respect to the natural scene.[64] Other have also denied the allegation of Shelley's 'weak grasp upon the actual', focusing on his accuracy with respect to natural data.[65]

Second, it has been argued that Leavis's criteria are not relevant to the kind of poetry that Shelley writes. F. W. Bateson writes in defence of the 'Ode to the West Wind' that 'Shelley's images are not meant to build up a landscape or effect a comparison. Their function is simply to add to the kaleidoscope of associations which surrounds the central symbol.'[66] Why should we call flawed a poetry which gives the immediate impression that images feel right and associations work appropriately?

The 'kaleidoscope of associations' in Shelley is a vehicle to suggest the many-faceted objects of the phenomenal world. However, in *Prometheus* stress is equally laid on the ultimate unity of things beyond or behind the surface variety. Conceptual incoherence matters in *Prometheus* because Shelley makes it matter; he chose conceptual unity as his theme. His Platonic thrust cannot be sustained merely by using the word 'white' four times in six lines. If the play's theme of unity is made attractive only because of its contrast with a surface confusion of images and not by the resolution of disparate images into unity, then Shelley fails to offer what he says he is offering.

The play works syncretically. Prometheus is also Christ; Asia is also Venus. Associations of self-sacrifice and love, respectively, are brought together from both Christian and pagan traditions to create the characters. Fluidity is a principle of the drama, and individual identities and events tend to merge. When Earth recalls the torments which Zeus inflicted on the earth after Prometheus' curse, her speech gathers many allusions:

> Then—see those million worlds which burn and roll
> Around us: their inhabitants beheld
> My sphered light wane in wide Heaven; the sea
> Was lifted by strange tempest, and new fire
> From earthquake-rifted mountains of bright snow
> Shook its portentous hair beneath Heaven's frown;
> Lightning and Inundation vexed the plains;
> Blue thistles bloomed in cities; foodless toads
> Within voluptuous chambers panting crawled;
> When plague had fallen on man and beast and worm,
> And Famine, and black blight on herb and tree,
> And in the corn and vines and meadow grass
> Teemed ineradicable poisonous weeds
> Draining their growth, for my wan breast was dry
> With grief . . .
>
> (1. 163–77)

The associations in the passage range from the torments Zeus rains down on Prometheus at the end of Aeschylus' *Prometheus Bound*, to the curse on the Egyptians who held the Israelites captive, to Demeter's grief at the abduction of Persephone, to the moment of Christ's death, and to Shakespeare's descriptions of the earthquake before Caesar's assassination. All the allusions evoke calamity and are meant to convey the loss of hope and the ache of all our woe. Yet the allusions are not exact. The disparity of meanings in the stories and their different contexts keep them from functioning coherently. They do form a kaleidoscope of associations of devastating loss, but Shelley wants more: the assimilation of these stories to a central pattern of the oppressed spirit freeing itself by renouncing its bondage to hate.

When Prometheus refers to Jupiter as 'eyeless in hate', a different series of associations is called forth. The word has a Greek equivalent and occurs in Greek tragedy. But notable uses of the word in English literature are also present: *Lear*'s 'impetuous blasts, with eyeless rage' (3. 1) , 'Turne out that eyeless villain' (3. 7), and 'That eyeless head of thine' (4. 6)) as well as *Samson Agonistes*' 'Ask for this great Deliverer now, and find him Eyeless in Gaza' (ll. 38–9). The allusive force connects the exorbitant sufferings of Lear, Gloucester, and Samson with Prometheus. But when these parallels are examined, they move in different directions. Samson's heroic endurance of torment, Lear's suffering on the heath, and the putting out of Gloucester's eyes all contribute to associations of injustice and endurance. But again, Shelley is trying for more: to subsume these stories under the general category of the Mind first binding itself to and then freeing itself from its hate. He is trying for more than the stories allow. They do not support his theme, and he relies on our suspending critical attention for his effect.

There is a divorce between philosophy and technique in *Prometheus Unbound*. Shelley evolved a style expressive of myriad presences, of the multiple individuated particulars of a scene and particular allusive associations, rapidly shifting one to another. But it is not brought into a relation with the demands of his Platonizing. The two run concurrently but without the interplay necessary to resolve their competing demands. Why, though, should we not value the contradiction between them? I praised the ending of Hölderlin's 'Mnemosyne' because of its ability to do justice to an emotional and logical contradiction. Petrarch makes splendid poetry out of a contradiction; in 'Quanto più m'avicino al giorno estremo', for example, he compares ''l duro et greve l terreno incarco' ('the hard and grievous earthly burden') to 'fresca neve' ('fresh snow'), which is neither hard nor grievous, but light and beautiful. That contradiction is part of Petrarch's fundamental experience of being torn between this world and the next, a tension in evidence throughout the sonnets as well the major theme of the *Secretum*. The division between the phenomenal and noumenal worlds in Shelley is conceptually analogous. It is evident stylistically in the descriptions of nature that are dense with epithets and placed alongside instances of white unity; a style abruptly shifting among things is joined to a style correlative to the apprehension of oneness, as historical and mythological exempla are combined under a single ethical precept. But it is the nature of the combination that is important, and Shelley combines them without relating them. He uses an Aeschylean style of parataxis and compounds not to oppose, or resist, or deny the demands his thought would impose on it, but to evade them.

Unlike Shelley, Swinburne in *Atalanta in Calydon* (1865) imitates the form as well as the language of Greek tragedy. The play moves from prologue and parodos through five episodes and stasimons to the exodus. The last episode presents the characteristic Greek messenger's speech, and the exodus includes a kommos, a lament sung alternately by the chorus and actors. Moreover, the language of *Atalanta* reproduces characteristic aspects of Greek dramatic poetry. An early reviewer wrote that Swinburne's study of the Attic dramatists had enabled him 'to reproduce felicitously many of their terms of expression. The scholar is struck, every few lines, by some phrase which he can fancy a direct translation from the Greek . . .'[67] In my edition of the play, I tried to substantiate that claim.[68]

The reviewer none the less argued that the imitation was fundamentally flawed because Swinburne's 'modern habits of thinking and writing' did not accord 'with the solemn and severe stateliness of Attic tragedy'. Swinburne's mind was 'cast in a mould most unlike the Greek', a mould he went on to describe:[69]

A Greek poet is never confused, nor are his thoughts obscure, although they may seem so when they hint at something without wishing or being able to follow it out. It is his tendency to dwell upon insoluble problems, not a want of light and force in his own mind, that makes us think Aeschylus difficult. Himself, although in an inferior degree to Sophocles, he is definite, precise, subtle; his ideas are single and separate, often delicately interwoven in a complex web of thought, while yet each thread retains its individual colour, and is not blended undistinguishably in the whole. Modern habits of thinking and writing want this clear singleness, and Mr. Swinburne is wholly a modern. His images, metaphors, and allusions are heaped upon one another in a wild prodigal way which reminds us of Shelley or Browning more than of any ancient poet; he lays on stroke after stroke of colour till the last obliterate the first, and we are bewildered among thick-coming sensations. His metaphors are not often incongruous, but they follow so fast as to be confusing, and it is seldom that any distinct and vivid impression is left on the reader's mind.

The qualities the reviewer associated with classical Greece—'light', 'definite', 'precise', 'clear singleness'—were those of Winckelmann's Greece, which had saturated English aesthetic assumptions to such an extent that the critic was oblivious to what strikes the modern reader as the most obvious qualities of Aeschylean style. The allegedly 'wholly modern' style of wild and prodigal heaping up of images, metaphors, and allusions describes Aeschylus' style extremely well.

And since Aeschylus was Swinburne's constant touchstone for aesthetic excellence,[70] and since he called himself a disciple of Aeschylus, in explicit contrast to Arnold the disciple of Sophocles,[71] it is natural to ask what use Swinburne may have made of Aeschylus' language. Like Shelley and like Hopkins, Swinburne found in Aeschylus a language that can be used to express disintegration: fractured multiplicity in Shelley, abruption in Hopkins, and division in Swinburne. The major differences among them are due, in part, to the skill with which something is posed against disintegration: the Neoplatonic One in Shelley, Christ in Hopkins. In Swinburne division is not opposed but consummated in oblivion.

'Division' and its cognates are key words in *Atalanta*. The emotional climax of the play is Althaea's decision that her love for her brothers and the demand that they be avenged must outweigh her devotion to her son. She is divided between these loves. In her speech at lines 1729–61, she moves from outrage at her brothers' deaths to love for her son and finally to the sense of implacable duty requiring vengeance. These are the conflicting emotions of the episode. 'My spirit is strong against itself', she cries out at line 1704, like Milton's Samson; 'I am severed from myself' at line 1943. When she hears from the messenger that her son has killed her brothers, Althaea cries that the gods 'rend me, they divide me, they destroy' (l. 1506). The argument between Meleager and his uncles occurred over the division (l. 1515) of the spoil. The second messenger describes Meleager dying: 'as keen ice divided of the sun | His limbs divide' (ll. 1989–90). The chorus laments him:

> How art thou rent from us,
> Thou that wert whole
> As with severing of eyelids and eyes, as with sundering of body and soul.
>
> (2064–6)

At line 2171 the chorus invokes 'the gods who divide and devour'. In Meleager's last speech, he tells his mother that though his knees would worship, 'thy fire and subtlety, | Dissundering them, devour me' (ll. 2223–4).

The syntax as well as the vocabulary of *Atalanta* articulate division. Note, for example, how often Swinburne repeats a word but in a context that divides it from itself. 'The days dividing lover and lover' (l. 91); 'And man from man they fell, for ye twain stood God against god' (ll. 555–6); 'breaking of city by city; The dividing of friend against friend, The severing of brother and brother' (ll. 835–8). 'Arrow on arrow and wound on wound' (p. 1036) is an intensification, but it intensifies the agent of division. Only at the end of the play, with Meleager's last words to Atalanta, is there a joining:

> And stretch thyself upon me and touch hands
> With hands and lips with lips

$$(2300–1)$$

a consummation in death, achieved only when life no longer divides.

The most important way that Swinburne's syntax makes vivid the experience of division is a consequence of his diffuse style. That diffuseness is Swinburne's medium, not simply a defect but both defect and felicity combined. As T. S. Eliot argued, 'had Swinburne practised greater concentration his verse would be, not better in the same kind, but a different thing . . . his diffuseness is one of his glories'.[72] Often Swinburne is diffuse in his poetry in a very simple way, by the conjunction 'and' (less often, 'or'). Here are phrases from the first speech of *Atalanta*, that of the chief huntsman:

mistress of the months and stars (1)
dead men and dark hours (5)
all things fierce or fleet that roar and range (7)
gentler shafts than snow or sleep (8)
hear now and help and lift no violent hand (9)
favourable and fair as thine eye's beam | Hidden and shown in heaven (10–11)
killing the stars and dews | And dreams and desolation of the night (18–19)
burn and break the dark (21)
through all the roar and ripple of streaming springs (27)
reddening flakes and flying flowers (28)
shaken from hands and blown from lips of nymphs (29)
fair as the snow and footed as the wind (46)
firm hills and the fleeting sea (48)
roaring river and labouring sea (54)

He continually expands a single word (an adjective, noun, or verb) into two or more and frequently doubles phrases as well. Sometimes the effect is that of hendiadys. 'Dreams and desolation' is bolder than 'desolate dreams' and focuses greater attention on desolation. Similarly 'winter's rains and ruins' (l. 89), as hendiadys for 'winter's ruining rains', emphasizes the destructive power and allows the classical meaning of ruin (*ruo*, rush blindly into disaster) to bear on the phrase. More often the expanded and sometimes bifurcated expressions are not intrinsically to be defended but gain a cumulative weight as particular instances of the fundamental structural principle of his verse.[73] The play opens with an invocation to Artemis:

> Maiden, and mistress of the months and stars
> Now folded in the flowerless fields of heaven,
> Goddess whom all gods love with threefold heart,
> Being treble in thy divided deity,
> A light for dead men and dark hours, a foot
> Swift on the hills as morning, and a hand
> To all things fierce and fleet that roar and range
> Mortal, with gentler shafts than snow or sleep;
> Hear now and help and lift no violent hand . . .
>
> (1–9)

In this complex and formal invocation, the goddess is addressed first as 'maiden', then 'mistress', and then 'goddess', and then synecdochally and metaphorically as 'light', 'foot', and 'hand'. The six terms are added together in apposition; they expand and qualify each other. They differ from the parallel expressions quoted above because in the invocation each term after maiden is itself expanded by adjectives or an adjectival phrase or clause of varying size. The single word 'maiden' is syntactically equal to 'mistress of the months and stars Now folded in the flowerless fields of heaven', fourteen words; 'Goddess whom all gods love with threefold heart Being treble in thy divided deity', fourteen words; 'A light for dead men and dark hours', eight words; 'a foot Swift on the hills as morning', eight words; and 'a hand To all things fierce and fleet that roar and range Mortal, with gentler shafts than snow or sleep', twenty words. The adjectival expansions themselves may contain further expansions. The result is to remove any balanced parallels and to block any straightforward comprehension. It is not possible on the first readings to know the relation of the parts in these first lines, to recognize that six terms stand in apposition. As image follows image in rapid succession, the passage evades a clear syntactical ordering.

Consider next an elaborate, loosely Homeric simile:

> she thereat
> Laughed, as when dawn touches the sacred night

The sky sees laugh and redden and divide
Dim lips and eyelids virgin of the sun,
Hers, and the warm slow breasts of morning heave,
Fruitful, and flushed with flame from lamp-lit hours,
And maiden undulation of clear hair
Colour the clouds; so laughed she from pure heart . . .

(1524–31)

The lines are difficult to grasp because the parts are of such unequal size. Eventually the reader realizes that, when dawn touches the night, the sky sees three things happen: lips and eyelids laugh and redden and divide, breasts heave, and hair colour the clouds. The emotive response, however, is not to grammar but instead to a succession of beautiful images that reveal the dawn as it happens; images take priority over syntax as unmediated experience takes priority over reflection.

Subordinating conjunctions are not common in *Atalanta*. Temporal, logical, concessive, etc. relations are far less frequent than either conjunction or disjunction. As in Shelley, a logic of images breaks out against syntactical ordering. Shelley manages this especially through the infoldings of relative clauses; Swinburne, especially through conjunction and apposition. In both poets, agglutination or accumulation produces rapid cuts among images and perspectives. This is what the *Saturday Review* critic censured as un-Greek and what readers of Aeschylus find so Aeschylean.

The style of *Atalanta*—agglutinative, rapidly shifting—is Swinburne's greatest achievement because it embodies the central themes and emotional pattern of his work: division and oblivion. The effort to work out the meaning is a crucial part of the experience of reading Swinburne: the reader is divided between haltingly making sense of the words and being impelled forward by the rhythm. This divided and frustrated state is the formal embodiment of man's fate, divided as we are by our loves and by the irreconcilable demands of the gods. That frustration is an intrinsic part of the experience; it is the inability to master experience, and it characterizes both Meleager and Althaea, divided beings.

The invocation to Artemis in the first lines of the play in its difficulty suggests the difficult and fraught relation of men to the gods. The complexity of the relations among the parts of the address is a means to indicate that our dealings with the gods are dangerous and hard to anticipate. Portentous and climactic events, like

Meleager and the golden fleece (ll. 583 ff.), the killing of the boar (ll. 230 ff.), Althaea's loves for her son and brothers (ll. 1565 ff.), and many choruses are rendered in this style, which creates a sense of division by the adjectival expansion of grammatical elements to such an extent, and so variably, that the overall ordering of the syntax is obscured.

Parataxis, however, does not have to take the rough, variable form which threatens syntactic coherence. The parataxis of Homer, for example, works in a very different way; perhaps the most famous imitation of this style in English poetry is Matthew Arnold's, in *Sohrab and Rustum* (1853). Consider these lines:

> And, with a mournful voice, Rustum replied:—
> 'Fear not! as thou hast said, Sohrab, my son,
> So shall it be; for I will burn my tents,
> And quit the host, and bear thee hence with me,
> And carry thee away to Seistan,
> And place thee on a bed, and mourn for thee,
> With the snow-headed Zal, and all my friends.
> And I will lay thee in that lovely earth,
> And heap a stately mound above thy bones,
> And plant a far-seen pillar over all,
> And men shall not forget thee in thy grave . . .
>
> (795–805)

Simple conjunction dominates the passage; however, the elements that are conjoined are of roughly equal length, and they are all clearly ordered by the syntax. This is the style of the 'Grecian taste', of the dominant strand of British hellenism. Swinburne adopts this style too, though inflecting it in his own way: he makes it grammatically correlate with the state of oblivion.

He does this by successively removing, not adding, elements. As in the last stanza of 'The Garden of Proserpine':

> Then star nor sun shall waken
>   Nor any change of light:
> Nor sound of waters shaken,
>   Nor any sound or sight:
> Nor wintry leaves nor vernal,
> Nor days nor things diurnal;
> Only the sleep eternal
>   In an eternal night.

Parallel negations also suggest or enforce oblivion throughout *Atalanta*:

> And when night comes the wind sinks and the sun,
> And there is no light after, and no storm,
> But sleep and much forgetfulness of things.
>
> (294–96)

> Lands indiscoverable in the unheard-of west,
> Round which the strong stream of a sacred sea
> Rolls without wind for ever, and the snow
> There shows not here white wings and windy feet,
> Nor thunder nor swift rain saith anything,
> Nor the sun burns, but all things rest and thrive
>
> (511–56)

> I am gone down to the empty weary house
> Where no flesh is nor beauty nor swift eyes
> Nor sound of mouth nor might of hands and feet.
>
> (2295–97)

In Swinburne's understanding, it is in the nature of things that the gods place competing demands on us that cannot be harmonized; we choose, or do not choose, and are destroyed. After our destruction follows the quiet of oblivion. 'For silence after grievous things is good' (l. 1197).

Destruction and oblivion are embodied in both these styles, one in which the parts are amplified diversely, creating division and confusion; and one where the monotony of parts signals the unchanging nature of the dead. The 'and' in such examples is as much a mark of division as it is of addition. It indicates that disjunct things are combined, with division, complication, and destruction as a result. It comes at a cost, however, because it is diffuse; semantic density, the intrinsic weight of the particular word, the *mot juste*, are rarely to be found in the kind of poetry Swinburne is writing.

In England, Greece was seen as the locale where mind and body like man and god constituted a unity that the moderns had lost but must strive for. By offering a version of Greece dominated by the fact of division, Swinburne drastically undercut that ideal. The play was celebrated by critics who would later object to *Poems and Ballads*, though both are blasphemous in similar ways; the blasphemy of *Atalanta* was shielded, that is it failed to be perceived, by the cultural insulation provided by the dominant model of ancient Greece.

Both Shelley and Swinburne drew on Greek mythology and reimagined Greek tragedy. Hopkins loathed Greek mythology.[74] Even so, Aeschylus was as important to Hopkins as he was to the other two, though he was far from inspiring Hopkins to invoke Greece. And though he was important, Aeschylus was hardly uniquely important to him; Keats and Shakespeare mattered more to him. Indeed, Shakespeare mattered more to Shelley and Swinburne, too; in all studies of influence there is the danger that isolating one element unduly emphasizes it. Sometimes the very fact that a single factor can be isolated as an influence is tantamount to admitting that it is not the deepest stimulus because it has not been most fully absorbed.

So it would be misleading to impute a direct line of transmitted influence from Aeschylus to Hopkins. Both are known for their bold compound words (see Chapter 4); Hopkins's hyperbaton 'the rólling level úndernéath him steady aír' is like Aeschylus' χθόνα βάκτροις ἐπικρούσαντας Ἀτρείδας ('earth with staves striking sons of Atreus', *Agamemnon* 202–3). Even so, Hopkins was treating English with a freedom he believed it had intrinsically as a Germanic language, rather than trying to beat English into a Greek shape.

The most important parallel between Hopkins and Aeschylus is a style in which images are rapidly merged and metaphors abruptly shifted. But even in this respect, Aeschylus is not uniquely important; in addition to Shakespeare, there is the example of Pindar, notorious or celebrated for centuries because of his speed and the absence of logical connections in the odes. There are other reasons to adduce a Pindaric influence: the form of *The Wreck of the Deutschland* is a kind of Pindaric ode, celebrating spiritual rather than physical athletes and in which the physical afflictions of the nuns are subsumed in the celebration of their spiritual rightness. Wordsworth's immortality ode had already compounded the Pindaric form with spiritual celebration, by linking the origin of the Pindaric ode as a victory celebration with the Pauline injunction to seek an incorruptible, not corruptible, crown.[75] The flexible combinations in the Pindaric ode of narrative, prayer, and reflection occur also in Hopkins's poem.

One reason to emphasize Aeschylus over other Greek influences on Hopkins's style is Hopkins's own description of the dramatist.[76]

What a noble genius Aeschylus had! Besides the swell and pomp of words for which he is famous there is in him a touching consideration and manly tenderness; also an earnestness of spirit and would-be piety by which the man makes himself felt through the playwright. This is not so with Sophocles, who is only the learned and sympathetic dramatist, and much less with Euripides.

Earnestness is a constant criterion in Hopkins's criticism.[77] Homer lacks it; Bridges betrays it by his introduction of Athena on stage; but Aeschylus has 'earnestness of spirit'. This may be the most important word in Hopkins's criticism:

By the by inversions—As you say, I do avoid them, because they weaken and because they destroy the earnestness of the utterance.[78]

I hold that by archaism a thing is sicklied o'er as by blight. Some little flavours, but much spoils, and always for the same reason—it destroys earnest: we do not speak that way; therefore if a man speaks that way he is not serious . . . [79]

This leads me to say that a kind of touchstone of the highest or most living art is seriousness: not gravity but the being in earnest with your subject—reality.[80]

Earnestness in Hopkins is the proper relation of selfhood to reality. The abrupt, shifting style of Aeschylus was for him the pre-eminent classical example of such a relation. The style expressed both the manifold sensory presence of things and the uncertain or inconstant self finding its way to being in earnest with its subject.

Hopkins's earliest poetry is marked by hectic and centrifugal shifts of images.[81] 'A Vision of the Mermaids', for example, is dense with epithets; diverse colours, textures, and shapes fill the lines. This density of diverse description is put to use later in his Catholic poetry to stress the inscape of the natural world, the individuation, the dappling of things and creatures, bearing witness to God in their unknowing ways:

> Glóry be to God for dappled things—
>> For skies of couple-colour as a brinded cow;
>>> For rose-moles all in stipple upon trout that swim;
> Fresh-firecoal chestnut fálls; finches' wings;
>> Lándscape plotted and pieced—fold, fallow, and plough;
>>> And áll trádes, their gear and tackle and trim.

Yet for all the intensity, even ferocity, of his images, Hopkins does not abandon the logic of syntax in favour of the momentum gathered by imagistic associations; on the contrary, he uses syntax to direct that momentum to its proper place. All the images of 'Pied Beauty' are channelled into a final imperative that could not be syntactically simpler: 'Práise hím'. In the octet of 'As Kingfishers Catch Fire', selving, particularizing individuation, is expressed in the abruptly shifting sequence of images (kingfishers, dragonflies, wells, stones, string, bell's bow), but the sestet makes clear that human activity belongs to another realm. Turning on the designed insufficiency of the octet ('I say more: the just man justices'), it offers a vivid state-ment of doctrine, not a logic of images which it reveals to be limited and self-enclosed. It is graceful, syntactically and semantically, as it combines different registers and presents them as one. 'Goings' ('thát keeps all his goings graces') is both a colloquialism and echo of the Psalmist ('Hold up my goings in thy paths, that my footsteps slip not', 17: 5, cf. 40: 2, 140: 4). 'Grace' ranges in its implications from the beauty of the graceful body, to gracious behaviour, to the state of God's grace ('God's better beauty'), all present in the sestet, and superior to the state of nature which he had made so attractive in the octet.[82]

Not only nature but also selfhood is described in rapidly shifting imagery. Geoffrey Hill has called attention to the 'abrúpt sélf' of 'Henry Purcell', noting that Hopkins also uses the adjective to describe sprung rhythm.[83] 'Abrupt', then, is both a technical term of Hopkins's prosody and a word of selfhood. Abrupt cadences and abrupt language are means to make present a self that is labouring under great pressure. Hopkins' abrupt imagery is another means to this end.

Unlike the grace-full and therefore graceful man of the sestet of 'As Kingfishers Catch Fire', the abrupt self is marked by rapid and strenuous shifts of metaphor and images. The second quatrain of 'Carrion Comfort' runs:

> But ah, but O thou terrible, why wouldst thou rude on me
> Thy wring-earth right foot rock? lay a lionlimb against me? scan
> With darksome devouring eyes my bruisèd bones? and fan,
> O in turns of tempest, me heaped there; me frantic to avoid thee and
> flee?

Hopkins is represented as a wrestler; as a lion's quarry; carrion; and as a heap of grain. The inconstant, labile self is under great stress, vacillating yet utterly in earnest.

In *The Wreck of the Deutschland*, Hopkins writes:[84]

> I am sóft síft
> In an hourglass—at the wall
> Fast, but mined with a motion, a drift,
> And it crowds and it combs to the fall;
> I stéady as a wáter in a wéll, to a póise, to a páne,
> But roped with, always, all the way down from the tall
> Fells or planks of the voel, a vein
> Of the góspel próffer, a préssure, a prínciple, Chríst's gíft.
>
> (25–32)

The abrupt shift of image from hourglass to well, from dead sand to life-giving water, sets forth the abruptly shifting inconstancy of the self. In contrast to God, the 'Gróund of béing and gránite of it' (l. 254), the abrupt, moody self is an 'ócean of a mótionable mínd' (l. 253). In this way Hopkins unites parataxis and theology. The quickly changing images of self are also balanced by Christ, not subject to mutability. Hopkins fits a kaleidoscopic and paratactic imagery to the changeable self, but then rebukes that self by the syntax of his theology.[85]

Hopkins invented a metre and style expressive of the abrupt self; was he able to express with equal power the dilemmas faced by the selfhood of others? John Robinson argues that the last third of *The Wreck of the Deutschland* does not take seriously the question of why a loving God permits human suffering. Instead, the human suffering is merely elided in the strenuous assertion of divine favour. The transformation of storm flakes into flowers (l. 168) or drowning into bathing (l. 184) is crass, Robinson argues, and is possible only by relinquishing an imaginative grip on the reality of the situation.[86] He thinks that Hopkins's remark to Bridges about the death of Bridges's sister a year after her husband had been murdered is similarly callous.[87] 'But sufferings falling on such a person as your sister was are to be looked on as the marks of God's particular love and this is truer the more exceptional they are', Hopkins wrote in 1869, three years after his conversion.[88]

But Robinson is himself crass and unimaginative. Hopkins offers the 'scróll-leaved flówers' of the storm as the stylized flowers of pictorial martyrology. When he writes that the drowning nuns 'bathe' in St Francis's 'fall-gold mercies', he is no more callous than in the letter to Bridges: we experience God's love in suffering. Hopkins intends not to mitigate human suffering but to render the experience of divine mercy terrifying.

Yet to succeed Hopkins had somehow to acknowledge on its own terms the extremity of the suffering that is not finally important on its own terms. He failed to do this; instead, he replaced the nuns' physical and mental agony with its spiritual meaning. Their plight was 'wild-worst', they endured an 'extremity', but not for long. As one of them called Christ to herself, 'wild-worst' became her 'wild-worst Best'. The 'extremity' was saved in advance from being extreme because Christ was to 'cure the extremity where he had cast her'. The reward of their suffering, the 'jay-blue heavens' of 'pied and peeled May', was presented more abruptly and vividly than the actuality of wild-worst extremity; those images immediately followed their agony, mitigating the horror they endured.[89]

In the poem Hopkins maintained a contrast between the sister's heart's rightness and his own vacillating self; however, the contrast was also one in which she was exempted from the extremity of suffering and in which the uniqueness of his own distress was underlined. This damaged the poem; a lesser poem like 'Margaret Clitheroe' faced the suffering of another more unblinkingly. From the parataxis he learnt from Aeschylus, from English literature, from the centrifugal speech rhythms of his own time, Hopkins invented a powerful technique: embodying the earnest voice of his abrupt self, which despite its own recalcitrance assumed a proper place within a syntax of doctrinal statement; yet he was unable to imagine his suffering self in relation to other selves that suffer, having found their suffering more tractable than his own.

The pale afterlife of Victorian hellenism died along with the Homeric enthusiasms with which the First World War was greeted by the English public-school class. Yet Greek and Greece survived, though not in the Arnoldian formulation. After the publication of Hopkins's poems and the rediscovery of Hölderlin's, their parataxis played a major role in the development of modernist styles. For one modernist poet, Aeschylean Greek was a direct stimulus. In 1919 Ezra Pound wrote:[90]

One might almost say the Aeschylus' Greek is agglutinative, that his general drive, especially in choruses, is merely to remind the audience of the Trojan war; that syntax is subordinate, and, duly subordinated, left out ... certainly more sense and less syntax (good or bad) in translations of Aeschylus might be a relief.

Reading Aeschylus, Ronald Bush has shown,[91] was essential in the genesis of *The Cantos*; it helped Pound solve the problem of how to make a long poem out of imagistic principles. He discovered the ideogram only after he had already developed his technique, and found in it confirmation rather than inspiration. The free verse he evolved was likewise indebted to his reading of Greek lyric, based on certain recurring metrical shapes separated by syllables not counting in the scansion.[92] Pound's innovations were the most important continuation of English poetry under the spell of Greek. Those innovations, together with the new importance of archaic, pre-Periclean Greece in the arts, in anthropology, and in philosophy (a 'renaissance of the archaic' it has been called) renewed a hellenism that had become etiolated and was moribund, giving it a new life that lasted until after the Second World War, when things changed again.

Notes

CHAPTER ONE: MULTILINGUALISM IN LITERATURE

1. For an introduction to the topic, see John Edwards, *Multilingualism* (Harmondsworth: Penguin, 1995).
2. For a survey of historical research into multilingualism, see Peter Burke, 'The Social History of Language', *The Art of Conversation* (Ithaca, NY: Cornell University Press, 1993). Many of the examples in this paragraph are derived from that essay.
3. Known in several versions; first recorded in 1601. See H. Weinreich, *Wege der Sprachkultur* (Stuttgart: Deutsche Verlags-Anstalt, 1985), 190.
4. Quoted in Abram Tertz, *Strolls with Pushkin* (New Haven: Yale University Press, 1993), 154.
5. Quoted in Leonard Forster, *The Poets' Tongues: Multilingualism in Literature* (Cambridge: Cambridge University Press, 1970), 18. See Franz Grillparzer, *Sämtliche Werke*, ed. Albert Zipper (Leipzig: Reclam, 1902), vi. 195.
6. There are many linguistic studies of code-switching. See e.g. the issue of *World Englishes* devoted to the topic of 'Code-Mixing: English Across Languages', 8/3 (Winter 1989). Broader studies of the phenomenon include Carol Scotton and William Ury, 'Bilingual Strategies: The Social Functions of Code-Switching', *International Journal for the Sociology of Language*, 13 (1977), 5–20, and Carol Scotton, 'The Possibility of Code-Switching: Motivations for Maintaining Multilingualism', *Anthropological Linguistics*, 24 (1982), 432–44.
7. See E. Glyn Lewis, 'Bilingualism and Bilingual Education: The Ancient World to the Renaissance', in Joshua Freedman, *Bilingual Education* (Rowley, Mass.: Newbury House, 1976), 150–201, and L. A. Holford-Strevens, 'VTRAQUE LINGVS DOCTVS: Some Notes on Bilingualism in the Roman Empire', in H. D. Jocelyn with H. Hunt (eds.), *Tria Lustra* (Liverpool: Liverpool Classical Monthly, 1993), 203–13. Very recently the topic has been magisterially surveyed by J. N. Adams, *Bilingualism and the Latin Language* (Cambridge: Cambridge University Press, 2003); see also J. N. Adams, M. Janse, and S. Swain (eds.), *Bilingualism in Ancient Society* (Oxford: Oxford University Press, 2002).
8. Andrew L. Sihler, *New Comparative Grammar of Greek and Latin* (New York: Oxford University Press, 1995), 12.
9. The first line of Livius' *Odyssey*—'Virum mihi, Camena, insece versutum'—shows both faithfulness to Homer (the syntax, the word order, *insece* for ἔννεπε) and originality (the native Italian *Camena* rather than a Greek muse, *versutum* which plays with the etymology of πολύτροπον but has a quite different semantic range).

10. 'A worthless and unteachable race', Pliny, *Natural History* 29. 7. 14.

11. See esp. Simon Swain, *Hellenism and Empire: Language, Classicism, and Power in the Greek World, AD 50–250* (Oxford: Clarendon Press, 1996).

12. Unlike *bilinguis*, commonly used both in classical and medieval Europe, *multilinguis* has always been a rare word. In English, *bilingual* and *multilingual* are 19th-cent. coinages; previously, it was enough to call someone a *linguist* (Johnson: 'a man skillful in languages'). Recent studies of multilingualism in medieval England include Thorlac Turville-Petre, *England the Nation: Language, Literature, and National Identity, 1290–1340* (Oxford: Clarendon Press, 1996) and D. A. Trotter (ed.), *Multilingualism in Later Medieval Britain* (Rochester, NY: D. S. Brewer, 2000).

13. 'Grant translateur, noble Geffroy Chaucier' is the refrain of a ballad by Eustache Deschamps. Langland's 'macaronic sublime' is discussed by A. V. C. Schmidt in his introduction to his Everyman edn. of the poem (1995, p. xlviii).

14. Quoted as an epigraph to Warren Boutcher, 'Vernacular Humanism in the Sixteenth Century', in Jill Kraye (ed.), *The Cambridge Companion to Renaissance Humanism* (Cambridge: Cambridge University Press, 1996), 189.

15. Françoise Waquet, *Latin, or the Empire of a Sign: From the Sixteenth to the Twentieth Centuries*, tr. John Howe (London and New York: Verso, 2001).

16. Kristian Jensen, 'The Humanist Reform of Latin and Latin Teaching', in Kraye (ed.), *Cambridge Companion to Renaissance Humanism*, 63–81. See also Robert Black, *Humanism and Education in Medieval and Renaissance Italy* (Cambridge: Cambridge University Press, 2001).

17. Boutcher, 'Vernacular Humanism', 189–202.

18. The statistics are quoted in Waquet, *Latin*, 81–2. For German and Latin statistics in the 18th cent., see Bernhard Fabian, *The English Book in Eighteenth-Century Germany* (London: British Library, 1992), 45 and n. 24.The distribution by language of French and Latin printed books in France during the 16th cent., as well as the distribution by language (English and Latin) of 'O' books in Oxford and Cambridge from 1500 to 1800 and the distribution of books in Latin, German, and French printed in Germany from 1566 to 1795 are graphically charted in Henri-Jean Martin, *The French Book* (Baltimore: Johns Hopkins University Press, 1996), 25–7.

19. Anthony Grafton, 'The New Science and the Traditions of Humanism', Kraye (ed.), *Cambridge Companion to Renaissance Humanism*, 203–23.

20. Waquet, *Latin*, ch. 8, 'Class'.

21. Ibid. 47 and 63–5.

22. J. W. Binns, *Intellectual Culture in Elizabethan and Jacobean England* (Leeds: Francis Cairns, 1990), 216.

23. Christopher Stray, *Classics Transformed* (Oxford: Clarendon Press, 1998), 68–74.

24. The evidence is surveyed in John B. Gleason, *John Colet* (Berkeley, Calif.: University of California Press, 1989), 228.

25. On Greek in the Middle Ages, see Roberto Weiss, *Medieval and Humanist Greek* (Padua: Editrice Antenore, 1977), and also Walter Berschin, *Greek Letters and the Latin Middle Ages* (Washington, DC: Catholic University of

America, 1988); on the persistence of the 'myth of 1453', see Peter Burke, 'The Myth of 1453: Notes and Reflections', in Michael Erbe *et al.* (eds.), *Querdenken: Dissens und Toleranz im Wandel der Geschichte* (Mannheim: Palatium Verlag, 1996), 23–30; on the importance of 1423 in the recovery of Greek, see N. G. Wilson, *From Byzantium to Italy: Greek Studies in the Italian Renaissance* (Baltimore: Johns Hopkins University Press, 1992), 25.

26. For the position of Greek in the Renaissance, see Anthony Grafton and Lisa Jardine, 'The New Subject: Developing Greek Studies', in their *From Humanism to the Humanities* (Cambridge, Mass.: Harvard University Press, 1986); Peter Burke, 'The Renaissance', in K. J. Dover (ed.), *Perceptions of the Ancient Greeks* (Cambridge: Blackwell, 1992); and esp. N. G. Wilson, *From Byzantium to Italy: Greek Studies in the Italian Renaissance* (Baltimore: Johns Hopkins University Press, 1992). For 19th-cent. views of Greek in the Renaissance, recall George Eliot's *Romola*, in which Bardo's enthusiasm for Greek leads him to denigrate Latin literature as merely 'transplanted and derivative' in comparison (book i, ch. 6).

27. Wilson, *From Byzantium*, 158.

28. In the *Prose della Volgar Lingua*; see Pietro Bembo, *Prose e rime*, ed. Carlo Dionisotti (Turin: UTET, 1960), 85.

29. Baldassare Castiglione, *The Book of the Courtier*, tr. Thomas Hoby ([1561] London: J. M. Dent, 1928), book 1, p. 71.

30. *The Civilization of the Renaissance in Italy* (New York: Harper, 1958), i. 205.

31. Wilson, *From Byzantium*, 102, 130–1; Grafton and Jardine, *From Humanism*, 1–28 (but see Wilson, *From Byzantium*, 170 n. 5); Wilfred Mustard, *The Eclogues of Baptista Mantuanus* (Baltimore: Johns Hopkins, 1911), 21.

32. See Erika Rummel, *The Humanist–Scholastic Debate in the Renaissance and the Reformation* (Cambridge, Mass.: Harvard University Press, 1995) and *The Confessionalization of Humanism in Reformation Germany* (Oxford: Oxford University Press, 2000).

33. Kristian Jensen, 'The Humanist Reform of Latin and Latin Teaching', 78. Note, however, the letter by Bucer in which he calls the study of Greek, Hebrew, *and* Latin as 'eminently useful' (Rummel, *Confessionalization*, 41). Rummel also quotes (*Confessionalization*, 106) a parodic letter by Urbanus Rhegius in which the Roman see justifies its antipathy to Greek and Hebrew because its interests lie in ensuring that 'Germans read nothing but the [Latin] decretal'.

34. Rummel, *Confessionalization*, 115.

35. Most of the relevant data can be found in Emile Egger, *L'Hellénisme en France*, 1869. See too Linton C. Stevens, 'A Re-evaluation of Hellenism in the French Renaissance' in Werner L. Gundersheimer (ed.), *French Humanism: 1470–1600* (New York: Harper & Row, 1970).

36. Arthur Tilley, *Studies in the French Renaissance* ([1922] New York: Barnes & Noble, 1968), 165.

37. See J. B. Trapp, 'The "Conformity" of Greek with the Vernacular: The History of a Renaissance Theory of Languages', in J. B. Trapp, *Essays on the Renaissance and the Classical Tradition* (Aldershot: Variorum, 1990), 8–21.

38. George Huppert, *Public Schools in Renaissance France* (Urbana and Chicago: University of Illinois Press, 1984), 127. Roger Zuber, 'France 1640–1790', in Dover, *Perceptions of the Ancient Greeks*, 150.

39. M. L. Clarke, *Greek Studies in England 1700–1830* (Cambridge: Cambridge University Press, 1945), 3. Clarke, who quotes those lines by Crabbe, also describes a connection between medicine and Greek studies in this period.

40. Stray, *Classics Transformed*, 66.

41. Quoted by Eric A. Blackall in the 2nd edn. of *The Emergence of German as a Literary Language* (Ithaca, NY: Cornell University Press, 1978), 10–11. Blackall assembles many expressions in the 18th cent. of the desirability of German imitating Greek: see pp. 143–4, 165, 286, 316–17, 326–7, 361, 425, 457.

42. Stray, *Classics Transformed*, 25–6.

43. Joachim Wohlleben, 'Germany 1750–1830', in Dover, *Perceptions of the Ancient Greeks*.

44. Anthony Grafton, 'Germany and the West 1830–1900', in Dover *Perceptions of the Ancient Greeks*; W. Jens, 'The Classical Tradition in Germany: Grandeur and Decay', *Upheaval and Continuity: A Century of Germany History* (London: Wolff, 1973).

45. J. Mordaunt Crook, *The Greek Revival* ([1972] London: John Murray, 1995); on Romantic hellenism, see Timothy Webb, *English Romantic Hellenism 1700–1824* (New York: Barnes & Noble, 1982) and 'Romantic Hellenism', in Stuart Curran (ed.), *The Cambridge Companion to British Romanticism* (Cambridge: Cambridge University Press, 1993), 148–76, as well as Bernard Herbert Stern, *The Rise of Romantic Hellenism in English Literature, 1732–1786* (Brooklyn, NY: Banta, 1940).

46. R. M. Ogilvie, *Latin and Greek* (London: Routledge & Kegan Paul, 1964), 82–5.

47. Stray, *Classics Transformed, passim*; Gaisford's statement is quoted and discussed on p. 60.

48. On the Victorian domestication of Greece see Richard Jenkyns, *The Victorians and Ancient Greece* (Cambridge, Mass.: Harvard University Press, 1980) and Frank M. Turner, *The Greek Heritage in Victorian Britain* (New Haven: Yale University Press, 1981). On George Grote, the historian who played a key role in that domestication, see M. L. Clarke, *George Grote* (London: Athlone Press, 1962) and A. D. Momigliano, 'George Grote and the Study of Greek History', *Studies in Historiography* (New York: Harper's, 1966).

49. Elizabeth Barrett Browning, *Aurora Leigh*, book 2, ll. 76–7. George Eliot, *Middlemarch*, ch. 7. Besides helping to enforce distinctions among the genders, it also was a way to demarcate class divisions, as observed in Thomas Hardy, *Jude the Obscure* and *A Pair of Blue Eyes*.

50. J. W. Mackail, *Lectures on Greek Poetry* (London: Longman's, 1911), p. xvi; *What is the Good of Greek?* (1923, quoted in Stray, *Classics Transformed*, 288), 6.

51. On this topic, the best work with which I am familiar includes Forster, *Poets' Tongues*; Dorothy Gabe Coleman, *The Gallo-Roman Muse* (Cambridge:

Cambridge University Press, 1979); John Hale, *Milton's Languages* (Cambridge: Cambridge University Press, 1997); and occasional essays in the *Acta Conventus Neo-Latini*.

52. Ann Moss, 'Being in Two Minds: The Bilingual Factor in Renaissance Writing', in Rhoda Schnur (ed.), *Acta Conventus Neo-Latini Hafniensis* (Binghamton, NY: Medieval and Renaissance Text and Studies, 1994), 61–74.

53. I draw on Waquet's discussion of Montaigne, *Latin*, 50–1.

54. I allude to Donald Davidson, 'On the Very Idea of a Conceptual Scheme', *Inquiries into Truth and Interpretation* (Oxford: Clarendon Press, 1984).

55. Forster, *Poets' Tongues*, 19.

56. Geneviève Demerson, 'Joachim Du Bellay traducteur de lui-même', in Grahame Castor and Terence Cave (eds.), *Neo-Latin and the Vernacular in Renaissance France* (Oxford: Clarendon Press, 1984), 113–24; Ellen S. Ginsberg, 'Translation, Imitation, Transformation: Du Bellay as Self-Translator', in Schnur (ed.), *Acta Conventus Neo-Latini Hafniensis*, 429–36; E. Ginsberg, 'Joachim Du Bellay's Latin Poem Patriae desiderium and his Vernacular Poetry', Jean Claude Margolin (ed.), *Acta Conventus Neo-Latini Turonensis* (Paris: J. Vrin, 1980); Yvonne Hoggan, 'Aspects du bilinguisme littéraire chez Du Bellay: Le Traitement poétique des thèmes de l'exil dans les *Poemata* et *Les Regrets*', *Bibliothèque d'Humanisme et Renaissance*, 44 (1982), 65–79.

57. *Œuvres poétiques*, vii. *Œuvres latines: Poemata*, ed. Geneviève Demerson (Paris: Nizet, 1984), 79.

58. There is a large literature on self-translation, especially as concerns Beckett and Nabokov.

59. Forster, *Poets' Tongues*, 65, 69.

60. See Frank Stack, *Pope and Horace* (Cambridge: Cambridge University Press, 1985). Stack takes as the point of departure for his book 'the fact that Pope printed alongside his Imitations of Horace the texts of the original Horatian poems on which they were based' (p. xiii). See too ch. 6 of James McLaverty, *Pope, Print, and Meaning* (Oxford: Oxford University Press, 2001); the quotation appears on p. 157 of McLaverty.

61. Hale, *Milton's Languages*, 19–66.

62. W. Hilton Kelliher, 'The Latin Poetry of George Herbert', in *The Latin Poetry of English Poets*, ed. J. W. Binns (London: Routledge & Kegan Paul, 1974), 48. The dissatisfactions expressed by Herbert H. Huxley with the scholarly and critical literature on Herbert's neo-Latin poems ('The Latin Poems of George Herbert (1593–1633)', in P. Tuynman, G. C. Kuiper, and E. Kessler (eds.), *Acta Conventus Neo-Latini Amstelodamensis* (Munich: W. Fink, 1979), 560–5) have not, to my knowledge, been adequately addressed.

63. See Siegried Wenzel, *Macaronic Sermons* (Ann Arbor: University of Michigan Press, 1994). The edn. of Folengo's *Baldus* by Emilio Faccioli (Turin: Einaudi, 1989) discusses works devoted to Folengo and also to macaronic literature on pp. xli–xliv. The genre is surveyed by Jozef IJsewijn in *Companion to Neo-Latin Studies* (Louvain: Leuven University Press, 1990–8), i. 1 60 and ii. 136–8.

64. 'It is well known that at Caieta Faustina picked her love affairs from among sailors and gladiators', from 'Marcus Antoninus', *Historia Augusta* 19. 7.

65. 'Exhausted by men but not satisfied she withdrew', Juvenal 6. 130.

66. On Gibbon's footnotes, see Anthony Grafton, *The Footnote* (Cambridge, Mass.: Harvard University Press, 1997), 1–4, 97–104 (nothing in *The Decline and Fall of the Roman Empire* 'did more than its footnotes to amuse his friends and enrage his enemies').

67. Contrast Eliot's 'daemonic, chthonic powers' (in 'The Dry Salvages'), a phrase as domesticated as Pound's is foreign.

68. 'A most subtle question, whether a chimera bombinating in the vacuum can consume second intentions.' William Chillingworth, who seems to have invented the angels-on-a-pin question, linked it to Rabelais's question in *The Religion of Protestants: A Safe Way to Salvation* (1638); see *Notes and Queries* (18 Oct. 1890), 314. Voltaire lent fame to the bombinating chimera in his article on 'Authority' in the *Philosophical Dictionary*.

69. *Finnegans Wake*, 281; adaptations of the quotation are found at pp. 14–15, 236, and 615. Ingeborg Landuyt and Geert Lernout (*Joyce Studies Annual*, 6 (1995), 99–138) identified Joyce's immediate source in Léon Metchnikoff's *Les Grandes Fleuves historiques* rather than in Quinet's *Introduction à la philosophie de l'histoire de l'humanité*. Clive Hart gives an inventory of the echoes of Quinet in the *Wake* in his *Structure and Motif in Finnegans Wake*. It is translated and discussed in Richard Ellmann, *James Joyce*, rev. edn. (New York: Oxford University Press, 1982), 664.

70. In a BBC lecture ('The Lost Senecan Voice in English Poetry') delivered on 30 Sept. 1999.

71. Christopher Ricks, *T. S. Eliot and Prejudice* (Berkeley and Los Angeles: University of California Press, 1988), 192.

72. Louis L. Martz, *The Poetry of Meditation* (New Haven: Yale University Press, 1974), 105–8.

73. The sources of Swinburne's Latin titles are given in my edn. of *Poems and Ballads* (London: Penguin, 2000).

74. Gérard Genette, *Paratexts* (Cambridge: Cambridge University Press, 1997), 144–9.

75. From the manuscript description of the 1st edn., with autograph corrections, of Coleridge's *Poems on Various Subjects* in the British Library.

76. Allen Josephs, *For Whom the Bell Tolls: Ernest Hemingway's Undiscovered Country* (New York: Twayne, 1994); 'Appendix: On Language' thoughtfully examines what have been taken as Hemingway's extensive errors in Spanish grammar and idiom.

77. Ch. 2 of the first book of *Hard Times* (entitled 'Murdering the Innocents'), ch. 13 of *Bleak House*, and ch. 11 of *Dombey and Son*.

78. Geoffrey Hughes, *Swearing* (London: Penguin, 1998), 78.

79. Stack, *Pope and Horace*, 235.

80. C. Ricks, *Allusion to the Poets* (Oxford: Oxford University Press, 2002), 153–5.

81. Tom McArthur, 'Foreignism', and Garland Cannon and Tom McArthur, 'Loanword', in Tom McArthur (ed.), *The Oxford Companion to the English Language* (New York: Oxford University Press, 1992).

82. Vol. v., ch. 42.
83. Book viii, l. 7.

CHAPTER TWO: VARIETIES OF LANGUAGE PURISM

1. The examples are Guy Davenport's, from 'Zukofsky's English Catullus', *Maps*, 5. According to C. C. Bombaugh, *Oddities and Curiosities of Words and Literature* (3rd edn., 1890; abridged and reprinted, New York: Dover, 1961), 184, 43% of the words in Johnson's dictionary derive from Latin, 30% from French, 11% from Saxon, and 7% from Greek.

2. Geoffrey Hughes, *A History of English Words* (Oxford: Blackwell, 2000), 97.

3. All the examples are taken from the article 'Bisociation' by Tom McArthur in his *Oxford Companion to English Literature* (New York: Oxford University Press, 1992), 131–2. For extensive lists of such pairs, see John Earle, *English Prose* (London: Smith, Elder, & Co., 1891).

4. Thomas Finkenstaedt, *Ordered Profusion; Studies in Dictionaries and the English Lexicon* (Heidelberg: C. Winter, 1973), 64. However, bear in mind that the doubling of words has a long history in English and is evident in the 'redundancy' of Old English formulaic diction as well as in later medieval and early modern English prose. On the latter, see E. K. Chambers, 'The Continuity of English Prose from Alfred to More and his School', in *Harpsfield's Life of More* (London: Early English Text Society, 1932), cxix: 'During the bilingual period, a writer of English naturally often coupled his English word with a Romance synonym. When English prose reasserts itself there is therefore an inevitable tendency to tautology'.

5. Sylvia Adamson, 'Literary Language', in Roger Lass (ed.), *The Cambridge History of the English Language* (Cambridge: Cambridge University Press, 1999), iii. 574. Subsequently abbreviated as *CHEL*.

6. The topic was exhaustively studied in Jürgen Schäfer, *Shakespeares Stil: Germanisches und Romanisches Vokabular* (Frankfurt a. M.: Athenäum Verlag, 1973). In 'Anhang II', Schäfer lists 'germanische-romanische Synonympaare' in Shakespeare. For instances of one way that Latin and Saxon are combined but not contrasted, see Bryan A. Garner, 'Latin-Saxon Hybrids in Shakespeare and the Bible', in Vivian Salmon and Edwina Burness (eds.), *A Reader in the Language of Shakespearean Drama* (John Benjamins, 1987), 229–34.

7. Geoffrey Hughes, *Swearing* (Harmondsworth: Penguin, 1998), 24.

8. For an overview of the topic, see Tom McArthur, 'English in Tiers', *English Today*, 6/3 (July 1990), 15–20.

9. Peter Rickard, *A History of the French Language* (London: Hutchinson & Co., 1974), 93.

10. Ibid. 101. This was a continuation and intensification of late medieval trends. The quotation by Ronsard appears here.

11. *Essays* (Oxford: Clarendon Press, 1889), i. 119–20. Pattison also insists that the French disgust at pedantry 'prevents French writing from ever rising above the level of good drawing-room conversation'.

12. I summarize Jacques Barzun, *An Essay on French Verse* (New York: New Directions, 1990), 21–2.

13. Wendy Ayres-Bennett, *Vaugelas and the Development of the French Language* (London: MHRA, 1987), 123–32 and 201–28.

14. Sylvia Adamson, 'Literary Language', *CHEL* iii. 617.

15. Ibid. 619.

16. Terttu Nevalainen, 'Early Modern English Lexis and Semantics', *CHEL* iii. 341. See Bryan A. Garner, 'Shakespeare's Latinate Neologisms', in Salmon and Burness (eds.), *A Reader in the Language of Shakespearean Drama* (John Benjamins, 1987), 207–28.

17. Finkelstaedt, *Ordered Profusion*, 47.

18. See Susie I. Tucker, *Protean Shape: A Study in Eighteenth-Century Vocabulary and Usage* (London: Athlone Press, 1967), 39–46, for attacks on latinisms and latinate diction in the second half of the 18th cent.

19. Sylvia Adamson, 'Literary Language', *CHEL* iii. 596.

20. Josephine Miles, *Poetry and Change* (Berkeley: University of California Press, 1974), 107. These new expectations for the adjective were influential first in poetry, and then, later in the 18th cent. and in the early 19th cent., they were true also for prose.

21. Josephine Miles, *Eras and Modes in English Poetry* (Berkeley: University of California Press, 1964), table 2.

22. In *Don Sebastian* (1690), Act 5, Dryden uses the word to describe hell, 'that irremeable burning Gulph'.

23. I summarize and quote from Bruce Redford, 'Hearing Epistolick Voices: Teaching Johnson's Letters' in David R. Anderson and Gwin J. Kolb (eds.), *Approaches to Teaching the Works of Samuel Johnson* (New York: MLA, 1993), 83.

24. W. K. Wimsatt, jun., *Philosophic Words* (New Haven: Yale, 1948), 104–13. By the way, why isn't *marcescent* used more often in a metaphoric sense?

25. Donald Davie, 'The Language of Science and the Language of Literature 1700–1740', reprinted in *Older Masters* (New York: Continuum, 1993).

26. *Lady Alimony* (1659) 'your acrimonious spirit'; Smollett (1751) 'acrimonious expressions' (twice), 'acrimonious remonstrance'; Aaron Hill (1753) 'envy's acrimonious rage'; Richard Glover (1761) 'acrimonious taunt'; Smollett (1762) 'acrimonious remonstrance'; Walter Harte (1767) 'vindictive plaints and acrimonious strains'; David Garrick (1774) 'proud, acrimonious, sarcastic expression'.

27. Donald Davie, *Purity of Diction in English Verse* (1952; reprinted by Penguin, 1992), 6.

28. *Rambler*, 168 (26 Oct. 1751).

29. Pope, note to *Iliad* 11. 668.

30. According to the *OED*, American *ass* in the sense of British *arse* dates from 1860.

31. Hughes, *Swearing*, 3, 20.

32. H. L. Mencken, *The American Language* (New York: Knopf, 1921), 149.

33. Hughes, *Swearing*, 3, 242.

34. I have discussed this at greater length in 'John Dryden: Classical or Neoclassical?', *Translation and Literature*, 10/1 (2001).

35. Hopkins, letter to Bridges (6 Nov. 1887), *Letters of Gerard Manley Hopkins to Robert Bridges* (London and New York: Oxford University Press, 1955), 267–8. Housman, 'The Name and Nature of Poetry', in *Collected Poems and Selected Prose*, ed. Christopher Ricks (London: Penguin, 1988), 359.

36. Addison objects to the homeliness of Milton's 'No fear lest Dinner coole' (*Paradise Lost*, 5. 396) and 'For this we may thank *Adam*' (10. 736) because certain obvious phrases 'contract a Kind of Meanness by passing through the Mouths of the Vulgar'. Discussed and quoted in Sylvia Adamson, 'Literary Language', *CHEL* iii. 617.

37. Sylvia Adamson, 'Literary Language', *CHEL* iii. 615.

38. Paul Auster, *Random House Book of Twentieth-Century French Poetry* (New York: Random House, 1982), pp. xxxi–xxxii.

39. Vernon Rendall, *Wild Flowers in Literature*, is particularly harsh about Pope, whose reference to 'ev'n the wild heath' in *Windsor Forest* 'is the nearest he gets to mentioning a flower in the 434 lines of the poem'. Flowers were thematically central to much 19th-cent. French poetry; see Philip Knight, *Flower Poetics in Nineteenth-Century France* (Oxford: Clarendon Press, 1986).

40. R. S. Thomas, *Selected Prose* (Bridgend: Poetry Wales Press, 1983), 84.

41. See William Empson's essay on the 'double irony' of *Tom Jones*, reprinted in *Fielding*, ed. Ronald Paulson (New York: Prentice-Hall, 1962), 123–45.

42. That is, if Chadwyck-Healey can be trusted. Both grunts had existed for a century in drama before appearing in non-dramatic prose. The *OED* article for *ugh* is unusually inadequate, which dates it from 1765; the vocable had appeared in drama from the mid-17th cent., and represented weeping and grunting as well as coughing.

43. Davie, *Purity of Diction in English Verse*, 68. Geoffrey Hill, 'Style and Faith', *TLS* 4630 (27 Dec. 1991). The phrase 'antepast of heaven' also occurs in Traherne's 'Innocence', which was probably not known to Wesley.

44. Alexander Pope, *Imitations of Horace* (New Haven: Yale, 1961), ed. John Butt, vol. iv, p. xix.

45. Geoffrey Hill, *The Lords of Limit* (Oxford: Oxford University Press, 1984), 78.

46. Manfred Görlach, 'Regional and Social Variations', *CHEL* iii. 479–80. The quotation from Cheke is found in his prefatory letter to Hoby's translation of Castiglione.

47. Quoted in Suzanne Romaine, 'Introduction', *CHEL* iv. 21.

48. Rosemond Tuve, 'Ancients, Modern, and Saxons', *ELH* 6/3 (Sept. 1939), 165–90; see pp. 179–80. See also Richard Foster Jones, *The Triumph of the English Language* (Stanford, Calif.: Stanford University Press, 1953), 214–71.

49. See Tucker, *Protean Shape*, 33–8 and 104–13.

50. *Spectator*, 165 (8 Sept. 1711).

51. Boswell, in year 1763 of the *Life*: 'Why, Sir, his style is not English; the structure of his sentences is French.'

52. See the preface to the *Dictionary*, esp.

53. i. 190–1. Birkbeck Hill edn. of the *Lives*. See also Johnson's comments about

the great excellencies and great faults of Thomas Browne's style: 'His style is, indeed, a tissue of many languages; a mixture of heterogeneous words!' (Boswell, *Life*, 1756). 'A Babylonish Dialect' is a quotation from Samuel Butler, *Hudibras*, canto i, l. 93.

54. Purley and Webster are quoted in A. D. Horgan, *Johnson on Language* (New York: St Martin's Press, 1994), 106.

55. Macaulay, 'Review of Croker's Boswell', published in 1831; in *Works of Lord Macaulay* (London: Longmans Green, 1898), viii. 56–111.

56. C. J. Wells, *German: A Linguistic History to 1945* (Oxford: Oxford University Press, 1985), 394. See esp. Alan Kirkness, *Zur Sprachreinigung im Deutschen 1781–1871* (Tübingen: Narr, 1975).

57. On Murray, see Katharine Maud Elisabeth Murray, *Caught in the Web of Words: James A. H. Murray and the Oxford English Dictionary* (New Haven: Yale, 1977); on Furnivall, see William Benzie, *Dr. F.J. Furnivall: Victorian Scholar Adventure* (Norman, Okla.: Pilgrim, 1983). Two books by Richard Chenevix Trench were particularly influential in popularizing and moralizing philology: *On the Study of Words* (London, 1859) and *English: Past and Present* (London, 1877). See also Cary H. Plotkin, *The Tenth Muse: Victorian Philology and the Genesis of the Poetic Language of Gerard Manley Hopkins* (Carbondale, Ill.: Southern Illinois University Press, 1989).

58. John Hookham Frere, *The Monks and the Giants* (1817), prologue, vi. 6. In *Works* (London, 1874), ii. 220.

59. Sylvia Adamson, 'Literary Language', *CHEL* iv. 609.

60. See Markham L. Peacock, jun., *The Critical Opinions of William Wordsworth* (Baltimore: Johns Hopkins University Press, 1950), 69; David Crystal and Hilary Crystal, *Words on Words* (Chicago: University of Chicago Press, 2000), 11: 19.

61. Knud Sørenson, *Charles Dickens: Linguistic Innovator* (Aarhus: Arkona, 1985).

62. Listed on p. 42 of Anne Carson, 'Translator's Foreword', *Electra* (Oxford: Oxford University Press, 2001).

63. About which T. S. Eliot offers the finest criticism; see *John Dryden* (New York: Holliday, 1932), 30–1. Quoted and discussed in Christopher Ricks, *T. S. Eliot and Prejudice* (Berkeley, University of California, 1988), 159–62.

64. It is no use pointing out that Thomson cut the line when he published the play three years later; or that Shakespeare's Coriolanus cries 'Oh my Mother, Mother: Oh!' The contemporary mockery, Fielding's jab, and Johnson's relish in telling the story have made the line eternally Thomson's.

65. Herbert Spencer, *The Philosophy of Style* (Boston, 1892), 4.

66. Jones, *Triumph*, 237–40.

67. George Gascogine, *Certayne Notes of Instruction* (1575), in G. Gregory Smith (ed.), *Elizabethan Critical Essays* (Oxford, 1904), i. 51; George Puttenham, *The Arte of English Poesie* (1589) in *Elizabethan Critical Essays*, ii. 80, 83, and 129; Roger Ascham, *The Scolemaster* (1570), in *Elizabethan Critical Essays*, i. 30; William Webbe, *A Discourse of English Poetrie* (1586), in *Elizabethan Critical Essays*, i. 281; King James VI, *Ane Schort Treatise* (1584), in *Elizabethan Critical Essays*, i. 215; William

Camden, *Remaines Concerning Britain* (1605), in *The English Language*, ed. W. F. Bolton (Cambridge: Cambridge University Press, 1973), i. 63; Thomas Campion, *Observations in the Art of English Poesie* (1602) in *Elizabethan Critical Essays*, ii. 333.

68. C. S. Lewis's description of Campion, in *English Literature in the Sixteenth Century Excluding Drama* (Oxford: Oxford University Press, 1954), 365.

69. Letter to Cromwell, 25 Nov. 1710. A few years before, Pope had expressed the same sentiment, but allowed for greater versatility: '*Monosyllable-Lines*, unless very artfully managed, are stiff, or languishing: but may be beautiful to express Melancholy, Slowness, or Labour', letter to Walsh, 22 Oct. 1706.

70. 'On the Poems of Lydgate', *Works*, ed. Edmund Gosse (London: Macmillan, 1884), i. 396.

71. This is the conclusion of Calvin S. Brown, 'Monosyllables in English Verse', *SEL* 3 (1963), 473–91, from whom I have taken several examples and all the statistics.

72. Gascoigne, in *Elizabethan Critical Essays*, i. 51; Puttenham, in *Elizabethan Critical Essays*, i. 83; Thomas Nashe, *Summers Last Will and Testament* (1600), l. 675; Richard Carew, in *Elizabethan Critical Essays*, ii. 288; William Camden, in *The English Language*, i. 63. For debates on quantity, see Richard Helgerson, *Forms of Nationhood* (Chicago: University of Chicago, 1992).

73. Dryden, 'Discourse of Satire', in *Works* (Berkeley, Calif.: University of California Press, 1974), iv. 88; Swift, *Tatler*, 230 (28 Sept. 1710).

74. Mrs Lovechild, *Fables in Monosyllables* (1790) was perhaps the first such influential book for children, followed by Mrs Barbauld, *Easy Lessons for Children* (1810), E. S., *Short Stories in Words of One Syllable* (1822), and adaptations of *Robinson Crusoe* and *Gulliver's Travels* into 'words of one syllable' by the indefatigable Lucy Aitken (under the pseudonym Mary Godolphin).

75. Spencer, *Philosophy of Style*, 5.

76. 'On Wordsworth's Poetry', *Tait's Magazine* (1845).

77. G. K. Chesterton, *The Victorian Age in Literature* (New York: Holt, 1913), 94.

78. See n. 74. Occasionally monosyllabic sermons would be published in the 19th cent.; see J. Gill, 'A Sermon in words of one syllable only by a Manchester layman' (1860) and Henry C. Leonard, 'Great truths in small words: "God is love". A sermon in words of one syllable' (1870). A poem 'Monosyllabics' consisting of two sonnets was published in *Princeton Magazine* and signed by B. Short in 1850; the first sonnet was reprinted anonymously in *Eclectic Magazine* in 1862 under the title 'Beauty of Words with One Syllable'; reprinted without a title and attributed to Dr J. Addison Alexander in Alfred H. Welsh, *Development of English Literature and Language* (1888); both sonnets were printed by C. C. Bombaugh in *Gleanings for the Curious from the Harvest Fields of Literature* under the title 'The Power of Short Words'.

79. Bodleian Library MS Tanner 169, fo. 79ʳ; facs. in R. S. M. Hirsh, 'The Works of Chidiock Tichborne', *English Literary Renaissance*, 16 (1986), 309–10; first printed in *Verses of Prayse and Joye* (1586).

80. Aurel Stein, *The House of Death* (Baltimore: Johns Hopkins University Press, 1986), 75–83.

81. William Loe, *The Songs of Sion*, in *Miscellanies of The Fuller Worthies' Library*, ed. Alexander Grosart, 1870.

CHAPTER THREE: THE INTERFERENCE OF LATIN WITH ENGLISH
LITERATURE

1. Ezra Pound's definition, in 'Marianne Moore and Mina Loy' (1918), *Selected Prose: 1909–65* (New York: New Directions, [1950] 1973), 424.

2. 'Epilogue to the Satires', ll. 73–4.

3. Recall Bishop Thomas Sprat's famous praise of the 'close, naked, natural way of speaking, positive expressions, clear senses, a *native* easiness' in his history of the Royal Society (my emphasis). Sprat, *History of the Royal Society*, ed. J. I. Cope and H. W. Jones (St Louis: Washington University Press, 1959), 113.

4. *Letters of Gerard Manley Hopkins to Robert Bridges* (London and New York: Oxford University Press, 1955), 267–8. Donald Davie, *Purity of Diction in English Verse* ([1952] London: Penguin, 1992), 150.

5. Letter to Boehlendorff on 4 Dec. 1801.

6. Uriel Weinreich, *Languages in Contact* ([1953] The Hague: Mouton, 1967), 1. Weinreich offers an extensive discussion of the linguistic and social reasons why phonic, grammatical, and lexical interference may be promoted or resisted. However, neither literary examples nor written ones formed part of his discussion; he was interested in interference in speech (the result of an individual speaker's knowledge and performance) and not interference in language (in which it has become stable or even normative, the result of the frequent production of interference by speakers): 'In speech, interference is like sand carried by a stream; in language, it is the sedimented sand deposited on the bottom of a lake' (ibid. 11). See, too, 'The Concept of Interference', in Ilse Lehiste, *Lectures on Language Contact* (Cambridge, Mass.: MIT Press, 1988), 1–27.

7. I follow in the footsteps of D. S. Carne-Ross, especially his article 'Jocasta's Divine Head: English with a Foreign Accent', *Arion*, 3rd ser., 1/1 (1989), 106–41.

8. *Lives of the Poets*, ed. Birkbeck Hill (Oxford: Clarendon Press, 1905), i. 190. (The 'Babylonish Dialect' alludes to Samuel Butler, *Hudibras*, 1. 1. 93.) See further on that page: 'Such is the power of his poetry that his call is obeyed without resistance, the reader feels himself in captivity to a higher and a nobler mind, and criticism sinks in admiration'.

9. Such writing by no means always imitates classical models. Keats identified two specimens of 'very extraordinary beauty' that are unique to Milton's particular genius: 'which cost Ceres all that pain' (4. 271) and 'Nor could the Muse defend Her son' (7. 37–8); neither instance of contained grief invokes foreign expressions.

10. Discussed at greater length in my 'Milton's Language, Milton's Languages', *Literary Imagination*, 2/1 (Winter 2000), 93–100.

11. See ' Milton I' (1936) and 'Milton II' (1947) in *On Poetry and Poets* (New York: Farrar, Straus & Cudahy: 1957), 161–2 and 178–9.
12. Joyce's difficult style also eased the book past its censors. My reading of *Finnegans Wake* follows Guy Davenport, 'Ariadne's Dancing Floor', *Every Force Evolves a Form* (San Francisco: North Point Press, 1987), 53–63.
13. Jed Rasula and Steve McCaffery (eds.), *Imagining Language* (Cambridge, Mass.: MIT Press, 1998), p. x; E. H. Gombrich, *Art and Illusion* (New York: Pantheon Books, 1960); Michel Serres, *Hermes: Literature, Science, Philosophy* (Baltimore: Johns Hopkins University Press, 1982), tr. Josué V. Harari and David F. Bell; Martin Heidegger, 'Why Poets?', *Off the Beaten Track* (Cambridge: Cambridge University Press, 2002), tr. Julian Young and Kenneth Haynes.
14. David Norton, *A History of the English Bible as Literature* (Cambridge: Cambridge University Press, 2000), 45 n. 12; Ronald A. Knox, *On Englishing the Bible* (London: Burns Oates, 1949), 44.
15. Norton, *History of English Bible*, 26, 28.
16. Knox (*Englishing*, 47) believes that the reason why the Catholic Bible, even after it was extensively revised by Challoner, sounds 'barbarous and exotic' to Protestants is that the King James version 'won' in a country 'with a totalitarian prose tradition'.
17. James G. Carleton, *The Part of Rheims in the Making of the English Bible* (Oxford: Clarendon Press, 1902).
18. Preface to the King James Bible (1611). The Rheims translation gave rise to a wide polemic, recently studied by Ellie Gebarowski-Shafer in her master's thesis under the auspices of the Editorial Institute at Boston University, *The Rheims New Testament Controversy: Biblical Annotation and Polemics in Elizabethan England* (2002). The most influential figures in the dispute were Gregory Martin and William Fulke, on whom see Norton, *History of English Bible*, 49–52.
19. Preface to the 'Rheims' New Testament.
20. Norton lists a half-dozen opponents of the Rheims translation who supplied different lists of unacceptable terms; see *History of English Bible*, 46 n. 13 and 51.
21. See the index to McKerrow's edn. of Nashe's works under 'fustian', 'inkhorn', and 'gallimafrey', and Nashe, *Works*, i. 316 (*Foure Letters Confuted*) for a list of inkhorn terms in Harvey. For Harvey's list, see *Pierces Supererogation* in Gabriel Harvey, *Works*, ed. Alexander B. Grosart ([1884] New York: AMS Press, 1966), ii. 265. See also the index of Nashe's *Works* for 'pedantism'. For a description of Harvey's humanism in action, see Lisa Jardine and Anthony Grafton, ' "Studied for Action": How Gabriel Harvey Read his Livy', *Past and Present*, 129 (1990), 30–78.
22. Nashe, *Works*, i. 270 (*Foure Letters Confuted*).
23. Harvey, *Works*, ii. 265 (*Peirces Supererogation*).
24. Nashe, *Works*, iii. 90–1 (*Have with You to Saffron-Walden*).
25. McKerrow's defense of Harvey's Third Letter: 'If we can tolerate the strange jargon in which, like almost everything else of [Harvey's], it is written, we shall find it to contain a great deal of sound sense. *Works*, v. 85.
26. Nashe, *Works*, iii. 78 and 80 (*Have with You to Saffron-Walden*).

27. Harvey, *Works*, ii. p. 275, 265 (*Peirces Supererogation*).

28. Early in his career, Nashe admired 'the man whose extemporall veine in any humour will excell our greatest Art-maisters deliberate thoughts' (*Works*, iii. 312); in *Have with You to Saffron-Walden*, he boasted that we would be able to give 'suddaine extemporall answeres' to the 'Paraliticke Quacksaluer'.

29. See 'An ynkehorne letter' in Thomas Wilson, *The Arte of Rhetorique* (1553); it is printed on pp. 327–8 in the edn. by Thomas J. Derrick (New York and London: Garland, 1982). In 1589, George Puttenham discussed inkhorn terms in *The Arte of English Poesie*; see p. 145 of the edn. by Gladys Doidge Willcock and Alice Walker (Cambridge: Cambridge University Press, 1936), who discuss the controversy over such terms on pp. xci–xcii of their introduction. The controversialists could draw on the example of Erasmus' *Praise of Folly* (409A).

30. The *OED*'s first citation for *posteriors* in the sense of *buttocks* is dated 1619; however, the 1592 tragedy *Solyman and Perseda* has the line 'And with his pointed dart prickt my posteriors.'

31. *Letters of Thomas Carlyle to Mill, Sterling and Browning* ([1923] New York: Haskell House, 1970), 191–2 (letter dated 4 June 1835).

32. John Holloway, *The Victorian Sage* ([1953] New York: Norton, 1965), 69–70.

33. Discussed by D. S. Carne-Ross in 'Jocasta's Divine Head'.

34. See Ronald Bush, 'A Great Digest', *Essays in Criticism*, 49/2 (April 1999), 190–2.

35. Mary Paterson Cheadle, *Ezra Pound's Confucian Translations* (Ann Arbor: University of Michigan Press, 1997), 197–8.

36. D. M. MacKinnon, *The Problem of Metaphysics* (Cambridge: Cambridge University Press, 1974), 167–8.

37. Jaroslav Pelikan, 'Pernicious Amnesia: Combating the Epidemic', Jacques Barzun Award Lecture, 8 Nov. 1997, p. 6.

38. Christopher De Hamel, *A History of Illuminated Manuscripts* (London: Phaidon, [1986] 1994), 165.

39. 'The Spanish original was, by our standards, an impudent forgery, purporting to be a contemporary life of the great emperor discovered in Cosimo de Medici's library: the real Meditations being then, and till 1539, safely unknown', C. S. Lewis, *English Literature in the Sixteenth Century Excluding Drama* (Oxford: Clarendon Press, 1954), 150, where the remark about the sentences and the style is also quoted.

40. The *OED* article on *who* conflates English and Latin usages in a way similar to that of the article on *there*. Subsection 8(a) is devoted to instances where the pronoun is used 'as compound relative in the nominative, of persons (less freq. a person): The persons (or person) that'. The expression is called archaic, and it is further explained that it is 'chiefly a latinism; esp. in 'There are who . . .' = L. *Sunt qui . . .*' In the early quotations, from 1596 to 1605, *who* is used to mean *he who*. One example comes from *Macbeth*: *Who was the Thane, liues yet*. Yet why should we call it a latinism? Especially when there are so few latinisms in Shakespeare's syntax? See E. A. Abbot, *A Shakesperian Grammar*. (New York: Dover, 1966 [1870]), 304–6.

41. *Tudor to Augustan English* (London: Deutsch, 1969), 54.
42. It occurs at least twice in the works of major novelists after 1700: in ch. 15 of vol. v of Sterne's *Tristram Shandy*, where the hero praises the power of music and incidentally declines *there are who* in the three English cases ('there is—whom I could sit and hear whole days,—whose talents lie in making what he fiddles to be felt,—who inspires me with his joys and hopes'); and in the epigraph to ch. 38 of Eliot's *Daniel Deronda*.
43. Shakespeare has recourse to it in *Henry VIII*, in the first scene of Act 5:

> *Louell*: . . . Th' Archbyshop
> Is the Kings hand, and tongue, and who dare speak
> One syllable against him?
> *Gard*. Yes, yes, Sir *Thomas*,
> There are that Dare . . .

In contrast, *there are that* in Fanshawe's translation from Petronius (l. 246), Grainger's translation from Tibullus (1. 1. 122), and Yalden's translation of Ovid's *Art of Love* (2. 459) sounds a Latin note. I note it also in Vaughan's 'The Proffer' (l. 37) and Philips's *Cyder* (2. 287); but not subsequently.
44. Heywood: *The Art of Loue*, 3. 365. Sandys: *Metamorphosis*, 8. 833. Dryden: 'Of the Pythagorean Philosophy', l. 574; *Ovid's Art of Love: Book I*, l. 806; 'The Sixth Satyr of Juvenal', l. 483; *Æneis*, 5. 478, 7. 561, 9. 58.
45. Before Milton, the phrase is rare. In the 1607 edn. of *Certaine Smalle Workes* (1607), Samuel Daniel includes the 'Funerall Poeme upon the Earle of Devonshire', with the line 'There were, who did aduise him . . .' George Sandys includes a commendatory poem at the beginning of his translation of Ovid's *Metamorphoses* (1632), 'Urania to the Queen', which has 'There be who our Delights despise . . .' In 1656, Abraham Cowley published a Pindaric ode to Dr Scarborough, who is contrasted in it with another kind of physician: 'There are who all their *Patients* chagrin have . . .'
46. In Latin, 'think not God' is not uncommon; see e.g. Seneca, *Epistle* 95 ('Primus deorum cultus est deos credere'; there is a closer parallel in Greek, Plato's *Laws* 885c (ἡμῶν οἱ μὲν τὸ παράπαν θεοὺς οὐδαμῶς νομίζομεν, 'some of us do not believe in [think] gods at all').
47. Before Pope, Oldisworth makes use of the phrase in his translation of *Odes* 1. 1 (1719). After Pope, it becomes almost de rigueur: it is found in Philip Francis, in one of the most popular (and best) translations of Horace; Duncombe; Smart; and others.
48. In 1840 Wordsworth wrote that he 'never read a word of German metaphysics, thank Heaven' (letter to Robinson, 16 Mar.; *Letters*, iv. 49); still, Coleridge was intently theorizing about duty around this time (see e.g. n. 3026 from 1807 in the *Notebooks*).
49. See Christopher Ricks, 'George Crabbe's Thoughts of Confinement', *Essays in Appreciation* (Oxford: Clarendon Press, 1996), 67–89.
50. David Crystal, *Language Play* (London: Penguin, 1998).
51. As in Raymond Queneau's *Exercises de style* (1947), 'Hellénismes': 'Dans un hyperautobus plein de pétrolonautes . . .'

CHAPTER FOUR: SOME GREEK INFLUENCES ON ENGLISH POETRY

1. See D. S. Carne-Ross, 'Jocasta's Divine Head: English with a Foreign Accent', *Arion*, 3rd ser., 1/1 (Winter 1990), 117–20; F. T. Prince, *The Italian Element in Milton's Verse* (Oxford: Clarendon Press, 1954), 145–68; and John Hale, *Milton's Language: The Impact of Multilingualism on Style* (Cambridge: Cambridge University Press, 1997), 180–93.

2. For an overview of the morphology of adjective compounds, see Randolph Quirk (ed.), *A Comprehensive Grammar of the English Language* (Harlow: Longman, 1985), 1576–8. Compound words may be hyphenated, combined as a single word, or printed as two words with no hyphen; see the 'General Explanations' at the head of the *OED*: 'not only is the use of the hyphen a matter of indifference in an immense number of cases, but in many where it is habitually used, the combination implies no unity of signification; while others, in which there is a distinct unity or specialization of meaning, are not hyphenated'. Poets themselves sometimes adopt inconsistent practices. Tennyson e.g. in his early verse combined words without hyphens, but came to change his mind about the practice: 'I had an idiotic hatred of hyphens in those days', he subsequently wrote (quoted in the headnote to 'Œnone' in *Tennyson: A Selected Edition*, ed. Christopher Ricks (Berkeley and Los Angeles: University of California Press, 1898), 36. Christopher Ricks discusses hyphens in Geoffrey Hill's poetry, attending also to them in Coleridge, Tennyson, Dickinson, and Eliot, in *The Force of Poetry* (Oxford and New York: Oxford University Press, 1987), 326–55.

3. The φυσίζοος αἶα (*Iliad* 3. 243), which inspired Ruskin's eloquence in *Modern Painters*.

4. The letter (to Johann von Botzheim) was published in 1523 as *Catalogus omnium Erasmi Roterodami lucubrationum*; it was later expanded and revised. It is translated in *Collected Works of Erasmus* (Toronto: Toronto University Press, 1974–), ix. 293–64.

5. See book ii, ch. 6, of the *Deffence*; and the 'Épitre-Préface' to his translation of books 4 and 6 of the *Aeneid* (*Œuvre poétiques*, ed. Henri Chamard, vi/2, 'Traductions', 251–2).

6. '. . . pourueu qu'ils soyent gratieux & plaisans à l'oreille'. *Œuvres complètes*, ed. Paul Lamonier (Paris: Marcel Didier, 1949), xiv. 31.

7. *La Précellence du langage françoise*, 152–65. On p. 163, he urges French poets to use discretion in using these epithets, to 'sow with the hand, not with the whole sack' (quoting the Greek of Corinna).

8. Marc-Antoine de Muret, *Commentaires au Premier Livre des Amours de Ronsard*, ed. Jacques Chomarat, Marie-Madeleine Fragonard, and Gisèle Mathieu-Castellani ([1553] Geneva: Librairie Droz, 1985). See also 'Aime-laine, aime-fil, aime-estain' from Ronsard's 'La Quenoille' (1559); 'chasse-peine, | Donne-vie, oste-soin' from 'Hynne de l'or' (1556); etc. In the *Abbregé* (1565), Ronsard advised poets to avoid using more than two epithets of any sort, except for rare occasions of *gaillardise* (*Œuvres complètes*, xiv. 18).

9. *Abbregé: Œuvres complètes*, xiv. 17. See Paul Laumonier, *Ronsard poète lyrique* (Paris: Hachette, 1923), 325–7 ('Les épithètes'); and, in general,

Isidore Silver, *Ronsard and the Hellenic Renaissance in France* (St Louis: Washington University, 1961). The use of compound words by the poets of the Pléiade is discussed by Henri Chamard, *Histoire de la Pléiade* (Paris: Henri Didier, 1939), iv. 69–74; he notes on p. 72 several instances where Ronsard removed compound epithets when he revised his poems. The compound words of the Pléiade are listed in Charles Marty-Laveaux, *La Pléiade françoise* ([1896] Geneva: Slatkine Reprints, 1966), ii. 253–340.

10. Josuah Sylvester balks at transmitting Du Bartas's compounds: 'The nimble, flaming, bright, light, heat-full Fire, | Fountaine of Life . . .' and 'All haile faire Earth, bearer of Townes and Towers, | Of Men, Gold, Graine, Phisike, and Fruites, & Flowers.'

11. *Babilon, A Part of the Seconde Weeke of Gvillavme de Salvste Seignevr dv Bartas, with the Commentarie, and Marginall Notes of S. G. S.* (London, 1595).

12. Veré L. Rubel briefly discusses Grimald's effectiveness in forming compounds in *Poetic Diction in the English Renaissance* (New York: MLA, 1941), 86; though Rubel notes that most of his compounds are Saxon, Niilo Peltola identifies a number of compounds which Grimald translated from classical sources (*The Compound Epithet and its Use in American Poetry from Bradstreet through Whitman* (Helsinki: Suomalaisen Tiedeakatemian toimituksia, 1956), 35.

13. A. H. Upham, *French Influence in English Literature* (New York: Octago, 1909), lists translations from 1584 to 1641. Sidney's translation of Du Bartas is lost.

14. Aristotle, *Rhetoric* 3. 5 and 7 (1406^{a-b} and 1408^{b}).

15. Sidney, *Astrophel and Stella*, i. 8, C. 11, Seventh Song 17; Spenser, *The Fairie Queene*: 2. 7. 22. 3, 4. 5. 45. 1, 5. 4. 47. 1; Shakespeare, *King Lear*, 4. 1, 4. 3, 5. 3 (First Quarto).

16. In distinguishing between enargeia and energia, Puttenham divides poetical ornaments into two sorts: the first 'to satisfy & delight th'eare onely by a goodly outward shew set vpon the matter with wordes, and speaches smothly and tunably running', a quality the Greeks call enargeia, 'of this word *argos*, because it geueth a glorious lustre and light'; the second, 'by certaine intendments or sence of such words & speaches inwardly working a stirre to the mynde', which the Greeks called energeia, 'of *ergon*, because it wrought a strong and vertuous operation' (*The Arte of English Poesie*, ch. 3 of book iii).

17. Sidney, *Astrophel and Stella*: LXXV. 10 and XCIX. 10; Spenser, *The Fairie Queen*: 2. 12. 23. 6; Shakespeare, *Venus and Adonis*, 697, 703. Keats' reaction to Spenser is recalled by Charles Cowden Clarke: see Hyder Edward Rollins, ed., *The Keats Circle* (Cambridge, Mass.: Harvard University Press, 1948), ii. 149. *Sea-shouldring Whales* is not typical of Spenser's compound epithets, which are more often 'rather tame and colorless' (Frederick M. Padelford and William C. Maxwell, 'The Compound Words in Spenser's Poetry', *JEGP* 25 (1926), 509). On compound epithets generally, see Bernard Groom, *The Formation and Use of Compound Epithets in English Poetry from 1579* (Oxford: Clarendon Press, 1937), from whom I have taken some examples.

18. Padelford and Maxwell, 'Compound Words', 510–13, discuss the relation of Spenser's compound epithets to Greek.

19. See Peltola, *Compound Epithet*, 36: 'There was a marked contrast in the relationship of the English and French authors to the classics as the original source of compound epithets. A large proportion of those in the poetry of the Pléiade and Du Bartas can be traced back to classical models, while in English poetry instances of perfect agreement are infrequent.'

20. *The Poems of Alexander Pope*, vii. *The Iliad of Homer, Books I–IX*, ed. Maynard Mack (New Haven: Yale University Press, 1967), 10. See also pp. lxvii–lxviii.

21. *Réflexions critiques sur quelques passages du rheteur Longin*, IX; see *Œuvres complètes*, ed. Françoise Escal (Paris: Gallimard, 1966), 535. This occupied the first phase of the 'quarrel of the ancients and the moderns'; see Charles Perrault, *Parallèle des anciens et des modernes en ce qui regarde les arts et les sciences* (1692), iii. 59.

22. Milman Parry, *The Making of Homeric Verse*, ed. Adam Parry (Oxford: Clarendon Press, 1971).

23. *Complete Prose Works of John Milton*, i. ed. Don M. Wolfe (New Haven: Yale University Press, 1953), 891–92 (*An Apology for Smectymnuus*).

24. Samuel Johnson, *Lives of the English Poets*, ed. G. Birkbeck Hill (Oxford: Clarendon Press, 1905), i. 168.

25. Archie Burnett, 'Compound Words in Milton's English Poetry', *Modern Language Review*, 75/3 (July 1980). 499.

26. Ibid. 505.

27. See e.g. Kathy Eden, *Friends Hold All Things in Common* (New Haven: Yale University Press, 2002), 18–19.

28. Coleridge, *Biographia Literaria*, ed. James Engell and W. Jackson Bate (Princeton: Princeton University Press, 1983), 6–7.

29. *Essays of John Dryden*, ed. W. P. Ker (Oxford: Clarendon Press, 1900), i. 189 and 315; *Boswell's Life of Johnson*, i. 421. See also Johnson's objection that Gray was 'too fond of words arbitrarily compounded', *Johnson's Lives of the Poets*, ed. George Birkbeck Hill (Oxford: Clarendon Press, 1905), iii. 437.

30. I draw on J. W. Mackail, 'Collins, and the English Lyric in the Eighteenth Century', *Essays by Divers Hands*, NS 1, 1921 (Liechtenstein: Kraus Reprint, 1974), 18–19. See, too, Thomas Quayle, 'Compound Epithets in Eighteenth Century Poetry', in his *Poetic Diction: A Study of Eighteenth Century Verse* (London: Methuen & Co., 1924), 102–81.

31. B. W. A. Massey, *The Compound Epithets of Shelley and Keats* (Poznań: Poznańskie towarzystwo przyjaciol nauk, 1923), 98, 103.

32. Thomas Taylor, *Selected Writings*, ed. Kathleen Raine and George Mills Harper (London: Routledge & Kegan Paul, 1969), 165.

33. Massey counted 134 of them, *Compound Epithets*, 95.

34. Shelley translates ταννσίπτερον, the epithet of the moon in the first line of the Homeric hymn to the moon, as 'wide-wingèd' (he also mistranslates δοριπετῆ φόνον in *Cyclops* 305, as 'weapon-wingèd murder' in l. 294 of his version).

35. Compare e.g. the 'bee-pasturing isle' of *Hellas* 170 with Euripides, *Trojan*

Women 799: μελισσοτρόφου Σαλαμῖνος. See the list in Massey, *Compound Epithets*, 48–52. Contemporary reviewers noted the profusion of compound epithets and compared them to Greek practice; see James E. Barcus (ed.), *Shelley: The Critical Heritage* (London: Routledge & Kegan Paul, 1975), 231, 244. Reviewers were divided as to whether Shelley possessed a talent for manufacturing 'villianous compounds' or for felicitously compounding them.

36. Discussed as a still life in Guy Davenport, *Objects on a Table* (Washington, DC: Counterpoint, 1998), 95–101.

37. The epithet derives some of its power through its closeness to the Homeric 'far-famed', which occurs half a dozen times in Cowper's translation of the *Iliad* and the *Odyssey*.

38. 'Azure-lidded sleep', 'Eve of St. Agnes', 262; 'far-foamed sands', *Hyperion*, book ii, 172; 'soft-conched ear', 'Ode to Psyche', 4; 'cirque-couchant', *Lamia*, part 1, l. 46. See Christopher Ricks, *Keats and Embarrassment* (Oxford: Clarendon Press, 1984), 115–42 ('Taste and Distaste'). See, in general, David Watson Rannie, 'Keats's Epithets', *Essays and Studies*, iii, ed. by W. P. Ker (Oxford: Clarendon Press, 1912), 92–113.

39. George H. Ford, *Keats and the Victorians* (London: Archon Books, 1962), 40. See too Groom, *Formation*, 314.

40. John Ruskin, *Works*, ed. E. T. Cook and Alexander Wedderburn (London: Allen, 1903–12), vii. 107–8 ('Modern Painters').

41. In April 1818, Keats was planning to learn Greek, but by Sept. 1819 had abandoned the ambition. See Keats, *Letters*, ed. Hyder Edward Rollins (Cambridge, Mass.: Harvard University Press, 1958), i. 274 and ii. 212.

42. Simon Goldhill, *Who Needs Greek?* (Cambridge: Cambridge University Press, 2002), 186.

43. Charles Cowden Clarke's phrase from 'A few memoranda of the early life of John Keats', in *The Keats Circle: Letters and Papers 1816–1878*, ed. Hyder Edward Rollins (Cambridge, Mass.: Harvard University Press, 1948), 147.

44. Massey, *Compound Epithets*, 198–200, gives Greek parallels to Keats's compound epithets and on 232–4 lists all the compound epithets used with Greek figures of myth.

45. Ruskin, *Works*, xix. 309 ('The Queen of the Air').

46. Groom, *Formation*, 312: 'But among his compound epithets there are several which owe their charm to a power of myth suggestion. There is clearly the gem of a myth in such descriptive phrases as "tress-lifting waves", "chilly-finger'd spring", "Hush'd cool-rooted flowers, fragrant-eyed" . . . Such phrases give glimpses into the very core of Keats's imaginative life. They offer the clearest parallel in our literature to the embedded mythology in the diction of Homer.'

47. William Sharp, *The Life and Letters of Joseph Severn* (London, 1892), 29.

48. Douglas Bush, *Mythology and the Romantic Tradition in English Poetry* (Cambridge, Mass.: Harvard University Press, 1937), 112.

49. Helen Vendler, *The Odes of John Keats* (Cambridge, Mass.: Harvard University Press, 1983), 50–1.

50. Wilfred P. Mustard, *Classical Echoes in Tennyson* ([1904] New York: Haskell House, 1971); Theodore Redpath, 'Tennyson and the Literature of

Greece and Rome', in Hallam Tennyson (ed.), *Studies in Tennyson* (Totowa, NJ: Barnes & Noble, 1981), 105–30.

51. George Steiner discusses a line of the translation and points to the effective power of a phrase which might be read as a compound (since compounds are not necessarily hyphenated): 'But he was athlete to me—huge, grace breathing', Cassandra cries, recalling her rape by Apollo; Browning recreates both the violence and the mystery of the event; see *After Babel* (Oxford: Oxford University Press, 1975), 314–15. There are not many such instances. Browning's compound epithets and their relation to Greek are studied in B. W. A. Massey, *Browning's Vocabulary: Compound Epithets* (Poznań: Poznańskie towarzystwo przyjaciol nauk, 1931).

52. 'One way of salvaging its beauty is to treat the mythology allegorically; so treated, it "gives rise to the most beautiful results."' See the letter to R. W. Dixon on 23 Oct. 1886 in *The Correspondence of Gerard Manley Hopkins and Richard Watson Dixon*, ed. Claude Colleer Abbot (London: Oxford University Press, 1970), 145–7. Compare the letter to Robert Bridges on 17 May 1885, *The Letters of Gerard Manley Hopkins to Robert Bridges*, ed. Claude Colleer Abbot (London and New York: Oxford University Press, 1955), 216–17.

53. *Letters to Bridges* (22 Oct. 1879), 95.

54. *Further Letters of Gerard Manley Hopkins*, ed. Claude Colleer Abbott, 2nd edn. (London: Oxford University Press, 1956), 306–7 (letter to Patmore, 24 Sept. 1883) and 381–2 (letter to Patmore, 20 Oct. 1887).

55. 'Dun Scotus' Oxford' gives a nostalgic evocation of an idealized Middle Ages. The agglutinative force of the five consecutive compound epithets, each meant to be charming, not vehement—'Cuckoo-echoing, bell-swarmèd, lark-charmèd, rook-racked, river-rounded'—introduce an energy which the sonnet does not absorb or direct.

56. On the death-bed in Victorian literature, see Michael Wheeler, *Death and the Future Life in Victorian Literature and Theology* (Cambridge: Cambridge University Press, 1990), 28–47. On the Victorian experience of death, see J. S. Curl, *The Victorian Celebration of Death* (Detroit: Partridge Press, 1972); Geoffrey Rowell, *Hell and the Victorians* (Oxford: Clarendon Press, 1974); and Patricia Jalland, *Death in the Victorian Family* (New York: Oxford University Press, 1996), esp. ch. 2, 'Revival and Decline of the Good Christian Death'. Finally, see the chapter on death by Gerhard Joseph and Herbert F. Tucker in Herbert F. Tucker, ed., *A Companion to Victorian Literature and Culture* (Malden, Mass.: Blackwell, 1999), 110–24. Hopkins parodied the clichés of Robert Bridges, 'On a Dead Child', in *Letters to Bridges* (26 Jan. 1881), 122.

57. For an overview of negative composition in Greek, see A. C. Moorhouse, *Studies in the Greek Negatives* (Cardiff: University of Wales Press, 1959), 47–68.

58. See e.g. the comment by Simon Pulleyn on *Iliad* 1. 316 in his *Iliad: Book One* (New York: Oxford University Press, 2000).

59. That is, he would have had it in mind as a linguistic form, not a semantic equivalent. 'Unpastured' probably means 'unfed', despite the fact that the *OED* and generations of readers have taken it to mean 'not used as pasture'.

A few lines before this one, Ocean tells Apollo that 'the loud deep calls me home even now to feed it | With azure calm'. Timothy Webb points out that 'unpastured' means 'unfed' in *Adonais* 238 and that Shelley thought the system of pasturage was wasteful (his views are summarized by Kelvin Everest and Geoffrey Matthews in their edn. of Shelley).

60. For discussion and examples of these in Greek tragedy, see Fraenkel's commentary to Aeschylus, *Agamemnon* 1142 and Barrett's commentary to Euripides, *Hippolytus* 1144. This kind of oxymoron was not restricted to poetic diction in the 19th century but appeared as well in essays and novels. In his essay 'Detached Thoughts on Books and Reading' (*Last Essays of Elia*, 1833) Charles Lamb refers to '*books which are no books—biblia a-biblia*'; George Gissing echoes Lamb in *New Grub Street* (1891) in ch. 23, 'books that are no books—*biblia abiblia*'; and in the essay 'Books within Books' (1914), Max Beerbohm too takes over the phrase.

61. *Paradise Lost*, 2. 185 ('Unrespited, unpitied, unrepreevd'), 3. 231 ('unprevented, unimplor'd, unsought'), 5. 898–9 ('unmov'd | Unshak'n, unseduc'd, unterrifi'd'); *Paradise Regained*, 3. 429 ('Unhumbl'd, unrepentant, unreform'd'); and *Samson Agonistes* 1424 ('dishonourable, impure, unworthy').

62. Sophocles, *Antigone* 1071: ἄμοιρον, ἀκτέριστον, ἀνόσιον νέκυν; Euripides, *Iphigenia in Tauris* 220: ἄγαμος, ἄτεκνος, ἄπολις, ἄφιλος; Euripides, *Hecuba* 669: ἄπαις, ἄνανδρος, ἄπολις.

63. Walter MacKellar, the editor of the Variorum Commentary on *Paradise Regained* (New York: Columbia University Press, 1975), adds two examples from Greek prose: Plato, *Phaedrus* 240: ἄγαμον, ἄπαιδα, ἄοικον and Demosthenes, *Philippic* 1. 36: ἄτακτα, ἀδιόρθωτα, ἀόρισθ' ἄπαντα. Cf. Spenser, *Faerie Queene* 7. 7. 46. 5: 'Vnbodied, vnsoul'd, vnheard, vnseene'; Shakespeare, *Hamlet*, 1. 5: 'Cut off euen in the Blossomes of my Sinne, | Vnhouzzled, disappointed, vnnaneld'; Fairfax, *Godfrey of Bulloigne*, 2. 16. 8 'Vnseene, vnmarkt, vnpitied, vnrewarded' ('o non visto, o mal noto, o mal gradito').

64. Pope expands two Greek negatives into three English ones in *Iliad* 22. 483–4: 'Divine *Patroclus*! Death has seal'd his eyes; | Unwept, unhonour'd, uninterr'd he lies!' Thomson, though interrupting the sequence with 'and,' has 'unblessed, untended, and unmourned' in *Summer*, 1086. Goldsmith has 'Unenvied, unmolested, unconfined' in *The Deserted Village*, 258. Other examples, and possibly many more, will have escaped my notice.

65. 3. 245: 'careless youth, unburdened, unalarmed' in the 14-book *Prelude* was 'Unburthen'd, unalarm'd, and unprofan'd' at 3. 245 of the 13-book *Prelude* (both stages). 6. 41: 'Unbiassed, unbewildered, and unawed' (6. 54 in the AB-stage and 6. 45 in the C-stage of the 13-book *Prelude*). 6. 506: 'Unchastened, unsubdued, unawed, unraised' (6. 442 in the AB-Stage and 6. 517 in the C-stage of the 13-book *Prelude*). 10. 168: 'for Society's unreasoning herd' in the 14-book *Prelude* was 'Unquenchable, unsleeping, undismayed' at 10. 148 at the AB-stage of the 13-book *Prelude*; it was changed at the C-stage (10. 192). 14. 134: 'unchecked, unerring, and untired'.

66. Thomas N. Corns, *Milton's Language* (Oxford: Basil Blackwell, 1990), 84–6.

67. Massey, *Browning's Vocabulary*, 270. James Milroy, *The Language of Gerard Manley Hopkins* (London: André Deutsch, 1977), 77. On Hopkins's *disremembering*, see Geoffrey Hill, 'Common Weal, Common Woe', forthcoming in *Style and Faith* (Counterpoint, 2003).

68. Geoffrey Hill, *The Triumph of Love* (Boston: Haughton Mifflin, 1998), xxiii.

69. The best account of the 'Beauty of Buttemere', by Florence Verducci in *Ovid's Toyshop of the Heart* (Princeton: Princeton University Press, 1985), 6–19, describes the poetic tact—and bias—of Wordsworth's portrayal: 'chaste, discreetly laundered, even bleached'.

70. John Buxton, *The Grecian Taste* (London: Macmillan Press, 1978), 158–9.

71. Timothy Webb, 'The Unascended Heaven: Negatives in "Prometheus Unbound"' in Kelvin Everest (ed.), *Shelley Revalued* (Leicester: Leicester University Press, 1983), 37–62.

72. See Paul Fussell, jun., *Theory of Prosody in Eighteenth-Century England* (New London, Conn.: Connecticut College, 1954), 101–57.

73. 'Among Swinburne's technical achievements the most conspicuous, if not the greatest, was his development of anapaestic verse. It was he who first made the anapaest fit for serious poetry . . . True, the anapaestic rhythm, even when invested by a master with these alluring splendours, is not, in English, the best vehicle for poetry': A. E. Housman in *Collected Poems and Selected Prose*, ed. Christopher Ricks (London: Penguin, 1988), 283–4.

74. Gibbon, *The Decline and Fall of the Roman Empire*, ch. 66: 'In their lowest servitude and depression, the subjects of the Byzantine throne were still possessed of a golden key that could unlock the treasures of antiquity; of a musical and prolific language, that gives a soul to the objects of sense, and a body to the abstractions of philosophy.' Cowper, preface to the 1st edn. of his translation of the *Iliad*: 'Our language is indeed less musical than the Greek, and there is no language with which I am at all acquainted that is not.'

75. Carne-Ross, 'Jocasta's Divine Head', 129–30.

76. See, in addition to the dispute between Arnold and Newman, *The Cambridge History of English and American Literature* (Cambridge: Cambridge University Press, 1907–21), xviii/1, ch. 7, s. 14 ('The hexameter controversy').

77. *Charles Kingsley: His Letters and Memories of his Life*, ed. Frances Kingsley (London: Kegan Paul, 1878), i. 338–49.

78. In G. Hermann, *Elementa doctrinae metricae* (1816), it is defined as a syllable or syllables 'extra tempus ante primum pedem'. In his commentaries on Sophocles, Jebb defines it the part of a verse 'preliminary to the regular metre'. The entry in the *OED* under 'anacrusis' is unfortunate because its quotations do not correspond to the definition. The word suffered from another meaning in the period, being also taken as the unstressed beat with which a rhythm begins (it is in this sense that the word is used in the quotations here and under 'anacrustic' and can therefore be offered as a synonym for 'thesis' in the quotations offered there).

79. Harlan Henthorne Hatcher, *The Versification of Robert Browning* ([1928] New York: Phaeton Press, 1968), 46–7, 62–74; Armin Kroder, *Shelley's*

Verskunst (Erlangen and Leipzig: Deichert, 1903), 64–5; Joseph B. Mayor, *Chapters on English Metre* ([1901] New York: Greenwood, 1968), 231.

80. *The Classical Tradition in Poetry* (London: Oxford University Press, 1927), 108 n. 1.

81. One guide to English prosody identifies Sir W. Watson's *Hymn to the Sea* as 'the best example of English elegiacs'. Christopher Middleton's translation of Goethe's 'Euphrosyne' is a convincing recent attempt to recreate the metre in English. On German elegiacs, see e.g. Theodore Ziolkowski, *The Classical German Elegy: 1795–1950* (Princeton: Princeton University Press, 1980) and David Constantine, *Hölderlin* (Oxford: Clarendon Press, 1988), 182–210. On the development of elegiac couplets in Russian, the 'poor relation' of the Russian hexameter, see Michael Wachtel, *The Development of Russian Verse: Meter and its Meanings* (Cambridge: Cambridge University Press, 1998), 171–205.

82. T. S. Osmond, *English Metrists* ([1921] New York: Phaeton Press, 1968), 96–7; Paull Franklin Baum, *The Principles of English Versification* (Cambridge, Mass.: Harvard University Press, 1924), 76–7; Brewster Ghiselin, 'Paeonic Measures in English Verse', *Modern Language Notes*, 57/5 (May 1942), 336–41. See also the chapter on paeonic verse in Enid Hamer, *The Metres of English Poetry* (London: Methuen, 1930).

83. It is, however, retained in the *OED*'s definition of sapphics, pherecreteans, glyconics, etc. No specialized vocabulary in the dictionary is in greater need· of revision than that relating to prosody; neither current nor historical meanings of prosodic terms are reliable. In the glossary to *Greek Metre* (Oxford: Clarendon Pressm 1982) Martin West writes that in the 19th cent. *logaoedic* was 'extended to all verse of assymetric rhythm; in the twentieth abandoned in disgust'.

84. Donald Davie, *Purity of Diction in English Verse and Articulate Energy* ([1952 and 1955] London: Penguin Books, 1992), 129.

85. Thomas Hardy, 'A Singer Asleep'.

86. *Seven Against Thebes* 229, κριμναμενᾶν νεφαλᾶν ὀρθοῖ. See Carne-Ross, 'Jocasta's Divine Head', 124, 126, on Swinburne and Shelley. W. H. Gardner, *Gerard Manley Hopkins*, ii. (London: Oxford University Press, 1949), 98–106, makes the most of the Greek influence on Hopkins's rhythms.

87. *Nineteenth-Century Minor Poets* (New York: Dell, 1965), 22–3.

CHAPTER FIVE: APOLLO, DIONYSUS, AND NINETEENTH-CENTURY
ENGLISH AND GERMAN POETRY

1. See e.g. Julian Young, *Nietzsche's Philosophy of Art* (Cambridge: Cambridge University Press, 1992), chs. 1 and 2, and *Heidegger's Philosophy of Art* (Cambridge: Cambridge University Press, 2001), ch. 1.

2. Mario Praz, *On Neoclassicism* (Evanston, Ill.: Northwestern University Press, 1969), 49.

3. It was an effort to impute to goodness an active motivation by arguing that

it attracted to some extent in the affective way that beauty attracted; it was therefore concerned to determine the relative roles of feeling and reason in moral action. See Robert E. Norton, *The Beautiful Soul* (Ithaca, NY: Cornell University Press, 1995).

4. Humphrey Trevelyan, *Goethe and the Greeks* (Cambridge: Cambridge University Press, 1941). Hugh Lloyd-Jones summarizes the relation in his preface to the 1981 edn. of the volume.

5. Hamann radically altered the picture of the Enlightenment Socrates. See James C. O'Flaherty, *Hamann's Socratic Memorabilia* (Baltimore: Johns Hopkins Press, 1967), 57–60.

6. F. J. Lamport, *German Classical Drama* (Cambridge: Cambridge University Press, 1990), 164.

7. G. Schottelius, the most important German grammarian of the 17th cent., asserted the affinity in his *Lingua ipsa Germanica*. Quoted by Eric A. Blackall in the 2nd edn. of *The Emergence of German as a Literary Language* (Ithaca, NY: Cornell University Press, 1978), 10–11. Blackall assembles many instances in the 18th cent. of the desirability of German imitating Greek: see pp. 143–4, 165, 286, 316–17, 326–7, 361, 425, 457.

8. As it is in Kleist's *Penthesilea*. Lamport refers, *Drama*, 166, to its 'tortuousness of syntax and word-order' and suggests the direct influence of ancient Greek.

9. 5. 20, tr. by H. M. Hubbell in the Loeb Cicero (1939).

10. *Institutio Oratoria* 10. 1. 66–8.

11. For an 18th-cent. contrasting of Aeschylus with Homer (rather than Sophocles), see John Brown, *A Dissertation on the Rise, Union, and Power, the Progressions, Separations, and Corruptions, of Poetry and Music* (London, 1763), 171: 'For Homer is equal, large, flowing, and harmonious: Eschylus is uneven, concise, abrupt, and rugged: The one leads you through the grand but gentle Declivities of Hill and Dale; the other carries you over a continued Chain of Rocks and Precipices.'

12. Linda M. Paterson, *Troubadours and Eloquence* (Oxford: Clarendon Press, 1975), 2–4, indicates that troubadour rhetoric is more complex than this simple division. I include it because I wish only to indicate a possible use of the smooth and rough styles.

13. P. E. Easterling, 'Plain Words in Sophocles', in Jasper Griffin (ed.), *Sophocles Revisited* (Oxford: Oxford University Press, 1999), 95–107.

14. For the poetry of 'nature asleep' after Alcman, see also *Aeneid* 4. 522. In the edn. of *Aeneid*, 4, by Arthur Stanley Pease (Cambridge: Harvard University Press, 1935), a long note on this line documents the topos.

15. Friedrich Hölderlin and Eduard Mörike, *Selected Poems*, tr. Christopher Middleton (Chicago: Chicago University Press, 1972), 238.

16. *Mitgeborne* (22) = σύγγονος; *göttergleich* (45) = ἀντίθεος (or other equivalent expressions); *unwirtbar* (142) = ἄξενος (used in Euripides *Iphigenia in Tauris* 94 and 341); *weit verbreiten* (555) = πολυσπερής; *Wechselmut* (973) = ἀλληλοφόνους μανίας (Aeschylus *Agamemnon* 1557). Identified by H. B. Cotterill in his edn. of *Iphigenie auf Tauris* (London: Macmillan, 1899).

17. See Joachim Angst and Fritz Hackert, *Erläuterungen und Dokumente: Johann Wolfgang Goethe*, Iphigenie auf Tauris (Stuttgart: Reclam, 1991).

198 NOTES TO PAGES 144-150

18. Lamport, *Drama*, 81, and Nicholas Boyle, *Goethe: The Poet and his Age* (Oxford: Oxford University Press, 1992), 272.
19. See George Steiner, *Antigones* (Oxford: Clarendon Press, 1984), 45–8.
    Erich Heller discusses the relation of Iphigenia and Antigone in *The Disinherited Mind* ([1957] New York: Harcourt Brace Jovanovich, 1975), 43–6.
20. Quoted in Angst and Hackert, *Erläuterungen*, 57 and 58.
21. Quoted by H. B. Cotterill in his edn. of the play (London: Macmillan, 1899), 174.
22. 'Denn die Unsterblichen lieben der Menschen | Weit verbreite gute Geschlechter' (554–5).
23. Theodor W. Adorno, 'On the Classicism of Goethe's *Iphigenie*', *Notes to Literature*, ii (New York: Columbia University Press, 1992), 154.
24. 'Mit seltner Kunst flichst du der Götter Rat | Und deine Wünsche klug in eins zusammen' (740–1).
25. Cf. 258–9, 1645, 1680–1, and 1795–6.
26. Cf. 164, 300, and 450.
27. Cf. 1257 and 1381.
28. Heller, *Disinherited Mind*, 41.
29. Adorno, 'Classicism', 153–70.
30. Norton, *Beautiful Soul*, 249–64.
31. Translated by Christopher Middleton in *The Poet's Vocation* (Austin, Tex.: Humanities Research Center, 1967), 27.
32. See e.g. his letter to Friedrich Wilmans, 28 Sept. 1803.
33. Geoffrey Hill, 'Little Apocalypse', *New and Collected Poems* (Boston and New York: Houghton Mifflin, 1994), 33.
34. David Constantine, *Hölderlin* (Oxford: Clarendon Press, 1990), 237.
35. David Constantine, 'Hölderlin's Pindar: The Language of Translation', *Modern Language Review* (1978), 825–34, discusses the translations and includes references to the large secondary material on the subject.
36. Constantine, *Hölderlin*, 238.
37. Steiner, *Antigones*, 66–106; Jochen Schmidt, 'Tragödie und Tragödientheorie: Hölderlins Sophoklesdeutung', *Hölderlin Jahrbuch*, 31 (1994–5), 64–82; Richard Stoneman, ' "A Crazy Enterprise": German Translators of Sophocles, from Opitz to Boeckh', in Jasper Griffin, *Sophocles Revisited*, 307–29.
38. For the latter, consider especially how Pindar's triad was finely suited for use in Hölderlin's late hymns, where the triad is an effective vehicle to express the dialectic of the *former* presence of divinity which is *now* absent but might *later* return.
39. As they are in his translations; Christopher Middleton noted of Hölderlin's translation of Pindar's *Pythian* 12 that the compound epithets are often even longer (by a syllable) than the original.
40. Constantine, *Hölderlin*, 171.
41. Michael Hamburger, *Contraries* (New York: Dutton, 1970), 29.
42. Blackall, *Emergence*, 347.
43. Friedrich Hölderlin, *Hymns and Fragments*, tr. Richard Sieburth (Princeton: Princeton University Press, 1984), 29–30.

44. Rilke's triply repeated 'denn' at the beginning of the first *Duino Elegy* in contrast is didactic: the initiate is speaking to outsiders. Adorno, in 'Parataxis: On Hölderlin's Late Poetry' (in *Notes to Literature*, iii. 340), gives a different interpretation of the particles. He suggests that they are a pseudologic, offering the appearance of synthesis that the sequence does not permit, the 'restitution phenomenon' of psychoanalysis.

45. Contrast the 'Stuttgart' edn. of Hölderlin by Friedrich Beissner (ii. 193–8 and 816–30) with the new 'Frankfurt' edn. by D. E. Sattler (viii. 734–40); cf. Jochen Schmidt, 'Hölderlins Hymne "Mnemosyne"', *Editio*, 5 (1991), 122–57.

46. He identifies the 'sinister side' of Dionysus in 'A Study of Dionysus' and refers to the 'unlovelier side, grotesque, unhellenic, unglorified by art' in 'Demeter and Persephone', both published in 1876 and then reprinted in *Greek Studies* (1895). On Pater and Nietzsche, see Billie Andrew Inman, *Walter Pater's Reading* (New York: Garland, 1981).

47. The phrase 'sweetness and light' was originally Swift's, from the *Battle of the Books* (1704). In *Culture and Anarchy* (1869) Arnold refers to the Greek 'ideal of beauty and sweetness and light, and a human nature complete on all its sides' and understands life under the ideal of hellenism to be 'full of what we call sweetness and light'.

48. See e.g. John Buxton, *The Grecian Taste* (London: Macmillan Press, 1978); Richard Jenkyns, *The Victorians and Ancient Greece* (Cambridge, Mass.: Harvard University Press, 1980); Frank M. Turner, *The Greek Heritage in Victorian Britain* (New Haven: Yale University Press, 1981); Timothy Webb, *English Romantic Hellenism: 1700–1824* (Manchester: Manchester University Press, 1982).

49. 'Colloquialism and Naive Style in Aeschylus', in *'Owls to Athens'*, ed. E. M. Craik (Oxford: Clarendon Press, 1990).

50. John Jones, *On Aristotle and Greek Tragedy* (New York: Oxford University Press, 1962), 119.

51. Perhaps most famously in the relation of the 'eagle's feast' (138) to the other slaughters of the play; see D. S. Carne-Ross, 'The Beastly House of Atreus', *Kenyon Review*, NS 3/2 (Spring 1981), 20–60.

52. Thomas G. Rosenmeyer, *The Art of Aeschylus* (Berkeley and Los Angeles: University of California Press, 1982), 88–9 (on *Agamemnon* 140–55).

53. Donald H. Reiman and Sharon B. Powers, *Shelley's Poetry and Prose* (New York: Norton, 1977), 192.

54. William Hazlitt in *Table Talk* (1821). In James E. Barcus, *Shelley: The Critical Heritage* (London: Routledge & Kegan Paul, 1975), 148.

55. The unsigned review in *The Literary Gazette, and Journal of the Belles Lettres* (9 Sept. 1820) in Barcus, *Shelley*, 228.

56. W. S. Walker in *The Quarterly Review* (October 1821). In Barcus, *Shelley*, 258

57. James Russell Lowell, in *North American Review* (1866). In Barcus, *Shelley*, 269.

58. The unsigned review in *The Literary Gazette, and Journal of the Belles Lettres* (9 Sept. 1820). In Barcus, *Shelley*, 230.

59. One of the major revaluations performed by Romantic critics was to see

Shakespearean and Greek drama *together* as constituting genuine tragedy; see George Steiner, *The Death of Tragedy* ([1961] New York: Oxford University Press, 1980), 190–2.

60. Doubts about the authorship of *Prometheus Bound* were first raised several decades after Shelley's death. See Mark Griffith, *The Authenticity of Prometheus Bound* (Cambridge: Cambridge University Press, 1977).

61. Shelley does not work the relative clause in this way only in poems with a Greek setting or concerned with the philosophical theme of unity and diversity. Near the beginning of *The Triumph of Life*, for example, he describes his vision of a stream of people hurrying on a public way:

> And weary with vain toil and faint for thirst
> Heard not the fountains *whose melodious dew*
>
> *Out of their mossy cells forever burst*
> Nor felt the breeze *which from the forest told*
> *Of grassy paths, and wood lawns interspersed*
>
> *With overarching elms and caverns cold,*
> And violet banks *where sweet dreams brood*, but they
> Pursued their serious folly as of old . . .
>
> (66–73)

The relative clauses are almost all descriptive; they set up a counterpoint to the desolate stream of people. The abrupt shifts between the desolation and the flowers and forests permit Shelley to move between harsh satire and utopian vision.

62. In Barcus, *Shelley*, 254.

63. F. R. Leavis, *Revaluation* (New York: Steward, 1947), 205, 207. For the similarities between the contemporary criticism of Shelley and modernist criticism, see Barcus, *Shelley*, 29–30.

64. *A Preface to Shelley* (Harlow: Longman, 1985), 117.

65. See e.g. Carl Grabo, *A Newton among Poets* (Chapel Hill, NC: University of North Carolina Press, 1930).

66. *English Poetry: A Critical Introduction* (London: Longman, 1950), 213 n. The kaleidoscope was not new to Shelley criticism; it had been invoked in an hostile unsigned review of Shelley's *Prometheus*, quoted in Barcus, *Shelley*, 231.

67. Unsigned review, *Saturday Review* (6 May 1865), xix. 540–2. Reprinted in Clyde K. Hyder (ed.), *Swinburne: The Critical Heritage* (New York: Barnes & Noble, 1970), 9–16.

68. *'Atalanta in Calydon' and 'Poems and Ballads'* (London: Penguin, 2000).

69. Hyder, *Critical Heritage*, 11.

70. See Clyde K. Hyder (ed.), *Swinburne as Critic* (London: Routledge & Kegan Paul, 1972), 126, 147, 260, 295, 297, and 305.

71. *The Swinburne Letters*, ed. Cecil Y. Lang. 6 vols. (New Haven: Yale University Press, 1959–62), iii. 53.

72. *The Sacred Wood* ([1920] New York: Methuen, 1983), 145.

73. And of his prose, too, as W. Brook Drayton Henderson has pointed out, quoting Swinburne in 'August Vaquerie': 'The *weight and edge* of his

trenchant and pungent style, the *point and balance* of this *vivid and virile* prose . . . are never used but to the direct end wanted, in *swift and loyal* service of the immediate need'. Henderson relates it to the prose style of Landor (he gives Landor's sentence: 'If it were allowable for me to *disdain or despise* even the *wickedest and vilest* of God's creatures, in which condition a king peradventure as easily as any other may be, I think I could, without much *perplexity or inquiry*, find something in the multitude of his blessings quite as *reasonable and proper* to thank him for') and to the whole tradition of English anti-ciceronianism. See W. Brooks Drayton Henderson, *Swinburne and Landor* (London: Macmillan, 1918), 200 n. 65.

74. See Ch. 4, n. 52.

75. Wordsworth writes in the 1807 *Ode*: 'Another race hath been, and other palms are won', an allusion to *1 Cor.* 24: 'Know ye not that they which run in a race run all, but one receiveth the prize? So run that ye may obtain. And every man that striveth for the mastery is temperate in all things. Now they do it to obtain a corruptible crown; but we an incorruptible.'

76. *Letters to Bridges* (30 July 1887), 256.

77. Walter E. Houghton discusses intellectual, moral, religious, and economic aspects of earnestness among the Victorians in *The Victorian Frame of Mind 1830–1870* (New Haven: Yale University Press, 1957), 208–62.

78. *Letters to Bridges* (14 Aug. 1879), 89.

79. *Letters to Bridges* (12 May 1885), 218. The allusion is to *Hamlet*, 3. 1. 85.

80. *Letters to Bridges* (1 June 1886), 225.

81. J. Hillis Miller, *The Disappearance of God* (Cambridge, Mass.: Harvard University Press, 1963), 273–6.

82. For a prose gloss, see Gerard Manley Hopkins, *Sermons and Devotional Writings,* ed. Christopher Devlin, SJ (London: Oxford University Press, 1959), 239: 'The sun and the stars shining glorify God. They stand where he placed them, they move where he bid them. "The heavens declare the glory of God". They glorify God, but they do not know it. The birds sing to him, the thunder speaks of his terror, the lion is like his sweetness; they are somewhat like him, they make him known, they tell of him, they give him glory, but they do not know they do, they do not know him, they never can, they are brute things that only think of food or think of nothing. This then is poor praise, faint reverence, slight service, dull glory.'

83. Geoffrey Hill, *Lords of Limit* (New York: Oxford University Press, 1984), 98. In *The Correspondence of Hopkins and Dixon* (27 Feb. 1879), Hopkins writes: 'I should add that the word sprung which I use for this rhythm means something like abrupt and applies by rights only where one stress follows another running, without syllable between.'

84. I print *planks* rather than *flanks*, following the argument of R. J. C. Watt, 'Editorial Mumpsimus in the Poems of Gerard Hopkins', *The Library*, 21/4 (Dec. 1999), 361–8.

85. Closer than Aeschylus to Hopkins's purpose is Donne's sonnet 'Batter my heart', which moves rapidly through the metaphors of an artifact, a town, a lover, all expressive of his spiritual state and bearing witness to the changeable nature of the human heart.

86. *In Extremity* (Cambridge: Cambridge University Press, 1978), 118–21.

87. *In Extremity*, 8.
88. *Letters to Bridges* (29 April 1869), 25.
89. Christopher Ricks argued that the poem fails to do justice to the human predicament of the nuns, thereby failing also in its depiction of the divine significance of that predicament; see *English Poetry and Prose 1540–1674*, ed. Ricks (London: Sphere, 1970), 269–70. Yet Hopkins illustrated effectively the intersection of human and divine within his own predicament.
90. Ezra Pound, 'Translators of Aeschylus', *Literary Essays*, ed. T. S. Eliot ([1954] Norfolk: New Directions, 1968), 273.
91. Ronald Bush, *The Genesis of Ezra Pound's* Cantos (Princeton: Princeton University Press, 1976), 181–2.
92. D. S. Carne-Ross, 'New Metres for Old: A Note on Pound's Metric', *Arion*, 6 (1967), 216–32.

Further Reading

Chapter One: Multilingualism in Literature

Adams, J. N., *Bilingualism and the Latin Language* (Cambridge: Cambridge University Press, 2003).

—— M. Janse, and S. Swain (eds.), *Bilingualism in Ancient Society* (Oxford: Oxford University Press, 2002).

Binns, J. W. (ed.), *The Latin Poetry of English Poets* (London: Routledge & Kegan Paul, 1974).

—— *Intellectual Culture in Elizabethan and Jacobean England* (Leeds: Francis Cairns, 1990).

Burke, Peter, *The Art of Conversation* (Ithaca, NY: Cornell University Press, 1993).

Clarke, M. L., *Greek Studies in England 1700–1830* (Cambridge: Cambridge University Press, 1945).

Dover, K. J. (ed.), *Perceptions of the Ancient Greeks* (Cambridge: Blackwell, 1992).

Edwards, John, *Multilingualism* (Harmondsworth: Penguin, 1995).

Forster, Leonard, *The Poets' Tongues: Multilingualism in Literature* (Cambridge: Cambridge University Press, 1970).

IJsewijn, Jozef (ed.), *Companion to Neo-Latin Studies* (Louvain: Leuven University Press, 1990–8).

Kraye, Jill (ed.), *The Cambridge Companion to Renaissance Humanism* (Cambridge: Cambridge University Press, 1996).

Ogilvie, R. M., *Latin and Greek* (London: Routledge & Kegan Paul, 1964).

Rummel, Erika, *The Confessionalization of Humanism in Reformation Germany* (Oxford: Oxford University Press, 2000).

Stray, Christopher, *Classics Transformed* (Clarendon Press: Oxford, 1998).

Trapp, J. B., 'The "Conformity" of Greek with the Vernacular: The History of a Renaissance Theory of Languages', in J. B. Trapp, *Essays on the Renaissance and the Classical Tradition* (Aldershot: Variorum, 1990).

Waquet, Françoise, *Latin, or the Empire of a Sign: From the Sixteenth to the Twentieth Centuries*, tr. John Howe (London and New York: Verso, 2001).

Weiss, Roberto, *Medieval and Humanist Greek* (Padua: Editrice Antenore, 1977).

Wilson, N. G., *From Byzantium to Italy: Greek Studies in the Italian Renaissance* (Baltimore: Johns Hopkins University Press, 1992).

Chapter Two: Varieties of Language Purism

Adamson, Sylvia, 'Literary Language', *The Cambridge History of the English Language*, iii. *1476 to 1776*, ed. Roger Lass (Cambridge: Cambridge University Press, 1999), 539–653.

—— 'Literary Language', *The Cambridge History of the English Language*, iv. *1776 to 1997*, ed. Richard M. Hogg (Cambridge: Cambridge University Press, 1998), 589–692.

Chambers, E. K., 'The Continuity of English Prose from Alfred to More and his School', in *Harpsfield's Life of More*, ed. E. K. Chambers (London: Early English Text Society, 1932).

Finkenstaedt, Thomas, *Ordered Profusion: Studies in Dictionaries and the English Lexicon* (Heidelberg: C. Winter, 1973).

Hughes, Geoffrey, *Swearing* (London: Penguin, 1998).

Jones, Robert Foster, *The Triumph of the English Language* (Stanford, Calif.: Stanford University Press, 1953).

Kirkness, Alan, *Zur Sprachreinigung im Deutschen 1781–1871* (Tübingen: Narr, 1975).

Miles, Josephine, *Poetry and Change* (Berkeley, Calif.: University of California Press, 1974).

Sørenson, Knud, *Charles Dickens: Linguistic Innovator* (Aarhus: Arkona, 1985).

Trench, Richard Chenevix, *On the Study of Words* (London, 1859).

—— *English: Past and Present* (London, 1877).

Tucker, Susie I., *Protean Shape: A Study in Eighteenth-Century Vocabulary and Usage* (London: Athlone Press, 1967).

Tuve, Rosemond, 'Ancients, Moderns, and Saxons', *ELH* 6/3 (Sept. 1939), 165–90.

Chapter Three: The Interface of Latin with English Literature

Carne-Ross, D. S., 'Jocasta's Divine Head: English with a Foreign Accent', *Arion*, 3rd ser. 1/1 (1989), 106–41.

Crystal, David, *Language Play* (London: Penguin, 1998).

Holloway, John, *Widening Horizons in English Verse* (Evanston, Ill.: Northwestern University Press, 1967).

Norton, David, *A History of the English Bible as Literature* (Cambridge: Cambridge University Press, 2000).

Rasula, Jed, and Steve McCaffery (eds.), *Imagining Language* (Cambridge, Mass.: MIT Press, 1998).

Weinreich, Uriel, *Languages in Contact* (1953, The Hague: Mouton, 1967).

Chapter Four: Some Greek Influences on English Poetry

Baum, Paull Franklin, *The Principles of English Versification* (Cambridge, Mass.: Harvard University Press, 1924).

Burnett, Archie, 'Compound Words in Milton's English Poetry', *Modern Language Review*, 75/3 (July 1980), 492–506.

Ghiselin, Brewster, 'Paeonic Measures in English Verse', *Modern Language Notes* 57/5 (May 1942), 336–41.

Groom, Bernard, *The Formation and Use of Compound Epithets in English Poetry from 1578* (Oxford: Clarendon Press, 1937).

Hamer, Enid, *The Metres of English Poetry* (London: Methuen, 1930).

Osmond, T. S., *English Metrists* (1921, New York: Phaeton Press, 1968).

Padelford, Frederick M., and William C. Maxwell, 'The Compound Words in Spenser's Poetry', *JEGP* 25 (1926), 498–516.

Quayle, Thomas, 'Compound Epithets in Eighteenth-Century Poetry', *Poetic Diction: A Study of Eighteenth-Century Verse* (London: Methuen & Co., 1924), 102–81.

Webb, Timothy, 'The Unascended Heaven: Negatives in "Prometheus Unbound"', in Kelvin Everest (ed.), *Shelley Revalued* (Leicester: Leicester University Press, 1983), 37–62.

Chapter Five: Apollo, Dionysus, and Nineteenth-century English and German Poetry

Adorno, Theodor W., 'On the Classicism of Goethe's Iphigenie', *Notes to Literature*, ii (New York: Columbia University Press, 1992), 153–70.

—— 'Parataxis: On Hölderlin's Late Poetry', *Notes to Literature*, ii (New York: Columbia University Press, 1992), 109–49.

Buxton, John, *The Grecian Taste* (London: Macmillan Press, 1978).

Constantine, David, *Hölderlin* (Oxford: Clarendon Press, 1990).

Heller, Erich, 'Goethe and the Avoidance of Tragedy', *The Disinherited Mind* (1957; New York: Harcourt Brace Jovanovich, 1975), 35–63.

Jenkyns, Richard, *The Victorians and Ancient Greece* (Cambridge, Mass.: Harvard University Press, 1980).

Norton, Robert E., *The Beautiful Soul* (Ithaca, NY: Cornell University Press, 1995).

Pound, Ezra, 'Translators of Aeschylus', *Literary Essays*, ed. T. S. Elliot (1954; Norfolk: New Directions, 1968).

Steiner, George, *Antigones* (Oxford: Clarendon Press, 1984).

Stoneman, Richard, '"A Crazy Enterprise": German Translators of Sophocles, from Opitz to Boeckh', in Jasper Griffin (ed.), *Sophocles Revisited* (Oxford: Oxford University Press, 1999), 307–29.

Trevelyan, Humphrey, *Goethe and the Greeks* (Cambridge: Cambridge University Press, 1941).

Turner, Frank M., *The Greek Heritage in Victorian Britain* (New Haven: Yale University Press, 1981).

Webb, Timothy, *English Romantic Hellenism: 1700–1824* (Manchester: Manchester University Press, 1982).

,

Index